DREAMING
OUT LOUD

To Shawn Bousiquot, writer & friend

DREAMING OUT LOUD

African American Novelists at Work

edited by

HORACE A. PORTER

Best wishes

UNIVERSITY OF IOWA PRESS

IOWA CITY

University of Iowa Press, Iowa City 52242
Copyright © 2015 by Horace A. Porter
www.uiowapress.org
Printed in the United States of America
Design by Sara T. Sauers

The University of Iowa Press is a member of Green Press
Initiative and is committed to preserving natural resources.
Printed on acid-free paper

Library of Congress Cataloging-in-Publication Data
Dreaming out loud : African American novelists at work /
[edited by] Horace Porter.
    pages   cm
Includes bibliographical references and index.
ISBN 978-1-60938-335-0 (pbk)
ISBN 978-1-60938-336-7 (ebk)
1. American fiction—African American authors.
2. African Americans in literature. 3. Fiction—
Authorship. 4. Race awareness in literature.
I. Porter, Horace A., 1950–editor.
PS508.N3D68 2015
810.8'0896073—dc23   2014034888

To Ralph Ellison (1913–1994)
&
James Alan McPherson

Contents

Preface

THIS BOOK WAS inspired by my own youthful dream of becoming a novelist, and by teaching, for thirty-six years, courses involving the novelists included in this anthology. In 1968, when I was a freshman at Amherst College, I read Ralph Ellison's *Invisible Man*. I have said elsewhere, "The book shook me with the force of an earthquake. It was a perfect book for me, coming, as if by magic, precisely when I needed it. Like its nameless narrator I was also a student and a black southerner who had recently arrived in the North."[1] The narrator's revelatory encounters were scenes of instruction, staged, or so it felt, just for me. When Ellison lectured at Amherst the next year, I discussed *Invisible Man* with him. I had never met a writer, let alone a famous one. After our first conversation, I no longer wanted to become a doctor. I decided I would write novels, move to New York, sip sparkling champagne at fashionable cocktail parties, and live happily ever after.

The next year I enrolled in my one and only creative writing class. Tillie Olsen, Amherst's visiting writer, taught the course. Olsen, known for her short story collection *Tell Me a Riddle*, conducted a mini writer's workshop for perhaps a dozen aspiring poets and novelists. With Olsen as an exemplary guide, we put aside our competitive mode of sharp analysis and scathing critique. We discussed the strengths of our classmates' short stories and poems and suggested ways to make improvements. We listened to Professor Olsen's advice. Keep a journal. Write every day. She said there would be bad days, good days, and splendid days when sentences would come streaming out of our minds as though from a divine source. She told us not to worry about the bad days, that even the best writers had their doubts. Emphasizing the point one day, Olsen read a quote from

Henry James' story "The Middle Years": "We work in the dark—we do what we can—we give what we have. Our doubt is our passion and our passion is our task. The rest is the madness of art."

After Olsen's class and during my remaining years at Amherst, I started thinking of myself as a literary intellectual. I stopped taking science courses—no chemistry, no math. I published a short story in the *Amherst Literary Magazine* and sometimes wrote essays and editorials about racial matters for the *Amherst Student*. While I still kept a journal, I didn't write much fiction. Instead, I wrote a senior honors thesis on Jean Toomer and Wallace Thurman, two writers of the Harlem Renaissance.

I decided to become a professor and applied to graduate school. While pursuing my Ph.D. in American studies at Yale, I still yearned to write novels. Whenever writers came to campus, I went to hear them. I vividly recall the poet Robert Hayden tearing up and taking a lengthy pause as he read his poem "Runagate Runagate."

In 1979, I began teaching in Dartmouth College's English Department. Many writers—including Mary McCarthy, Saul Bellow, William Styron, Chinua Achebe, and Toni Morrison—came to Dartmouth as Montgomery Fellows. They stayed at Montgomery House (a beautiful residence reserved for celebrated authors and distinguished guests) for short or longer visits. I met Achebe and Morrison. I had a private talk with William Styron about his friend James Baldwin. I was writing a book on Baldwin. It was an enlightening conversation about the period when Baldwin was working on *Another Country* (1962). I also met James Alan McPherson. I later tried convincing Ralph Ellison to give a lecture at Dartmouth. He informed me that he had already visited years before and was hard at work on his novel. I reminded him of the beauty and privacy of Montgomery House and said he would receive an attractive honorarium. He said, "Tell them that at my age, time is more important than money."

I was insistent because I wanted Ellison to speak to my class, a freshman seminar called "Writers at Work." I offered the course several times at Dartmouth and years later at Stanford. The course title was taken from one of the books on my syllabus, *Writers at Work*, a collection of interviews with major writers—including E. M. Forster, Dorothy Parker, and William Faulkner. The interviews were first published in the *Paris Review*. The first series was edited by Malcolm Cowley and included his introduction—"How Writers Write"—in which he describes "the four distinct stages" a writer faces when writing a story.[2]

Each interview was preceded by a copy of a manuscript page from one of the writer's works. The manuscript pages revealed how individual authors made revisions. This era predated the use of personal computers. Therefore, each page was a literal record as well as a vivid snapshot that captured aspects of the writer's editing. Some writers changed a word or two. Others crossed out paragraphs. Some covered their pages with indecipherable handwriting.

As we approached the course's end, we read essays that explored various difficulties writers faced. I also wanted my students to glimpse how writers experience—day by day—a range of intense emotions. In his anthology *The Writer's Craft*, John Hersey includes letters from Gustave Flaubert to Louise Colet. Flaubert corresponded with her while he was writing *Madame Bovary*. The novelist describes his painful emotions as well as sustained periods of creative pleasure: "I have plans for writing that will keep me busy till the end of my life, and though I sometimes have moments of bitterness that make me almost scream with rage (so acutely do I feel my own impotence and weakness), I have others when I scarcely contain myself for joy. Something deep and extra-voluptuous gushes out of me like an ejaculation of the soul."[3]

We read Norman Mailer's "The Last Draft of *The Deer Park*," his brutally honest account of the ugly scenes surrounding the composition of his third novel. Having published *The Naked and the Dead* when he was twenty-five, he describes the intense pressure brought on by his early commercial success and literary acclaim, his failing marriage, and his excessive use of alcohol and other drugs. Mailer also belatedly recognizes that he had made a crucial mistake in the novel's conception. He decides to rewrite it.

We discussed women and African American novelists. We read selections from Tillie Olsen's *Silences*. Olsen says, "I have had special need to learn all I could of this over the years, myself so nearly remaining mute and having to let writing die over and over again in me." Much of Olsen's book is dedicated to documenting "varieties" of silences, including the silences endured by women writers.[4] Since I also taught courses on African American literature, I included several selections from black novelists on their aesthetic challenges. For example, I assigned an interview with Ralph Ellison conducted by John Hersey. In "A Completion of Personality," Ellison refers to the symbiosis between novelist and novel: "Part of the pleasure of writing, as well as the pain, is involved in pouring into that thing which is being created all of what he cannot understand and cannot say and cannot deal with, or cannot even admit, in any other way. The artifact is a completion of personality."[5] Students usually responded to the interview by asking questions about Ellison's by then legendary but unpublished second novel.

I continued teaching and writing about African American novelists. I wrote *Stealing the Fire: The Art and Protest of James Baldwin* (1989) and *Jazz Country: Ralph Ellison in America* (2001). I also enjoyed the honor and rare privilege of correspondence and friendship with two writers: James Alan McPherson and Ralph Ellison. I tried keeping alive my dream of writing a novel. During the 1980s, I finally wrote a novel, *The Diamond Campaign*. It tells the story of Christopher Diamond, a black politician and aviator who runs for governor of Georgia in the seventies. He loses. I doubt that I will ever send the manuscript to a publisher. But Ralph Ellison read it, wrote extended comments, and said I had "a worthy tale to tell." He suggested that I get rid of my first-person narrator, rewrite the novel in the third person, and send it out. I didn't follow his advice. The manuscript has rested undisturbed for years in one of the boxes in our basement.

My experience teaching courses as well as writing about novelists, particularly African American authors, led me to edit this anthology. Furthermore, my efforts to bring characters alive on the page taught me something about the creative stamina, the heart, the passionate intensity that the genre demands. Any aspiring novelist, creative writing student, or interested reader will discover herein memorable stories that reveal the joys and challenges of writing novels. After all, Walter Mosley says in "For Authors, Fragile Ideas Need Loving Every Day" (included here), "Writing a novel is gathering smoke. It's an excursion into the ether of ideas." John Wideman uses another metaphor: "A story is a formula for extracting meaning from chaos, a handful of water we scoop up to recall an ocean."

Horace A. Porter
Iowa City, Iowa

Acknowledgments

FIRST, I THANK Jason Daniels, my research assistant, who helped throughout by doing various kinds of research in the library and online and by assisting with the word-processing, formatting, and copying of the manuscript. Props to you, Jason! During the summer of 2012, Donald "Field" Brown also tracked down a few sources for me. Sheri Gilbert did most of the permissions research and requests for the book, graciously tutoring me throughout the protracted process. I applaud her for her excellent work.

Elisabeth Chretien, my editor, made helpful suggestions that improved the book. I appreciate the support that Elisabeth Chretien; James McCoy, director of the University of Iowa Press; Amy Richard; Susan Hill Newton and other press staff have given me. I also thank Holly Carver, Joseph Parsons, and Charlotte M. Wright, former editors of the press, who also worked with me on the project. Christine Gever copyedited the manuscript with remarkable precision and patience.

Frank Moorer of Montgomery, Alabama, read the preface and introduction and made fine comments. I appreciate the moral support of my colleagues in American studies and African American studies—including Lena Hill, Michael Hill, Miriam Thaggert, and Deborah Whaley. However, I am responsible for the book's errors and omissions. As I prepared the final manuscript, Zachary Porter, my son, surprised me with a visit. He read the preface and introduction. Carla Carr, my spouse, helped, as with my previous books, in too many ways to spell out here. Her loyalty and love are my priceless jewels.

Finally, I thank the F. Wendell Miller Fund for payment of the permissions costs for most of the articles included herein.

Introduction

THIS ANTHOLOGY BRINGS together a group of living African American novelists and some from the early twentieth century who discuss writing novels. Similar anthologies that have focused on African American writers—including Jack O'Brien's *Interviews with Black Writers* (1973), Mari Evans' *Black Women Writers* (1984), and Claudia Tate's *Black Women Writers at Work* (1988)—have either been a series of interviews that include poets, novelists, and dramatists or general scholarly collections with articles by and about various writers.[6] While some of the writers included here are also accomplished poets and essayists, this anthology explores the novel as a genre. It allows the writers to tell us in their own words about becoming novelists and writing fiction. Some write about the art and stern discipline required to write novels. Others focus on family matters and professional obstacles. While the anthology is not a how-to guide—with chapters on writing dialogue or the pros and cons of using first-person narration—readers will find some references to craft. They will also discover inspiring accounts of vocational dedication.

The book includes essays by novelists who have won major national and international prizes, including James Alan McPherson and Alice Walker (Pulitzer Prize), and Ralph Ellison and Charles Johnson (National Book Award). Five novelists—James Alan McPherson, Ernest Gaines, John Wideman, Ishmael Reed, and Charles Johnson—have received coveted MacArthur Fellowships, or "genius" awards. It also contains essays by best-selling novelists, such as Terry McMillan and Walter Mosley. The twenty-one writers included here constitute roughly one hundred years of African American novelists at work. Living authors (five women and six men) wrote thirteen of the anthology's selections. The living novelists have written (in recent years) a remarkable range of works: short stories, literary essays, poetry collections, plays, and memoirs. Some have edited anthologies of their own and other writers' work. The novelists have produced an influential body of literature. The anthology comprises an honor roll of African American writers widely taught at colleges and universities. The chronological range and breadth of the selections will allow creative-writing students, instructors, and general readers to see how, over a century, very different novelists have dedicated themselves to a demanding vocation that occasionally ends in thwarted expectations and silences but often leads to literary prizes, fame, and good fortune. The anthology ends with Toni Morrison's 1993 Nobel Prize Lecture.

The Selection Process

I have chosen a mixture of complete essays, introductions, and excerpts from various authors. The authors selected have dedicated all or a considerable portion of their careers to writing novels and short stories. I searched for articles in which the novelists discuss both simple and complex questions about writing novels. For example: How much research do writers have to do before writing their novels? What happens if your first novel doesn't sell many copies? Does parenting necessarily get in the way of writing a novel? What audience should an African American novelist have in mind while writing her or his novel? Are African American novelists discriminated against in the publishing industry? Are there special hurdles that African American writers—whether men or women, straight, lesbian, or gay—must jump to become successful novelists?

I have chosen essays in which some novelists discuss their working habits—providing examples of sustained periods of creative joy, triumphant days of completion, and moments of serendipitous inspiration. Take, for instance, Alice Walker's inspiration for writing

The Color Purple: "I was hiking through the woods with my sister, Ruth, talking about a lover's triangle which we both knew. She said: '[A]nd you know, one day The Wife asked The Other Woman for a pair of her drawers.' Instantly the missing piece of the story I was mentally writing—about two women who felt married to the same man—fell into place. And for months, through illnesses, divorce, several moves, travel abroad, all kinds of heartaches and revelations—I carried my sister's comment delicately balanced in the center of the novel's construction I was building in my head."

In choosing my selections, I did not follow the democratic model of some anthologies—one or two specific representatives of various perspectives. Several writers included here have published essays addressing their own positions on matters related to gender, sexuality, or a particular aesthetic stance. Some of the essays have been included in their own books. However, the novelists are a diverse group. They hail from big cities and small towns, from the East and West Coasts, the South, the North, and the Midwest. They travel and live all over the world. Some of these places become the settings for their short stories and novels: rural towns in the South, New York City, Chicago, Los Angeles, Paris, London, Monrovia, Timbuktu. Several, including Richard Wright, James Baldwin, and Chester Himes, become expatriates.

The writers selected depict a variety of human types. They capture an astonishing range of emotional states, personal achievements, and predicaments: the ecstatic joys of courtship, a variety of sexual encounters, various marriages and infidelities. Nor do they shy away from raising difficult questions and depicting awkward and ugly truths: questions concerning the existence, gender, and presumed benevolence of God; depictions of child abuse, incest, rape, murder, incarceration, and electrocution.

I chose novelists who write in strikingly different styles. Their fictional styles range from naturalistic, to realistic, to epistolary, to magical realistic, to satiric. For example, among the living writers,

Ishmael Reed, Toni Morrison, and Charles Johnson have written about American slavery. In 1976, Ishmael Reed published *Flight to Canada*. Morrison and Johnson have each written two novels in which slavery is a central theme: Morrison has written *Beloved* (1987) and *A Mercy* (2008); Johnson has published *The Oxherding Tale* (1974) and *Middle Passage* (1990). A brief stylistic comparison of *Beloved*, *Middle Passage*, and *Flight to Canada* will be useful here: In *Beloved*, Morrison uses "magic realism," a straightforward blending of real situations and fantastic elements as organic aspects of the unfolding story. Beloved's ghost haunts the house at 124 Bluestone Road, where much of the novel takes place. Then one day Beloved unexpectedly appears on the front porch—fully embodied and conscious. Unlike the apparitional Banquo seen by Shakespeare's Macbeth, Beloved walks, talks, and indeed seduces. Morrison narrates the complex story from the third-person point of view—occasionally shifting perspectives to focus on the thinking of individual characters.

Rutherford Calhoun, the protagonist in Johnson's *Middle Passage*, tells his story in the first person. He keeps a journal. Readers are made privy to his encounters with various characters, including the love of his life, Isadora. Much of the story takes place on an ill-fated slave-trading ship, the *Republic*. The captive slaves from the Allmuseri tribe are brought on board along with a giant box housing a god of some sort. Johnson, a philosopher by training, uses this development as an aesthetic opportunity to allow Rutherford to engage in philosophical reflection and allegorical musings as he tries to fathom the meaning of Allmuseri values and cultural beliefs in relation to his own.

Reed's *Flight to Canada* is a satire of slavery and nineteenth-century America. Reed exploits the literary conventions of the slave narrative. The flight referred to in his title is not that of a runaway slave involved in the Underground Railroad. Ravens Quickskill simply boards a "jumbo jet" (in the 1860s) and flies to Canada. Reed includes other anachronisms such as television. He creates situations in which his invented characters encounter both nineteenth-century figures like Abraham Lincoln and living twentieth-century figures like Barbara Walters. Reed's allusive and dense style (including obscure references to abolitionists, etc.) allows him to poke fun at the ironies, contradictions, and moral absurdities of slavery.

Consider two other cases of stylistic difference—Ernest Gaines and James Baldwin. Both novelists' aesthetic choices are heavily influenced by their respective preoccupations with place. Gaines' novels usually deal with the mores and attitudes of racially segregated, rural, and Catholic parishes in Louisiana. When, for example, Gaines writes a scene set in a rural, segregated parish, he highlights the symbolic meaning of characters' actions in a deceptively straightforward manner. In *A Lesson Before Dying* (1993), Gaines uses a simple matter—asking a former employer for a favor—to deepen the layers of complexity in his plot and reveal the nature of interracial, class, and gender dynamics at work. How does a former Negro maid, "the help" for many years in a big house on a plantation, go about asking her former employers to assist her in helping her jailed nephew? Why does the maid decide to approach the wife although she knows the husband will make the final decision? Once she arrives at the house that she knows so well, where will the conversation take place? Will she be offered a glass of water or invited to sit?

Baldwin is preoccupied with place in another sense. New York and Paris invariably become anthropomorphic characters in his novels. He dramatizes clashes of cultures, triumphs, and defeats based on conflicting cultural assumptions. Like his idol Henry James, he frequently places relatively "innocent" Americans on foreign soil and allows the drama inspired by various encounters to unfold. In novels like *Giovanni's Room* (1956) and *Another Country* (1962), he uses big cities as places that highlight the bewildering fates of his characters—often gay or bisexual. His American characters in particular (both white and African American) discover that in

Europe's big cities people exist far beyond the confines of the American imagination.

Individual selections address different subjects—even when included in the same section of the book. For example, I include essays about two of Ernest Gaines' novels—*The Autobiography of Miss Jane Pittman* (1971) and *A Lesson Before Dying* (1993). The novels were published twenty-two years apart—the first about a black woman who lives to be one hundred years old and is a nonstop talker; the second about a young black man—surly, silent, and jailed, counting the days until he will sit in an electric chair.

I have also included two essays by James Baldwin, Langston Hughes, and John Wideman. The anthology's first section, "On Becoming African American Novelists," begins with "Why I Stopped Hating Shakespeare," one of Baldwin's rediscovered essays, about his "quarrel with the English language."[7] Baldwin eventually recognizes that African Americans had already created "a new idiom in an overwhelmingly hostile place." African American spirituals, the blues, and jazz become his exemplary aesthetic models. Baldwin discusses his early reading in the section included from *The Devil Finds Work*. The excerpt from Hughes' *The Big Sea* shows how supportive friends and patrons assisted him while writing his first novel. The second selection is "The Negro Artist and the Racial Mountain," his literary manifesto written during the Harlem Renaissance, to which subsequent writers and critics have often responded. The articles by Wideman are markedly different in content and form. Wideman's preface is the one piece that critically discusses rap music as a source and sound for a new cultural aesthetic. The excerpt from his memoir *Brothers and Keepers* (1984) allows us to see how an accomplished novelist wrestles with how to represent his incarcerated brother's own story without becoming a presumptuous and competitive intruder in the narrative.

The scope of this anthology was shaped by its format and other circumstances. I decided not to include interviews or articles about the writers, however compelling, written by others. Furthermore, while some novelists have been interviewed, they haven't to date written essays about how they write their novels. Other exemplary essays were not made available. Even among some of the stellar novelists included here, I could have chosen different selections. For example, Richard Wright has written an essay, "Blueprint for Negro Literature," in which he discusses some of the topics covered here. But I chose excerpts from *Black Boy* and "How Bigger Was Born." In *Black Boy*, we see the young, impoverished Wright reading day and night, desperately trying to keep himself "alive through transfusions from books." In "How Bigger Was Born," he vividly recalls the hard work he did as well as the creative joy he experienced while writing *Native Son* (1940). In some cases, the writing itself was the tie-breaker. Any editor would be hard-pressed to find a short article by Toni Morrison that surpasses the intellectual profundity, let alone the magisterial eloquence, of her Nobel Lecture.

Arrangement of Content

I have divided the book into three sections: part 1, "On Becoming African American Novelists"; part 2, "On Aesthetics, Craft, and Publication"; and part 3, "On Writing Major Novels." In part 1, the writers place their own literary lives in the spotlight. Several recount in compelling detail how and why they started writing fiction. The mixture of excerpts and complete essays allows readers to focus on specific and general matters. For example, several novelists discuss their early reading. Others address larger cultural and existential topics. While some writers focus on the beginning of their literary careers, others look back over several decades.

In part 2, the essays largely concern recurrent questions about aesthetic and practical matters. What are appropriate subjects for African American novelists? Are African American novelists inevitably forced to write for one audience or two—one black, the other white? What will publishers accept and reject (then and now) and why? Two essays are exclusively devoted to the craft of fiction.

In part 3, six case studies of novelists working on individual novels are included. In the specific cases of Richard Wright's *Native Son* (1940) and Ralph Ellison's *Invisible Man* (1952), I selected the concluding sections of their essays/introductions, in which the novelists directly address the actual writing and creative processes involved in producing their novels. I conclude the anthology with Toni Morrison's Nobel Lecture.

PART ONE

On Becoming African American Novelists

James Baldwin
(1924–1987)

WHEN *TIME* MAGAZINE put James Baldwin's dark, brooding face on its cover in 1963, he had already published three novels—*Go Tell It on the Mountain* (1953), *Giovanni's Room* (1956), and the controversial best seller *Another Country* (1962). However, it was his best-selling essay *The Fire Next Time* (1963) that landed him on the magazine's cover. Baldwin wrote the essay on the occasion of the one hundredth anniversary of the Emancipation Proclamation. The same year, Dr. Martin Luther King, Jr., delivered his famous "I Have a Dream" speech at the March on Washington for Jobs and Freedom, which Baldwin attended.

James Arthur Baldwin was born in New York City and grew up in Harlem. He graduated from DeWitt Clinton High School. Although he did not attend college, he started writing seriously while still in high school. In 1948, he published "The Harlem Ghetto," his first essay, in *Commentary* magazine. He returns to similar themes in *The Fire Next Time*, his prophetic analysis of the pent-up resentment and rage that many African Americans felt in the face of ongoing racial discrimination. Their collective sense of oppression, among other things, led to riots in major cities, including Los Angeles and Detroit. In earlier essay collections—*Notes of a Native Son* (1955) and *Nobody Knows My Name* (1961)—Baldwin speaks eloquently about the plight of African Americans.[8]

Some critics consider Baldwin one of the best essayists of the twentieth century. However, Baldwin was also dedicated to writing novels. He wrote with a framed portrait of Henry James, his idol, near his desk. After the commercial success and critical acclaim of *The Fire Next Time*, Baldwin published a collection of short stories,

Going to Meet the Man (1965), and three more novels—*Tell Me How Long the Train's Been Gone* (1968), *If Beale Street Could Talk* (1974), and *Just Above My Head* (1979). In his stories and novels, central themes about the roles and obligations of artists and writers reassert themselves—whether involving characters like Peter, a young actor, in "Previous Condition," his first published short story; an actual writer, like Leo Proudhammer, in *Tell Me How Long the Train's Been Gone*; or Arthur Montana, the famous singer, in his final novel, *Just Above My Head*.

Baldwin published twenty books—including a screenplay, a children's book, and one short volume of poems—during his lifetime. Most of his books were written while he lived abroad. In 1948, after Baldwin left New York City for Paris, he effectively became an expatriate. He lived in Paris, Switzerland, Istanbul, and eventually purchased a home in St. Paul de Vence, France. He died there in 1987. "Why I Stopped Hating Shakespeare" (1964) is taken from *The Cross of Redemption: Uncollected Writings* (2010), edited and with an introduction by Randall Kenan. In this essay, Baldwin reflects on the significance of Shakespeare in his writing career.

Why I Stopped Hating Shakespeare (1964)

Every writer in the English language, I should imagine, has at some point hated Shakespeare, has turned away from that monstrous achievement with a kind of sick envy. In my most anti-English days I condemned him as a chauvinist ("this England" indeed!) and because I felt it so bitterly anomalous that a black man should be forced to deal with the English language at all—should be forced to assault the English language in order to be able to speak—I condemned him as one of the authors and architects of my oppression.

Again, in the way that some Jews bitterly and mistakenly resent Shylock, I was dubious about Othello (what did he see in Desdemona?) and bitter about Caliban. His great vast gallery of people, whose reality was as contradictory as it was unanswerable, unspeakably oppressed me. I was resenting, of course, the assault on my simplicity; and, in another way, I was a victim of that loveless education which causes so many schoolboys to detest Shakespeare. But I feared him, too, feared him because, in his hands, the English language became the mightiest of instruments. No one would ever write that way again. No one would ever be able to match, much less surpass, him.

Well, I was young and missed the point entirely, was unable to go behind the words and, as it were, the diction, to what the poet was saying. I still remember my shock when I finally *heard* these lines from the murder scene in *Julius Caesar*. The assassins are washing their hands in Caesar's blood. Cassius says:

> Stop then, and wash.—How many ages hence
> Shall this our lofty scene be acted over,
> In states unborn and accents yet unknown!

What I suddenly heard, for the first time, was manifold. It was the voice of lonely, dedicated, deluded Cassius, whose life had never been real for me before—I suddenly seemed to know what this moment meant to him. But beneath and beyond that voice I also heard a note yet more rigorous and impersonal—and contemporary: that "lofty scene," in all its blood and necessary folly, its blind and necessary pain, was thrown into a perspective which has never left my mind. Just so, indeed, is the heedless State overthrown by men, who, in order to overthrow it, have had to achieve a desperate single-mindedness. And this single-mindedness, which we think of (why?) as ennobling, also operates, and much more surely, to distort and diminish a man—to distort and diminish us all, even, or perhaps especially, those whose needs and whose energy made the overthrow of the State inevitable, necessary, and just.

And the terrible thing about this play, for me—it is not necessarily my favorite play, whatever that means, but it *is* the play which I first, so to speak, discovered—is the tension it relentlessly sustains between individual ambition, self-conscious, deluded, idealistic, or corrupt, and the blind, mindless passion which drives the individual no less than it drives the mob. "I am Cinna the poet, I am Cinna the poet . . . I am not Cinna the conspirator"—that cry rings in my ears. And the mob's response: "Tear him for his bad verses!" And yet—though one howled with Cinna and felt his terrible rise, at the hands of his countrymen, to death, it was impossible to hate the mob. Or, worse than impossible, useless; for here we were, at once howling and being torn to pieces, the only receptacles of evil and the only receptacles of nobility to be found in all the universe. But the play does not even suggest that we have the perception to know evil from good or that such a distinction can ever be clear: "The evil that men do lives after them; The good is oft interred with their bones . . ."

Once one has begun to suspect this much about the world—once one has begun to suspect, that is, that one is not, and never will be, innocent, for the reason that no one is—some of the self-protective veils between oneself and reality begin to fall away. It is probably of some significance, though we cannot pursue it here, that my first real apprehension of Shakespeare came when I was living in France, and thinking and speaking in French. The necessity of mastering a foreign language forced me into a new relationship to my own. (It was also in France, therefore, that I began to read the Bible again.)

My quarrel with the English language has been that the language reflected none of my experience. But now I began to see the matter in quite another way. If the language was not my own, it might be the fault of the language; but it might also be my fault. Perhaps the language was not my own because I had never attempted to use it, had only learned to imitate it. If this were so, then it might be made to bear the burden of my experience if I could find the stamina to challenge it, and me, to such a test.

In support of this possibility, I had two mighty witnesses: my black ancestors, who evolved the sorrow songs, the blues, and jazz, and created an entirely new idiom in an overwhelmingly hostile place; and Shakespeare, who was the last bawdy writer in the English language. What I began to see—especially since, as I say, as I was living and speaking in French—is that it is experience which shapes a language; and it is language which controls an experience. The structure of the French language told me something of the French experience, and also something of the French expectations—which were certainly not the American expectations, since the French daily and hourly said things which the Americans could not say at all. (Not even in French.) Similarly, the language with which I had grown up had certainly not been the King's English. An immense experience had forged this language; it had been (and remains) one of the tools of a people's survival, and it revealed expectations which no white American could easily entertain. The authority of this language was in its candor, its irony, its density, and its beat: this was the authority of the language which produced me, and it was also the authority of Shakespeare.

Again, I was listening very hard to jazz and hoping, one day, to translate it into language, and Shakespeare's bawdiness became very important to me, since bawdiness was one of the elements of jazz and revealed a tremendous, loving, and realistic respect for the body, and that ineffable force which the body contains, which Americans have mostly lost, which I had experienced only among Negroes, and of which I had been taught to be ashamed.

My relationship, then, to the language of Shakespeare revealed itself as nothing less than my relationship to myself and my past. Under this light, this revelation, both myself and my past began slowly to open, perhaps the way a flower opens at morning, but more probably the way an atrophied muscle begins to function, or frozen fingers to thaw.

The greatest poet in the English language found his poetry where poetry is found: in the lives of the people. He could have done this only through love—by knowing, which is not the same thing as understanding, that whatever was happening to anyone was happening to him. It is said that his time was easier than ours, but I doubt it—no time can be easy if one is living through it. I think it is simply that he walked his streets and saw them, and tried not to lie about what he saw: his public streets and his private streets, which are always so mysteriously and inexorably connected; but he trusted that connection. And, though I, and many of us, have bitterly bewailed (and will again) the lot of an American writer—to be part of a people who have ears to hear and hear not, who have eyes to see and see not—I am sure that Shakespeare did the same. Only, he saw, as I think we must, that the people who produce the poet are not responsible to him: he is responsible to them.

That is why he is called a poet. And his responsibility, which is also his joy and his strength and his life, is to defeat all labels and complicate all battles by insisting on the human riddle, to bear witness, as long as breath is in him, to that mighty, unnameable, transfiguring force which lives in the soul of man, and to aspire to do his work so well that when the breath has left him, the people—*all people!*—who search in the rubble for a sign or a witness will be able to find him there.

Arna Bontemps
(1902–1973)

ARNA WENDELL BONTEMPS grew up in a strict Seventh Day Adventist household in Los Angeles, California. He attended Pacific Union College and graduated in 1923. He became a prolific writer and editor. He wrote poetry, plays, and essays and collaborated with Langston Hughes, his close friend, on several books for children. He edited several anthologies, such as *The Poetry of the Negro, 1746–1949* (1949). He earned a degree in library science from the University of Chicago in 1943 and served as Fisk University's head librarian for over a decade. Bontemps was one of the writers living and working in Harlem during the 1920s. He maintains that the harsh reality of the stock market crash in 1929 effectively brought the Harlem Renaissance to an end.

Bontemps' literary dedication and professionalism is thoroughly documented in over forty years of his correspondence with Langston Hughes. Their letters include an ongoing discussion of their individual books and those they co-authored.[9] They knew and discussed most prominent African Americans—including entertainers, politicians, and athletes. They made literary and personal assessments of other writers, including Robert Lowell, T. S. Eliot, and Ezra Pound. They wrote candidly to each other about African American writers as they started out and broke into print. Bontemps was a perceptive literary critic. The comments he made to Hughes about Ralph Ellison, especially the novelist's slow tempo of writing, turned out to be prophetic. In 1950, two years before the publication of *Invisible Man*, Bontemps wrote Hughes, "The difference between your situation and Ralph's is that Ralph is evidently making this one novel his life's work. That's one way to follow a literary career, but it requires a special kind of mentality. When one is producing such a book, the idea is not to finish it until one is tired of living. You, on the other hand, have formed the habit of finishing projects and that is what keeps you going."

Bontemps published three novels: *God Sends Sunday* (1931), *Black Thunder* (1936), and *Drums at Dusk* (1939). *The Old South: A Summer Tragedy and Other Stories of the Thirties* (1973) was published posthumously. Bontemps' introduction to *Black Thunder* included here captures the writer's principled dedication and desperate gamble to complete his second novel as the world seems to conspire against him, preventing him from feeding his growing family and cultivating his literary talent.

Introduction to *Black Thunder* (1968)

Time is not a river. Time is a pendulum. The thought occurred to me first in Watts in 1934. After three horrifying years of preparation in a throbbing region of the deep south, I had settled there to write my second novel, away from it all.

At the age of thirty, or thereabouts, I had lived long enough to become aware of intricate patterns of recurrence, in my own experience and in the history I had been exploring with almost frightening attention. I suspect I was preoccupied with those patterns when, early in *Black Thunder*, I tried to make something of the old majordomo's mounting the dark steps of the Sheppard mansion near Richmond to wind the clock.

The element of time was crucial to Gabriel's attempt, in historical fact as in *Black Thunder*, and the hero of that action knew well the absolute necessity of a favorable conjunction. When this did not occur, he realized that the outcome was no longer in his own hands. Perhaps it was in the stars, he reasoned.

If time is the pendulum I imagined, the snuffing of Martin Luther King, Jr.'s career may yet appear as a kind of repetition of Gabriel's

shattered dream during the election year of 1800. At least the oc-
currence of the former as this is written serves to recall for me the
tumult in my own thoughts when I began to read extensively about
slave insurrections and to see in them a possible metaphor of tur-
bulence to come.

Not having space for my typewriter, I wrote the book in longhand
on the top of a folded-down sewing machine in the extra bedroom
of my parents' house at 10310 Wiegand Avenue where my wife and
I and our children (three at that time) were temporarily and uncom-
fortably quartered. A Japanese truck farmer's asparagus field was
just outside our back door. From a window on the front, above the
sewing machine, I could look across 103rd Street at the buildings
and grounds of Jordan High School, a name I did not hear again
until I came across it in some of the news accounts reporting the
holocaust that swept Watts a quarter of a century later. In the vacant
lot across from us on Wiegand a friendly Mexican neighbor grazed
his milk goat. We could smell eucalyptus trees when my writing
window was open and when we walked outside, and nearly always
the air was like transparent gold in those days. I could have loved
the place under different circumstances, but as matters stood there
was no way to disguise the fact that our luck had run out.

My father and stepmother were bearing up reasonably well,
perhaps, under the strain our presence imposed on them, but only
a miracle could have healed one's own hurt pride, one's sense of
shame and failure at an early age. Meanwhile, it takes time to write
a novel, even one that has been painstakingly researched, and I do
not blame my father for his occasional impatience. I had flagellated
myself so thoroughly, I was numb to such criticism, when he spoke
in my presence, and not very tactfully, about young people with
bright prospects who make shipwrecks of their lives.

What he had in mind, mainly, I am sure, were events which had
brought me home at such an awkward time and with such uncertain
plans, but somehow I suspected more. At the age at which I made
my commitment to writing, he had been blowing a trombone in a

Louisiana marching band under the direction of Claiborne Williams. But he had come to regard such a career as a deadend occupation unworthy of a young family man, married to a schoolteacher, and he renounced it for something more solid: bricklaying. Years later when the building trades themselves began to fade as far as black workers were concerned, under pressure of the new labor unions, he had made another hard decision and ended his working years in the ministry.

He was reproaching me for being less resourceful, by his lights, and I was too involved in my novel to even reply. The work I had undertaken, the new country into which I had ventured when I began to explore Negro history, had rendered me immune for the moment, even to implied insults.

Had the frustrations dormant in Watts at that date suddenly exploded in flame and anger, as they were eventually to do, I don't think they would have shaken my concentration; but I have a feeling that more readers might then have been in a mood to hear a tale of volcanic rumblings among angry blacks—and the end of patience. At the time, however, I began to suspect that it was fruitless for a Negro in the United States to address serious writing to my generation, and I began to consider the alternative of trying to reach young readers not yet hardened or grown insensitive to man's inhumanity to man, as it is called.

For this, as for so much else that has by turn intrigued or troubled me in subsequent years, my three-year sojourn in northern Alabama had been a kind of crude conditioning. Within weeks after the publication of my first book, as it happened, I had been caught up in a quaint and poignant disorder that failed to attract wide attention. It was one of the side effects of the crash that brought on the Depression, and it brought instant havoc to the Harlem Renaissance of the twenties. I was one of the hopeful young people displaced, so to speak. The jobs we had counted on to keep us alive and writing in New York vanished, as some observed, quicker than a cat could wink. Not knowing where else to turn, I wandered into northern Alabama, on the promise of employment as a teacher, and hopefully to wait out the bad times, but at least to get my bearings. I did not stay long enough to see any improvement in the times, but a few matters, which now seem important, did tend to become clearer as I waited.

Northern Alabama had a primitive beauty when I saw it first. I remember writing something in which I called the countryside a green Eden, but I awakened to find it dangerously infested. Two stories dominated the news as well as the daydreams of the people I met. One had to do with the demonstrations by Mahatma Gandhi and his followers in India; the other, the trials of the Scottsboro boys then in progress in Decatur, Alabama, about thirty miles from where we were living. Both seemed to foreshadow frightening consequences, and everywhere I turned someone demanded my opinions, since I was recently arrived and expected to be knowledgeable. Eventually their questions upset me as much as the news stories. We had fled here to escape our fears in the city, but the terrors we encountered here were even more upsetting than the ones we had left behind.

I was, frankly, running scared when an opportunity came for me to visit Fisk University in Nashville, Tennessee, about a hundred miles away, get a brief release from tension, perhaps, and call on three old friends from the untroubled years of the Harlem Renaissance: James Weldon Johnson, Charles S. Johnson, and Arthur Schomburg. All, in a sense, could have been considered as refugees living in exile, and the three, privately could have been dreaming of planting an oasis at Fisk where, surrounded by bleak hostility in the area, the region, and the nation, if not indeed the world, they might not only stay alive but, conceivably, keep alive a flicker of the impulse they had detected and helped to encourage in the black awakening in Renaissance Harlem.

Each of them could and did recite by heart Countée Cullen's lines dedicated to Charles S. Johnson in an earlier year:

We shall not always plant while others reap
The golden increment of bursting fruit,
Not always countenance, abject and mute,
That lesser men should hold their brothers cheap;
Not everlastingly while others sleep
Shall we beguile their limbs with mellow flute,
Not always bend to some more subtle brute;
We were not made eternally to weep.

The night whose sable breast relieves the stark,
White stars is no less lovely being dark,
And there are buds that cannot bloom at all
In light, but crumple, piteous, and fall;
So in the dark we hide the heart that bleeds,
And wait, and tend our agonizing seeds.

Separately and with others we made my visit a time for declaring and reasserting sentiments we had stored in our memories for safekeeping against the blast that had already dispersed their young protégés and my friends and the disasters looming ahead.

Discovering in the Fisk Library a larger collection of slave narratives than I knew existed, I began to read almost frantically. In the gloom of the darkening Depression settling all around us, I began to ponder the stricken slave's will to freedom. Three historic efforts at self-emancipation caught my attention and promptly shattered peace of mind. I knew instantly that one of them would be the subject of my next novel. First, however, I would have to make a choice, and this involved research. Each had elements the others did not have, or at least not to the same degree, and except for the desperate need of freedom they had in common, each was attempted under different conditions and led by unlike personalities.

Denmark Vesey's effort I dismissed first. It was too elaborately planned for its own good. His plot was betrayed, his conspiracy crushed too soon, but it would be a mistake to say nothing came of it in Vesey's own time. The shudder it put into the hearts and minds of slaveholders was never quieted. *Nat Turner's Confession*, which I read in the Fisk Library at a table across from Schomburg's desk, bothered me on two counts. I felt uneasy about the amanuensis to whom his account was related and the conditions under which he confessed. Then there was the business of Nat's "visions" and "dreams."

Gabriel's attempt seemed to reflect more accurately for me what I felt then and feel now might have motivated slaves capable of such boldness and inspired daring. The longer I pondered, the more convinced I became. Gabriel had not opened his mind too fully and hence had not been betrayed as had Vesey. He had by his own dignity and by the esteem in which he was held inspired and maintained loyalty. He had not depended on trance-like mumbo jumbo. Freedom was a less complicated affair in his case. It was, it seemed to me, a more unmistakable equivalent of the yearning I felt and which I imagined to be general. Finally, there was the plan itself, a strategy which some contemporaries, prospective victims, felt could scarcely have failed had not the weather miraculously intervened in their behalf. Gabriel attributed his reversal, ultimately, to the stars in their courses, the only factor that had been omitted in his calculations. He had not been possessed, not even overly optimistic.

Back in Alabama, I began to sense quaint hostilities. Borrowing library books by mail, as I sometimes did, was unusual enough to attract attention. Wasn't there a whole room of books in the school where I worked—perhaps as many as a thousand? How many books could a man read in one lifetime anyway? We laughed together at the questions, but I realized they were not satisfied with my joking answers. How could I tell them about Gabriel's adventure in such an atmosphere?

Friends from the Harlem years learned from our mutual friends at Fisk that we were in the vicinity and began dropping in to say howdy en route to Decatur or Montgomery or Birmingham. There was an excitement in the state similar to that which recurred twenty-five years later when black folk began confronting hardened oppression by offering to put their bodies in escrow, if that was required. In 1931, however, the effort was centered around forlorn attempts to save the lives of nine black boys who had been convicted, in a travesty of justice, of ravishing two white girls in the empty boxcars in which all were hoboing.

The boyish poet Langston Hughes was one of those who came to protest, to interview the teen-age victims in their prison cells, and to write prose and poetry aimed at calling the world's attention to the enormity about to be perpetrated. It was natural that he should stop by to visit us. He and I had recently collaborated, mainly by mail, on the writing of a children's story, *Popo and Fifina: Children of Haiti*. He had the story and I had the children, so my publisher thought it might work. Perhaps it would not be too much to say they were justified. The story lasted a long time and was translated into a number of languages. The friendship between the two authors also lasted and yielded other collaborations over the next thirty-five years. But the association was anathema to the institution which had, with some admitted reluctance, given me employment.

As my year ended, I was given an ultimatum. I would have to make a clean break with the unrest in the world as represented by Gandhi's efforts abroad and the Scottsboro protests here at home. Since I had no connection or involvement with either, other than the fact that I had known some of the people who were shouting their outrage, I was not sure how a break could be made. The head of the school had a plan, however. I could do it, he demanded publicly, by burning most of the books in my small library, a number of which were trash in his estimation anyway, the rest, race-conscious and provocative. *Harlem Shadows*, *The Blacker the Berry*, *My Bondage and Freedom*, *Black Majesty*, *The Souls of Black Folk*, and *The Autobiography of an Ex-Coloured Man* were a few of those indicated.

I was too horrified to speak, but I swallowed my indignation. My wife was expecting another child, and the options before us had been reduced to none. At the end of the following term we drove to California, sold our car, and settled down in the small room in

Watts in the hope that what we had received for the car would buy food till I could write my book. By the next spring *Black Thunder* was finished, and the advance against royalties was enough to pay our way to Chicago.

Black Thunder, when published later that year, earned no more than its advance. As discouraging as this was, I was not permitted to think of it as a total loss. The reviews were more than kind. John T. Frederick, director of the Illinois Writers Project, read the book and decided to add me to his staff. He also commended it warmly in his anthology, *Out of the Midwest*, and in his CBS broadcasts. Robert Morss Lovett mentioned it in his class at the University of Chicago. But the theme of self-assertion by black men whose endurance was strained to the breaking point was not one that readers of fiction were prepared to contemplate at the time. Now that *Black Thunder* is published again, after more than thirty years, I cannot help wondering if its story will be better understood by Americans, both black and white. I am, however, convinced that time is not a river.

Langston Hughes
(1902–1967)

LANGSTON HUGHES IS appropriately best known as a poet. Some of his poems are often recited—"The Negro Speaks of Rivers" and "Harlem" come readily to mind. Hughes is one of the better-known writers of the Harlem Renaissance. But as Arnold Rampersad, Hughes' biographer, has documented, his literary career, unlike that of several of his peers, did not end with the Harlem Renaissance. Hughes continued writing at a steady pace until his death.[10]

Born in Joplin, Missouri, Hughes attended high school in Cleveland, Ohio. During his high school years, he also spent a year in Mexico with his father. Hughes attended Columbia University for one year. Thereafter, he traveled around the world. He documented his travels in his autobiography—*The Big Sea* (1940). He returned to college at Lincoln University in Pennsylvania and graduated in 1929.

Although poetry is a genre in which he clearly excelled, he also wrote short stories, plays, autobiographies, essays, children's books, and novels. As a writer of fiction, Hughes is widely known for his stories, many of which are humorous tales involving a recurrent character, Jesse B. Simple. Simple tells his stories with a combination of self-effacing humor and sharp social analysis. Hughes' novel *Not Without Laughter* (1930) depicts life for an African American family in Kansas at the beginning of the twentieth century. His essay "The Negro Artist and the Racial Mountain" (1926) anticipates issues, such as appropriate subjects and sources for African American writers, that have been revisited by many novelists, poets, and literary critics. The selection from *The Big Sea* that follows documents his start as a writer.

From *The Big Sea* (1940)

I was the Class Poet. It happened like this. They had elected all the class officers, but there was no one in our class who looked like a poet, or had ever written a poem. There were two Negro children in the class, myself and a girl. In America most white people think, of course, that *all* Negroes can sing and dance, and have a sense of rhythm. So my classmates, knowing that a poem had to have rhythm, elected me unanimously—thinking, no doubt, that I had some, being a Negro.

The day I was elected, I went home and wondered what I should write. Since we had eight teachers in our school, I thought there should be one verse for each teacher, with an especially good one for my favorite teacher, Miss Ethel Welsh. And since the teachers were to have eight verses, I felt the class should have eight, too. So my first poem was about the longest poem I ever wrote—sixteen verses, which were later cut down. In the first half of the poem, I said that our school had the finest teachers there ever were. And in the latter half, I said our class was the greatest class ever graduated. So at graduation, when I read the poem, naturally everybody applauded loudly.

That was the way I began to write poetry.

It had never occurred to me to be a poet before, or indeed a writer of any kind. But my mother had often read papers at the Inter-State Literary Society, founded by my grandfather in Kansas. And occasionally she wrote original poems, too, that she gave at the Inter-State. But more often, she recited long recitations like "Lasca" and "The Mother of the Gracchi," in costume. As Lasca she dressed as a cowgirl. And as Cornelia, the mother of the Gracchi, she wore a sheet like a Roman matron.

On one such occasion, she had me and another little boy dressed in half-sheets as her sons—jewels, about to be torn away from her by a cruel Spartan fate. My mother was the star of the program and the church in Lawrence was crowded. The audience hung on her words; but I did not like the poem at all, so in the very middle of it I began to roll my eyes from side to side, round and round in my head, as though in great distress. The audience tittered. My mother intensified her efforts, I, my mock agony. Wilder and wilder I mugged, as the poem mounted, batted and rolled my eyes, until the entire assemblage burst into uncontrollable laughter.

My mother, poor soul, couldn't imagine what was wrong. More fervently than ever, she poured forth her lines, grasped us to her breast, and begged heaven for mercy. But the audience by then couldn't stop giggling, and with the applause at the end, she was greeted by a mighty roar of laughter. When the program was over and my mother found out what had happened, I got the worst whipping I ever had in my life. Then and there I learned to respect other people's art.

Nevertheless, the following spring, at a Children's Day program at my aunt's church, I, deliberately and with malice aforethought, forgot a poem I knew very well, having been forced against my will to learn it. I mounted the platform, said a few lines, and then stood there—much to the embarrassment of my mother, who had come all the way from Kansas City to hear me recite. My aunt tried to prompt me, but I pretended I couldn't hear a word. Finally I came down to my seat in dead silence—and I never had to recite a poem in church again.

The only poems I liked as a child were Paul Laurence Dunbar's. And *Hiawatha*. But I liked any kind of stories. I read all of my mother's novels from the library: *The Rosary*, *The Mistress of Shenstone*, *Freckles*, Edna Ferber, all of Harold Bell Wright, and all of Zane Grey. I thought *Riders of the Purple Sage* a wonderful book and still think so, as I remember it.

In Topeka, as a small child, my mother took me with her to the little vine-covered library on the grounds of the Capitol. There I first fell in love with librarians, and I have been in love with them ever since—those very nice women who help you find wonderful books!

The silence inside the library, the big chairs, and long tables, and the fact that the library was always there and didn't seem to have a mortgage on it, or any sort of insecurity about it—all of that made me love it. And right then, even before I was six, books began to happen to me, so that after a while, there came a time when I believed in books more than in people—which, of course, was wrong. That was why, when I went to Africa, I threw all the books into the sea....

Patron and Friend

While I was at Lincoln, I spent several pleasant weekends in the spring or fall with Joel and Amy Spingarn at their country place, Troutbeck, that had once been the old farm of John Burroughs, the naturalist, where his trout pool is still preserved. I met the Spingarn sons and daughters, who were also in college or prep school. And I saw the beautiful medieval virgin in wood that Mrs. Spingarn had brought from Europe. She had there, too, a tiny hand press, and later published a small volume of my poems, in a limited edition on hand-made paper, a collection of lyrics called *Dear Lovely Death*.

The Spingarns were charming, quiet people. Joel Spingarn told me much about the early days of the National Association for the Advancement of Colored People, in which he had a great interest as one of the founders and later as its President. He told me, too, about his long acquaintanceship with Dr. Du Bois and other Negro leaders. And his brother, Arthur, who has one of the largest collections of Negro books in America, often spoke of the work of the older Negro authors like Chesnutt, my fellow Clevelander, and of others at the beginning of our literary history, of whom, until then, I had never heard.

During my years at Lincoln, on one of my week-end visits to New York, a friend took me to call on a distinguished and quite elderly white lady who lived on Park Avenue in a large apartment, with attendants in livery at the door and a private elevator-landing. I found her instantly one of the most delightful women I had ever met, witty and charming, kind and sympathetic, very old and white-haired, but amazingly modern in her ideas, in her knowledge of books and the theater, of Harlem, and of everything then taking place in the world.

Her apartment was many floors above the street and there was a view of all New York spread out beneath it. Her rooms were not cluttered with furniture or objects of art, but every piece was rare and beautiful. When I left, after a delightful evening, she pressed something into my hand. "A gift for a young poet," she said. It was a fifty-dollar bill.

From Lincoln, I wrote her and thanked her for the gift. In reply, she asked me to dine with her and her family on my next trip to New York. At dinner we had duck and wild rice. And for dessert, ice cream on a large silver platter, surrounded by fresh strawberries. The strawberries were served with their green stems still on them, the tiny red fruit being very pretty around the great mound of ice cream on the silver platter.

Carefully, I removed the green stems and put them on the side of my plate. But when I had finished eating the berries and ice cream, I noticed that no one else had any stems left on the plates. Their ice cream and all was gone. I couldn't imagine what they had done with their stems. What did one do with strawberry stems on Park Avenue? Or were these a very special kind of strawberry stem that you could eat? Or had I committed some awful breach of etiquette by removing my strawberry stems by hand and putting them in plain view of everyone on the side of my plate? I didn't know. I was worried and puzzled.

As the Swedish maids warmed the finger bowls, my curiosity got the best of me and I asked my hostess what had everyone else done with the strawberry stems. She smiled and replied that no one else had taken any—since they were all allergic to strawberries!

In the living room after dinner, high above Park Avenue with the lights of Manhattan shining below us, my hostess asked me about my plans for the future, my hopes, my ambitions, and my dreams. I told her I wanted to write a novel. She told me she would make it possible for me to write that novel. And she did by covering the expenses of my summer, so that I need do no other work during vacation.

That was the summer when I wrote a draft of *Not Without Laughter*. Then I went for a short vacation at Provincetown, where I saw the Wharf Players performing a version of Donald Ogden Stewart's *Parody Outline of History*. I liked the wide sandy beaches of Cape Cod, but I did not like Provincetown very much, because it was hard for a Negro to find a place to sleep, and at night the mosquitoes were vicious.

During my senior year at Lincoln, I rewrote my novel. And at graduation I was given a generous monthly allowance by my patron, who had read both drafts of the book, had helped me with it, and found it good. Then began for me a strange and wonderful year of economic freedom, starting with a boat trip up the Saguenay River to see the northern lights. (The boat trip would have been pleasant had I not been the only Negro on board in the midst of a crowd of Middle-Westerners and Southerners. The steward refused to give me a sitting in the dining-saloon except after all the whites had eaten. So I got off the boat somewhere in the wilds of Canada and came back to Montreal by train. The company refunded my money.)

In the fall I spent a few weeks with Jasper Deeter at Hedgerow Theater, writing my first play, *Mulatto*. Then I settled in Westfield, New Jersey, near New York, where I made the final revisions of my novel.

Richard Wright
(1908–1960)

RICHARD WRIGHT WAS born in rural Mississippi and grew up in Jackson under the watchful eye of his strict and religious maternal grandmother. He had a rough, impoverished childhood. Although Wright did not attend college, he read voraciously throughout his life. He also started writing stories during his teenage years. In 1938, he published *Uncle Tom's Children*, his first collection of stories. When his novel *Native Son* (1940) was published, it became a best seller.[11] Since its publication, it has been praised and criticized by writers and literary critics—including, most notably, James Baldwin, Irving Howe, and Ralph Ellison.

Wright's *Black Boy* (1945), his eloquent memoir of his boyhood days in the South, where he learned the tough lessons of "living Jim Crow," was also a critical and commercial success. Wright describes the psychological and emotional toll of racial segregation for all Southerners—blacks and whites. The 1945 edition of *Black Boy* excluded the substantial concluding section of Wright's original manuscript. The section that was left out dealt with Wright's early years in Chicago, especially his involvement with the John Reed Club, a group of communist literati, and his early attempts at writing.

Like Baldwin after him, Wright moved to Paris and became an expatriate. His later novels written in Paris—including *The Outsider* (1953), *Savage Holiday* (1954), and *The Long Dream* (1958)—lack the sensational power of *Native Son*. He continued publishing fiction and essays until his untimely death in 1960.

Wright was a prolific writer, publishing fifteen books—including novels, short stories, and essays—during his lifetime. He directly influenced James Baldwin and Ralph Ellison. *Eight Men* (1962), a collection of his short stories, was published posthumously. In *Black Boy*, Wright tells the story of his discovery of the transformative power of words. And he recalls both the immediate context and actual composition of *Native Son* in "How 'Bigger' Was Born."

From *Black Boy* (1945)

That afternoon I addressed myself to forging a note. Now, what were the names of books written by H. L. Mencken? I did not know any of them. I finally wrote what I thought would be a foolproof note: *Dear Madam: Will you please let this nigger boy*—I used the word "nigger" to make the librarian feel that I could not possibly be the author of the note—*have some books by H. L. Mencken?* I forged the white man's name.

I entered the library as I had always done when on errands for whites, but I felt that I would somehow slip up and betray myself. I doffed my hat, stood a respectful distance from the desk, looked as unbookish as possible, and waited for the white patrons to be taken care of. When the desk was clear of people, I still waited. The white librarian looked at me.

"What do you want, boy?"

As though I did not possess the power of speech, I stepped forward and simply handed her the forged note, not parting my lips.

"What books by Mencken does he want?" she asked.

"I don't know, ma'am," I said, avoiding her eyes.

"Who gave you this card?"

"Mr. Falk," I said.

"Where is he?"

"He's at work, at the M——— Optical Company," I said. "I've been in here for him before."

"I remember," the woman said. "But he never wrote notes like this."

Oh, God, she's suspicious. Perhaps she would not let me have the books? If she had turned her back at that moment, I would have ducked out the door and never gone back. Then I thought of a bold idea.

"You can call him up, ma'am," I said, my heart pounding.

"You're not using these books, are you?" she asked pointedly.

"Oh, no, ma'am. I can't read it."

"I don't know what he wants by Mencken," she said under her breath.

I knew now that I had won; she was thinking of other things and the race question had gone out of her mind. She went to the shelves. Once or twice she looked over her shoulder at me, as though she was still doubtful. Finally she came forward with two books in her hand.

"I'm sending him two books," she said. "But tell Mr. Falk to come in next time, or send me the names of the books he wants. I don't know what he wants to read."

I said nothing. She stamped the card and handed me the books. Not daring to glance at them, I went out of the library, fearing that the woman would call me back for further questioning. A block away from the library I opened one of the books and read a title: *A Book of Prefaces*. I was nearing my nineteenth birthday and I did not know how to pronounce the word "preface." I thumbed the pages and saw strange words and strange names. I shook my head, disappointed. I looked at the other book; it was called *Prejudices*. I knew what that word meant; I had heard it all my life. And right off I was on guard against Mencken's books. Why would a man want to call a book *Prejudices*? The word was so stained with all my memories of racial hate that I could not conceive of anybody using it for a title. Perhaps I had made a mistake about Mencken? A man who had prejudices must be wrong.

When I showed the books to Mr. Falk, he looked at me and frowned.

"That librarian might telephone you," I warned him.

"That's all right," he said. "But when you're through reading those books, I want you to tell me what you get out of them."

That night in my rented room, while letting the hot water run over my can of pork and beans in the sink, I opened *A Book of Prefaces* and began to read. I was jarred and shocked by the style, the clear, clean, sweeping sentences. Why did he write like that? And how did one write like that? I pictured the man as a raging demon, slashing with his pen, consumed with hate, denouncing everything American, extolling everything European or German, laughing at the weaknesses of people, mocking God, authority. What was this? I stood up, trying to realize what reality lay behind the meaning of the words . . . Yes, this man was fighting, fighting with words. He was using words as a weapon, using them as one would use a club. Could words be weapons? Well, yes, for here they were. Then, maybe, perhaps, I could use them as a weapon? No. It frightened me. I read on and what amazed me was not what he said, but how on earth anybody had the courage to say it.

Occasionally I glanced up to reassure myself that I was alone in the room. Who were these men about whom Mencken was talking so passionately? Who was Anatole France? Joseph Conrad? Sinclair Lewis, Sherwood Anderson, Dostoevski, George Moore, Gustave Flaubert, Maupassant, Tolstoy, Frank Harris, Mark Twain, Thomas Hardy, Arnold Bennett, Stephen Crane, Zola, Norris, Gorky, Bergson, Ibsen, Balzac, Bernard Shaw, Dumas, Poe, Thomas Mann, O. Henry, Dreiser, H. G. Wells, Gogol, T. S. Eliot, Gide, Baudelaire, Edgar Lee Masters, Stendhal, Turgenev, Huneker, Nietzsche, and scores of others? Were these men real? Did they exist or had they existed? And how did one pronounce their names?

I ran across many words whose meanings I did not know, and I either looked them up in a dictionary or, before I had a chance to do that, encountered the word in a context that made its meaning clear. But what strange world was this? I concluded the book with the conviction that I had somehow overlooked something terribly important in life. I had once tried to write, had once reveled in feeling, had let my crude imagination roam, but the impulse to dream had been slowly beaten out of me by experience. Now it surged up again and I hungered for books, new ways of looking and seeing. It was not a matter of believing or disbelieving what I read, but of feeling something new, of being affected by something that made the look of the world different.

As dawn broke I ate my pork and beans, feeling dopey, sleepy. I went to work, but the mood of the book would not die; it lingered, coloring everything I saw, heard, did. I now felt that I knew what the white men were feeling. Merely because I had read a book that had spoken of how they lived and thought, I identified myself with that book. I felt vaguely guilty. Would I, filled with bookish notions, act in a manner that would make the whites dislike me?

I forged more notes and my trips to the library became frequent. Reading grew into a passion. My first serious novel was Sinclair Lewis's *Main Street*. It made me see my boss, Mr. Gerald, and identify him as an American type. I would smile when I saw him lugging his golf bags into the office. I had always felt a vast distance separating me from the boss, and now I felt closer to him, though still distant. I felt now that I knew him, that I could feel the very limits of his narrow life. And this had happened because I had read a novel about a mythical man called George F. Babbitt.

The plots and stories in the novels did not interest me so much as the point of view revealed. I gave myself over to each novel without reserve, without trying to criticize it; it was enough for me to see and feel something different. And for me, everything was something different. Reading was like a drug, a dope. The novels created moods in which I lived for days. But I could not conquer my sense of guilt, my feeling that the white men around me knew that I was changing, that I had begun to regard them differently.

Whenever I brought a book to the job, I wrapped it in newspaper—a habit that was to persist for years in other cities and under other circumstances. But some of the white men pried into my packages when I was absent and they questioned me.

"Boy, what are you reading those books for?"

"Oh, I don't know, sir."

"That's deep stuff you're reading, boy."

"I'm just killing time, sir."

"You'll addle your brains if you don't watch out."

I read Dreiser's *Jennie Gerhardt* and *Sister Carrie* and they revived in me a vivid sense of my mother's suffering; I was overwhelmed. I grew silent, wondering about the life around me. It would have been impossible for me to have told anyone what I derived from these novels, for it was nothing less than a sense of life itself. All my life had shaped me for the realism, the naturalism of the modern novel, and I could not read enough of them.

Steeped in new moods and ideas, I bought a ream of paper and tried to write; but nothing would come, or what did come was flat beyond telling. I discovered that more than desire and feeling were necessary to write and I dropped the idea. Yet I still wondered how it was possible to know people sufficiently to write about them? Could I ever learn about life and people? To me, with my vast ignorance, my Jim Crow station in life, it seemed a task impossible of achievement. I now knew what being a Negro meant. I could endure the hunger. I had learned to live with hate. But to feel that there were feelings denied me, that the very breath of life itself was beyond my reach, that more than anything else hurt, wounded me. I had a new hunger.

In buoying me up, reading also cast me down, made me see what was possible, what I had missed. My tension returned, new, terrible, bitter, surging, almost too great to be contained. I no longer *felt* that the world about me was hostile, killing; I *knew* it. A million times I asked myself what I could do to save myself, and there were no answers. I seemed forever condemned, ringed by walls. . . .

What, then, was there? I held my life in my mind, in my consciousness each day, feeling at times that I would stumble and drop it, spill it forever. My reading had created a vast sense of distance between me and the world in which I lived and tried to make a living, and that sense of distance was increasing each day. My days and nights were one long, quiet, continuously contained dream of terror, tension, and anxiety. I wondered how long I could bear it.

James Baldwin

IN *THE DEVIL FINDS WORK* (1976), Baldwin remembers his boyhood reading of three novels: Dickens' *A Tale of Two Cities*, Dostoevski's *Crime and Punishment*, and Stowe's *Uncle Tom's Cabin*. He read Stowe's novel over and over. Baldwin read practically every book in Harlem's local library. During his high school years, he migrated downtown to the main branch of New York City's public library at 5th Avenue and 42nd Street. Since he never attended college, that library, guarded at its entrance by statues of two giant lions, became his Princeton or Yale.

From *The Devil Finds Work* (1976)

I read *Uncle Tom's Cabin* over and over and over again—this is the first book I can remember having read—and then I read *A Tale of Two Cities*—over and over and over again. Bill Miller takes me to see *A Tale of Two Cities*, at the Lincoln, on 135th Street. I am twelve.

    I did not yet know that virtually every black community in America contains a movie house, or, sometimes, in those days, an actual theater, called the Lincoln, or the Booker T. Washington, nor did I know why; any more than I knew why The Cotton Club was called The Cotton Club. I knew about Lincoln only that he had freed the slaves (in the South, which made the venture remote from me) and then had been shot, dead, in a theater, by an actor; and a movie I was never to see, called *The Prisoner of Shark Island*, had something to do with the murder of Lincoln. How I knew this, I do not remember precisely. But I know that I read everything I could get my hands on, including movie advertisements, and *Uncle Tom's Cabin* had had a tremendous impact on me, and I certainly reacted to the brutal conjunction of the words, *prisoner*, and *shark*, and *island*. I may have feared becoming a prisoner, or feared that I was one already; had never seen a shark—I hoped: but I was certainly trapped on an island. And, in any case, the star of this film, Warner Baxter, later, but during the same era, made a film with the female star of *A Tale of Two Cities*, called *Slave Ship*: which I did not see, either. . . .

The 1936 Metro-Goldwyn-Mayer production of *A Tale of Two Cities* ends with this enormity sprawled across the screen:

I am the resurrection and the life, saith the Lord: he that believeth in me, though he were dead, yet shall he live: and he that believeth in me shall never die.

I had lived with this text all my life, which made encountering it on the screen of the Lincoln Theater absolutely astounding: and I had lived with the people of *A Tale of Two Cities* for very nearly as long. I had no idea what *Two Cities* was really about, any more than I knew what *Uncle Tom's Cabin* was really about, which was why I had to read them both so obsessively: they had something to tell me. It was this particular child's way of circling around the question of what it meant to be a nigger. It was the reason that I was reading Dostoevsky, a writer—or, rather, for me, a messenger—whom I would have had to understand, obviously, even less: my relentless pursuit of *Crime and Punishment* made my father (vocally) and my mother (silently) consider the possibility of brain fever. I was intrigued, but not misled, by the surface of these novels—Sydney Carton's noble renunciation of his life on the spectacular guillotine, Tom's forbearance before Simon Legree, the tracking down of Raskolnikov: the time of my time was to reduce all these images to the angel dancing on the edge of the junkie's needle: I did not believe in any of these people so much as I believed in their situation, which I suspected, dreadfully, to have something to do with my own.

And it had clearly escaped everyone's notice that I had already been bull-whipped through the Psalms of David and The Book of Job, to say nothing of the arrogant and loving Isaiah, the doomed

Ezekiel, and the helplessly paranoiac Saint Paul: such a forced march, designed to prepare the mind for conciliation and safety, can also prepare it for subversion and danger. For, I was on Job's side, for example, *though He slay me, yet will I trust him,* and *I will maintain mine own ways before Him*—You will not talk to *me* from the safety of your whirlwind, never—and, yet, something in me, out of the unbelievable pride and sorrow and beauty of my father's face, caused me to understand—I did not understand, perhaps I still do not understand, and never will—caused me to begin to accept the fatality and the inexorability of that voice out of the whirlwind, for if one is not able to live with so crushing and continuing a mystery, one is not able to live. . . .

***

Since both the film for which I had been hired, and *Ché!* were controversial, courageous, revolutionary films, being packaged for the consumer society, it was hoped that our film would beat *Ché!* to the box-office. This was not among my concerns. I had a fairly accurate idea of what Hollywood was about to do with *Ché!*. (This is not black, bitter paranoia, but cold, professional observation: you can make a fairly accurate guess as to the direction a film is likely to take by observing who is cast in it, and who has been assigned to direct it.) The intention of *Ché!* was to make both the man, and his Bolivian adventure, irrelevant and ridiculous; and to do this, furthermore, with such a syrup of sympathy that any incipient Ché would think twice before leaving Mama, and the ever-ready friend at the bank. *Ché!*, in the film, is a kind of *Lawrence of Arabia,* trapped on the losing side, and unable, even, to understand the natives he has, mistakenly, braved the jungles to arouse. I had no intention of so betraying Malcolm, or *his* natives. Yet, my producer had been advised, in an inter-office memo which I, quite unscrupulously, intercepted, that the writer (me) should be advised that the tragedy of Malcolm's life was that he had been mistreated, early, by some whites, and betrayed (later) by *many* blacks: emphasis in the original. The writer was also to avoid suggesting that Malcolm's trip to Mecca could have had any political implications, or repercussions.

Well. I had never before seen this machinery at such close quarters, and I confess that I was both fascinated and challenged. Near the end of my Hollywood sentence, the studio assigned me a "technical" expert, who was, in fact, to act as my collaborator. This fact was more or less disguised at first, but I was aware of it, and far from enthusiastic; still, by the time the studio and I had arrived at this impasse, there was no ground on which I could "reasonably" refuse. I liked the man well enough—I had no grounds, certainly, on which to dislike him. I didn't contest his "track record" as a screenwriter, and I reassured myself that he might be helpful: he was signed, anyway, and went to work.

Each week, I would deliver two or three scenes, which he would take home, breaking them—translating them—into cinematic language, shot by shot, camera angle by camera angle. This seemed to me a somewhat strangling way to make a film. My sense of the matter was that the screenwriter delivered as clear a blueprint as possible, which then became the point of departure for all the other elements involved in the making of a film. For example, surely it was the director's province to decide where to place the camera; and he would be guided in his decision by the dynamic of the scene. However: as the weeks wore on, and my scenes were returned to me, "translated," it began to be despairingly clear (to me) that all meaning was being siphoned out of them. It is very hard to describe this, but it is important that I try.

For example: there is a very short scene in my screenplay in which the central character, a young boy from the country, walks into a very quiet, very special Harlem bar, in the late afternoon. The scene is important because the "country" boy is Malcolm X, the bar is Small's Paradise, and the purpose of the scene is to dramatize Malcolm's first meeting with West Indian Archie—the numbers man who introduced Malcolm to the rackets. The interior evidence of Malcolm's book very strongly suggests a kind of father-son relationship between

Archie and Malcolm: my problem was how to suggest this as briefly and effectively as possible.

So, in my scene, as written, Malcolm walks into the bar, dressed in the zoot-suit of the times, and orders a drink. He does not know how outrageously young and vulnerable he looks. Archie is sitting at a table with his friends, and they watch Malcolm, making jokes about him between themselves. But their jokes contain an oblique confession: they see themselves in Malcolm. They all have *been* Malcolm once. He does not know what is about to happen to him, but they do, because it has already happened to them. They have been seeing it happen to others, and enduring what has happened to them, for nearly as long as Malcolm has been on earth. Archie, particularly, is struck by something he sees in the boy. So, when Malcolm, stumbling back from the jukebox, stumbles over Archie's shoes, Archie uses this as a pretext to invite the boy over to the table. And that is all there is to the scene.

My collaborator brought it back to me, translated. It was really the same scene, he explained, but he had added a little action—thus, when Malcolm stumbles over Archie's shoes, Archie becomes furious. Malcolm, in turn, becomes furious, and the scene turns into a shoot-out from *High Noon*, with everybody in the bar taking bets as to who will draw first. In this way, said my collaborator (with which judgment the studio, of course, agreed) everyone in the audience could *see* what Archie saw in Malcolm: he admired the "country boy's" guts.

We are to believe, then, on the basis of the "translated" scene, that a group of seasoned hustlers, in a very hip Harlem bar, allow a child from the country whom nobody knows to precipitate a crisis which may bring the heat down on everybody, and in which the child, by no means, incidentally, may lose his life—while they take bets. West Indian Archie is so angry that a child stepped on his shoes that he forgets he has all that numbers money on him, and all those people waiting to be paid—both above and below the line.

34

And, furthermore, this was not at all what Archie saw in Malcolm, nor was it what I wanted the audience to see.

The rewritten scene was much longer than the original scene, and, though it occurs quite early in the script, derailed the script completely. With all of my scenes being "translated" in this way, the script would grow bulkier than *War and Peace*, and the script, therefore, would have to be cut. And I saw how that would work. Having fallen into the trap of accepting "technical" assistance, I would not, at the cutting point, be able to reject it; and the script would then be cut according the "action" line, and in the interest of "entertainment" values. How I got myself out of this fix doesn't concern us here—I simply walked out, taking my original script with me—but the adventure remained very painfully in my mind, and, indeed, was to shed a certain light for me on the adventure occurring through the American looking-glass.

Chester Himes
(1909–1984)

CHESTER HIMES ATTENDED Ohio State University—but not for long. He pulled a prank and was expelled before the end of his freshman year. His expulsion was indicative of his defiant nature. In 1928, after being convicted of armed robbery, he was sent to an Ohio state prison. He began his writing career while there.[12]

Born in Jefferson City, Missouri, in 1909, Himes became a prolific writer—eventually achieving international fame in Paris and later Spain. After a few early stories and articles were published while he was in prison, Himes continued writing consistently after his release. During the early 1940s, he moved to Los Angeles and worked as a screenwriter. Himes' first novels—*If He Hollers Let Him Go* (1945) and *Lonely Crusade* (1947)—were published during his screenwriting years. His novel *Cast the First Stone* (1952) dealt with homosexual life in prison. The original version of the novel, *Yesterday Will Make You Cry*, was published posthumously in 1998.

Himes decided to settle in Paris during the 1950s. Given his popular detective novels, he enjoyed a successful commercial career. He moved to Spain in 1969. He wrote detective novels that featured African American characters. His novels have been read as precursors to Walter Mosley's fiction, especially the Easy Rawlins novels. And long before Mosley's novels, like *Devil in a Blue Dress*, were filmed, several of Himes' novels—including *If He Hollers Let Him Go* and *Cotton Comes to Harlem* (1965)—were made into successful films.

Himes wrote many novels, a collection of short stories, and two autobiographies—*The Quality of Hurt* (1973) and *My Life of Absurdity* (1976).

He died in Moraira, Spain, in 1984. In the excerpt that follows, he discusses starting his professional career while still incarcerated.

From *The Quality of Hurt* (1973)

I began writing in prison. That also protected me, against both the convicts and the screws. The black convicts had both an instinctive respect for and fear of a person who could sit down at a typewriter and write, and whose name appeared in newspapers and magazines outside. The screws could never really kill a convict who was a public figure, or else convicts like Malcolm X and Eldridge Cleaver would never have gotten out of prison alive.

My first short stories were published in weekly newspapers and in magazines published by blacks: the *Atlanta World*, the *Pittsburgh Courier*, the *Afro-American*, the *Bronzeman*, *Abbott's Monthly*, and other similar publications. I sold my first short story, *Crazy in the Stir*, to *Esquire* magazine in 1934, and followed that same year with *To What Red Hell*, my story about the prison fire. I think *Esquire* had just begun to publish fiction the first of that year; before then it had been a men's-fashion magazine. After that, until I was released in May 1936, I was published only by *Esquire*.

I must admit that the convicts were unimpressed by my stories; anyway most of them never read them. But they were impressed by my name appearing in a national magazine which the prison newsboy, a lifer named Mack, was permitted to peddle about the prison. The screws could not kill me after my name began appearing in national publications, and they could not make me work as long as I drew compensation from the Ohio State Industrial Commission for total disability. But they punished me enough in other ways: Collectively I spent many months in solitary confinement—once I was in so long on starvation rations that my hair started coming out, my nails began falling off, and my body became weightless—I still bear the scars of the head whippings. They punished me in many more subtle ways which I have discovered to be peculiar to the white race. During my last year, when I was at the farm, the deputy warden, a sick man with a paralyzed arm, used to stand beside the dining-room door when we went to meals and wait for me so he could lean forward and grit his teeth at me. I then lost a year and a half of "good time" for "insubordination."

My first short stories, those I wrote in prison, were not racially oriented; I did not write about the lives of blacks in a white world. That was to come. In prison I wrote about crimes and criminals, mostly about the life in prison—*Crazy in the Stir, To What Red Hell, The Visiting Hour, Every Opportunity, The Night's for Crying, Strictly Business*, and such. . . .

When I returned to Cleveland that summer of 1936, I was on parole for the duration of my maximum sentence, a period of a little more than seventeen years. I found Jean, my sweetheart before I went to prison, and, obtaining the consent of my parole officer, married her. She was still in love with me, and I grew to love her too, desperately and completely. At the time I was living with my father in a couple of rented rooms on Ninety-third Street off Cedar Avenue, but after our marriage we went to live by ourselves in a series of shabby rented rooms. . . .

Eventually I was employed by WPA, at first as a laborer, digging sewers and dredging creeks in the snow and ice of the Cleveland suburbs, miles from where I lived, and then as a research assistant in the Cleveland Public Library, writing vocational bulletins for the Stevenson room, and lastly as a writer on the Ohio Writers' project.

It was while I was on the Writers' Project that I wrote a series of descriptive vignettes to "brighten up" the editorial page of the Cleveland *Daily News*, as the editor, N. R. Howard put it. Mr. Howard did not give me a by-line for these pieces, which were signed only CH, and accepted them personally, paying me one dollar each, for fear of difficulties with the union. At that time the Cleveland daily papers did not employ blacks, no doubt because there were no vacancies. As Louis B. Seltzer, editor of the Cleveland *Press*, put it, "I could not hire you if you were Jesus Christ reincarnated." But I have always considered Mr. Howard one of my best friends. He knew all about my prison record and he had read several of my stories in *Esquire* and knew I wanted to write fiction. And we talked of writing, among other things. We both liked Faulkner and we had both read Richard Wright's *Uncle Tom's Children*. I remember best Mr. Howard saying, "I am appalled at the number of mistakes I make each day." And it was Mr. Howard who said to me, "Chester, you have paid the penalty for your crime against society, now forget about it. You don't owe any more." That has been my attitude ever since; but there are some who think my debt should never end, and that I should pay it until my death. . . .

I needed desperately to leave Cleveland. I persuaded my parole officer to apply to Governor Harold Burton for the termination of my parole and the restoration of my citizenship; and when I got my sheepskin, making me a citizen for the first time, I registered with the Democratic Party in Cleveland. But before I had a chance to vote I left to work on Louis Bromfield's Malabar Farm in Pleasant Valley, Ohio.

The Jeliffes, a white couple who ran the Karamu settlement house and theater in the black ghetto, had interceded for me, and Mr. Bromfield knew of my past and my ambition. He took the trouble to read a long novel based on my prison observations, which I had entitled *Black Sheep*, and offered to help me to get it published.

This novel was the outcome of my personal hurts, which I have briefly documented, and did not contain any reference to my racial hurts. The publishers didn't want it. I have since learned that American publishers are not interested in black writers unless they bleed from white torture. I was beginning to bleed, but I had not bled enough by the time I wrote that book. This attitude might also apply to the white American readers of novels. I have never heard the phrase "It's a beautiful book" applied to a book written by a black writer unless the black characters have suffered horribly. I have heard scores of white people say of Richard Wright's books *Native Son* and *Black Boy* that they were "beautiful books." Of course, this does not mean the same thing to me as it does to these white people. The suffering of others does not fill me with any spiritual satisfaction. Nor do I revel in the anguish of my fellow human beings. I am not uplifted by other people's degradation. Perhaps in this respect I am not a good Christian. The suffering of Christ affects me with abhorrence, and I look upon his crucifixion, as upon all crucifixions, as a sadistic brutality.

Ishmael Reed
(1938–)

ALTHOUGH ISHMAEL REED was born in Chattanooga, Tennessee, he grew up in Buffalo, New York, and attended the State University of New York at Buffalo for several years. He later moved to New York City and eventually settled in California's Bay Area. Ishmael Reed's prose style has been deeply influenced by his early years as a writer/reporter for Buffalo's *Empire Star Weekly*. When one reads Reed's fiction, it can feel as though one is reading an original journal, in which the author presides as editor-in-chief. The definitive house style is characterized by its general tendency toward parody and satire, but it also includes predictable content. It features unusual human interest stories, whether about crooked politicians or about dead poets, and acerbic editorials in which the editor dissents from the left and the right.

Reed's original style is evident in his first novel. In 1967, he published *The Freelance Pallbearers*. He published, in swift succession, three more novels—*Yellowback Radio Broke-Down* (1969), *Mumbo Jumbo* (1972), and *Flight to Canada* (1976). *Mumbo Jumbo* was widely reviewed and was nominated for the National Book Award.[13] The book was praised for its striking originality and harshly criticized for its excesses. Reed has also published several volumes of poetry, including *Conjure* (1972). It too was nominated for a National Book Award. He has edited collections of his own essays as well as a wide range of anthologies.

Reed's latest works include a collection of essays, *Barack Obama and the Jim Crow Media: The Return of the Nigger-Breakers* (2010). His most recent novel, *Juice* (2011), is a satiric novel about the media's response to O. J. Simpson and race in America after what was called "the trial of the century." In 2012, he published *Going Too Far: Essays About America's Nervous Breakdown.*

In the following excerpt, "Boxing on Paper: Thirty-Seven Years Later," from *Writin' Is Fightin'* (1988), Reed recalls his early years as a journalist for Buffalo's *Empire Star Weekly.*

Boxing on Paper: Thirty-Seven Years Later (1988)

In 1953, I was working in a drugstore on William Street in Buffalo, New York. As I left one evening to go home, a man pulled up to the curb and told me that he needed somebody to help him deliver newspapers. There were stacks of them in the backseat of his old brown beat-up Packard, which was just a shade darker than he was. His name was A. J. Smitherman, editor of *The Empire Star Weekly,* a Buffalo newspaper. How would you like to have this job every week? he asked after we'd taken copies of his newspaper to all of the newsstands on his route. I had been writing before then, and date my first commissioned work to 1952, when my mother asked me to write a birthday poem for one of her fellow employees at Satler's Department Store on Fillmore.

As a youngster, living in the projects, I also composed mini-sermons that I'd deliver during Sunday School from the pulpit at Saint Luke's Church, an old Afro-American Episcopal Zion church located on Eagle Street. But working at *The Empire Star* brought me into contact with articulate black people like Mary Crosby, Mr. Smitherman, and his son, Toussaint. Within a year, they even let me try my hand at writing columns, and I wrote jazz articles in what was to become a pungent writing style.

I drifted away from the *Star* in high school, having other things on my mind and needing more spending money than Mr. Smitherman was able to pay me. He was a relentless man who was barely able to bring out his newspaper every week. When he died, *The Buffalo Evening News* noted that he had to struggle against adversity. That's one of the things I remember about this gentle, intellectual editor and poet. His calm in the face of calamity.

As fate would have it, in 1960, after I'd dropped out of college and found myself, a father, living in the Talbert Mall Projects, attempting to support a family on forty dollars per week, I volunteered to do some work for the *Star*, which was then edited by Joe Walker, a dynamic young militant who was causing a stir in the city because of his fight against segregated schools and on behalf of Black Power. It was then that the lively style of my writing was put to the test. Fighting for a traffic light for my Talbert Mall neighbors (it's still there); debating the current mayor, James Griffith, on the subject of school segregation; defending black prostitutes who'd been brutalized by the police; and, at the same time, writing poetry and plays. The *Star* folded.

An Irish-American poet named David Sharpe liked a play of mine, and I traveled to New York with him one weekend. We spent most of the time at Chumley's, a restaurant located on Bedford Street in the Village. I was impressed. The book jackets of authors who'd drunk there, including Edna Saint Vincent Millay, lined the wall, and years later I felt that I'd arrived because mine went up. A screenwriter read my play standing at the bar (a play that was later lost in an abandoned car); he liked it.

After that, there was no keeping me from New York, and a few weeks later, Dave and I went down on the Greyhound bus. I carried all of my belongings in a blue plastic bag I'd purchased for ten cents at the Laundromat, and noticing my embarrassment, Dave carried it for me. It was 1962.

In New York, I joined the Umbra Workshop, to which Amiri Baraka credits the origin of the type of black aesthetic that so influenced the Black Arts Repertory School. It was in that workshop that I began to become acquainted with the techniques of the Afro-American literary style.

In 1965, I ran a newspaper in Newark, New Jersey, where I featured some of the same issues I'd covered in the *Star*, including a controversial piece on a welfare mother, which offended some blacks because she didn't sport the proper coiffure. It was during my tenure as editor of the *Advance* newspaper that I wrote an article about the police. Under heavy criticism, they'd invited members of the community to travel with them as a way of monitoring their activities. Representatives from the local civil rights organizations refused, but, in the interest of fair play, I accompanied them on their rounds one Saturday night, and because I commented that they had a tough job, I was called a right-winger by some black intellectuals.

I don't have a predictable, computerized approach to political and social issues in a society in which you're either for it or agin' it. Life is much more complex. And so for my early articles about black-on-black crime, I've been criticized by the left, and for my sympathy with some "left-wing" causes I've been criticized by the right, though from time to time I've noticed that there doesn't seem to be a dime's worth of difference between the zealotry of the left and that of the right.

I think that a certain amount of philosophical skepticism is necessary, and so regardless of the criticisms I receive from the left, the right, and the middle, I think it's important to maintain a prolific writing jab, as long as my literary legs hold up, because even during these bland and yuppie times, there are issues worth fighting about. Issues that require fresh points of view.

It was quite generous, I thought, for critic Mel Watkins to compare my writing style with that of Muhammad Ali's boxing style. My friend the late Richard Brautigan even saluted me after the publication of *Mumbo Jumbo*, my third novel, with the original front-page description of Jack Johnson's defeat of Jim Jeffries, printed by the *San Francisco Daily*, 4 July 1910. This, too, amounted to overpraise. If I had to compare my style with anyone's it would probably be with that of Larry Holmes. I don't mince my words. Nor do I pull any punches, and though I've delivered some low blows over the years, I'm becoming more accurate, and my punches are regularly landing above the waistline. I'm not a body snatcher like Mike McCallum, and I usually aim for the head.

A black boxer's career is the perfect metaphor for the career of a black male. Every day is like being in the gym, sparring with impersonal opponents as one faces the rudeness and hostility that a black male must confront in the United States, where he is the object of both fear and fascination. My difficulty in communicating this point of view used to really bewilder me, but over the years I've learned that it takes an extraordinary amount of effort to understand someone from a background different from your own, especially when your life doesn't really depend upon it. And so, during this period, when black males seem to be on somebody's endangered-species list, I can understand why some readers and debating opponents might have problems appreciating where I'm coming from.

On a day in the 1940s, the story of the deportation of Jews to European concentration camps was carried in the back pages of a New York newspaper, while news of the weather made the front page. Apparently it was a hot day, and most people were concerned about getting to the beach. And so, during this period when American society begins to resemble those of feudal lore, where the income chasm between the rich and the poor is widening, when downtown developers build concrete and steel vanity monuments to themselves—driving out the writers, the artists, the poor, and leaving the neighborhoods to roaming drug-death squads (since all of the cops are guarding these downtown Brasilias)—it seems that most people are interested in getting to the beach and getting tanned so that they'll resemble the very people the media, the "educational" system, and the cultural leadership have taught them to despise (that's what I meant by blacks being objects of fear and fascination). The widespread adoption of such Afro-American forms as rock and roll can be viewed as a kind of cultural tanning.

And so as long as I can be a professional like Larry Holmes, that is, have the ability to know my way around my craft, I'll probably still be controversial. Arguing on behalf of the homeless, but at the same time defending Atlanta's middle-class leadership against what I considered to be unfair charges made by the great writer James Baldwin. . . . And as I continue to practice this sometimes uncanny and taxing profession, I hope to become humbler.

I've got a good shot. It's almost a miracle for a black male writer to last as long as I have, and though some may regard me as a "token," I'm fully aware that, regardless of how some critics protect their fragile egos by pretending that black talent is rare, black talent is bountiful. I've read and heard a lot of manuscripts authored by the fellas over the years. The late Hoyt Fuller was right when he said that for one published Ishmael Reed, there are dozens of talented writers in the ghettos and elsewhere, who remain unpublished. And having lasted this long, I've been able to witness the sad demise of a lot of "tokens" who believed what their literary managers told them. Who believed that they were indeed unique and unusual.

Just think of all the cocky boxers who got punched out by "nobodies" as they took on an unknown to warm up for their fight with the champion. In this business, spoilers are all over the place.

I was shocked to hear Secretary of State George Shultz acknowledge during the Iran-Contragate hearings what our cultural leadership, and "educational" defenders of Western civilization, fail to realize. That people are smart all over the world. I know that. I'm aware of the fellas, writing throughout the country in the back of beat-up trailers, in jails, on kitchen tables, at their busboy jobs, during the rest period on somebody's night shift, or in between term papers. All the guys burnt-out, busted, disillusioned, collecting their hundredth rejection slip, being discouraged by people who say they'll never be a champion, or even a contender. This is for them. Writin' is Fightin'.

46

James Alan McPherson
(1943–)

JAMES ALAN McPHERSON grew up in Savannah, Georgia, and moved to Atlanta to attend Morris Brown College. During his college summers, he found work as a dining car waiter for the Great Northern Railway. McPherson started writing short stories while at Morris Brown and continued writing while a student at Harvard Law School.

After receiving his law degree in 1968, McPherson decided to become a writer instead of an attorney. He enrolled in the University of Iowa's Writers' Workshop. His decision to write stories was influenced by the literary recognition he had begun receiving. The *Atlantic Monthly* awarded his story "Gold Coast" first prize in a competition. In 1969, McPherson published *Hue and Cry*, his first collection of short stories. The collection received good reviews and enthusiastic praise from critics and other writers, including Ralph Ellison. In some of the stories, like "Gold Coast" and "On Trains," he captures the complexity of American life through the eyes of sleeping-car porters.[14]

After receiving his M.F.A. from Iowa, McPherson taught at several universities before returning to Iowa to become a member of the workshop's faculty. In 1977, he published *Elbow Room*, for which he won the 1978 Pulitzer Prize for fiction. Among other awards, McPherson was, in 1981, one of the first recipients of a MacArthur Fellowship, or "genius award."

McPherson published *Crab Cakes* in 1998. The book is mostly a memoir that recounts the time he spent in Baltimore. McPherson also describes his trips to Japan and provides a comparative meditation on his attempt to understand the rituals of Japanese culture.

In 2000, McPherson published another collection of essays, *A Region Not Home*, which contains several autobiographical essays including "Gravitas," his homage to Ralph Ellison. One can see the novelist's or short story writer's discerning eye on display in such essays as "Disneyland," "El Camino Real," and "It Is Good to Be Shifty in a New Country," a piece that focuses on Mark Twain and the publication of a restored version of Twain's original manuscript of *The Adventures of Huckleberry Finn*. Another essay, "Grant Hall," focuses on the years during the late 1960s when McPherson attended the University of Iowa's Writers' Workshop. The essay includes a flashback to Grant Hall, his dormitory during his freshman year at Morris Brown College.

In "On Becoming an American Writer" (1978), McPherson discusses his background, including his matriculation and graduation from Harvard Law School. He tells us how his decision to write short stories is questioned by an older black friend. McPherson's friend harshly criticizes the writer for squandering opportunities that his Harvard law degree would have assured.

On Becoming an American Writer (1978)

In 1974, during the last months of the Nixon administration, I lived in San Francisco, California. My public reason for leaving the East and going there was that my wife had been admitted to the San Francisco Medical Center School of Nursing, but my private reason for going was that San Francisco would be a very good place for working and for walking. Actually, during that time San Francisco was not that pleasant a place. We lived in a section of the city called the Sunset District, but it rained almost every day. During the late spring Patricia Hearst helped to rob a bank a few blocks from our apartment, a psychopath called "the Zebra Killer" was terrorizing the city, and the mayor seemed about to declare martial law. Periodically the FBI would come to my apartment with pictures of the suspected bank robbers. Agents came several times, until it began to dawn on me that they had become slightly interested in why, of all the people in a working-class neighborhood, I alone sat at home every day. They never asked any questions on this point, and I never volunteered that I was trying to keep my sanity by working very hard on a book dealing with the relationship between folklore and technology in nineteenth-century America.

In the late fall of the same year a friend came out from the East to give a talk in Sacramento. I drove there to take him back to San Francisco. This was an older black man, one whom I respect a great deal, but during our drive an argument developed between us. His major worry was the recession, but eventually his focus shifted to people in my age group and our failures. There were a great many of these, and he listed them point by point. He said, while we drove through a gloomy evening rain, "When the smoke clears and you start counting, I'll bet you won't find that many more black doctors, lawyers, accountants, engineers, dentists. . . ." The list went on. He remonstrated a bit more, and said, "White people are very generous. When they start a thing they usually finish it. But after all this chaos, imagine how mad and tired they must be. Back in the fifties, when this thing started, they must have known anything could happen. They must have said, 'Well, we'd better settle in and hold on tight. Here come the niggers.'" During the eighteen months I spent in San Francisco, this was the only personal encounter that really made me mad.

In recent years I have realized that my friend, whom I now respect even more, was speaking from the perspective of a tactician. He viewed the situation in strict bread-and-butter terms: a commitment had been made to redefine the meaning of democracy in this country, certain opportunities and the freedom they provided. From his point of view, it was simply a matter of fulfilling a contractual obligation: taking full advantage of the educational opportunities that had been offered to achieve middle-class status in one of the professions. But from my point of view, one that I never shared with him, it was not that simple. Perhaps it was because of the differences in our generations and experiences. Or perhaps it was because each new generation, of black people at least, has to redefine itself even while it attempts to grasp the new opportunities, explore the new freedom. I can speak for no one but myself, yet maybe in trying to preserve the uniqueness of my experience, as I tried to do in *Elbow Room*, I can begin to set the record straight for my friend, for myself, and for the sake of the record itself.

In 1954, when *Brown v. Board of Education* was decided, I was eleven years old. I lived in a lower-class black community in Savannah, Georgia, attended segregated public schools, and knew no white people socially. I can't remember thinking of this last fact as a disadvantage, but I do know that early on I was being conditioned to believe that I was not *supposed* to know any white people on social terms. In our town the children of the black middle class were expected to aspire to certain traditional occupations; the children of the poor were expected not to cause too much trouble.

There was in those days a very subtle, but real, social distinction based on gradations of color, and I can remember the additional strain under which darker-skinned poor people lived. But there was also a great deal of optimism, shared by all levels of the black community. Besides a certain reverence for the benign intentions of the federal government, there was a belief in the idea of progress, nourished, I think now, by the determination of older people not to pass on to the next generation too many stories about racial conflict, their own frustrations and failures. They censored a great deal. It was as if they had made basic and binding agreements with themselves, or with their ancestors, that for the consideration represented by their silence on certain points they expected to receive, from either Providence or a munificent federal government, some future service or remuneration, the form of which would be left to the beneficiaries of their silence. Lawyers would call this a contract with a condition precedent. And maybe because they did tell us less than they knew, many of us were less informed than we might have been. On the other hand, because of this same silence many of us remained free enough of the influence of negative stories to take chances, be ridiculous, perhaps even try to form our own positive stories out of whatever our own experiences provided. Though ours was a limited world, it was one rich in possibilities for the future.

If I had to account for my life from segregated Savannah to this place and point in time, I would probably have to say that the contract would be no bad metaphor. I am reminded of Sir Henry Maine's observation that the progress of society is from status to contract. Although he was writing about the development of English common law, the reverse of his generalization is most applicable to my situation: I am the beneficiary of a number of contracts, most of them between the federal government and the institutions of society, intended to provide people like me with a certain status.

I recall that in 1960, for example, something called the National Defense Student Loan Program went into effect, and I found out that by my agreeing to repay a loan plus some little interest, the federal government would back my enrollment in a small Negro college in Georgia. When I was a freshman at that college, disagreement over a seniority clause between the Hotel & Restaurant Employees and Bartenders Union and the Great Northern Railway Company, in St. Paul, Minnesota, caused management to begin recruiting temporary summer help. Before I was nineteen I was encouraged to move from a segregated Negro college in the South and through that very beautiful part of the country that lies between Chicago and the Pacific Northwest. That year—1962—the World's Fair was in Seattle, and it was a magnificently diverse panorama for a young man to see. Almost every nation on earth was represented in some way, and at the center of the fair was the Space Needle. The theme of the U.S. exhibit, as I recall, was drawn from Whitman's *Leaves of Grass*: "Conquering, holding, daring, venturing as we go the unknown ways."

When I returned to the South, in the midst of all the civil rights activity, I saw a poster advertising a creative-writing contest sponsored by *Reader's Digest* and the United Negro College Fund. To enter the contest I had to learn to write and type. The first story I wrote was lost (and very badly typed); but the second, written in 1965, although also badly typed, was awarded first prize by Edward Weeks and his staff at the *Atlantic Monthly*. That same year I was offered the opportunity to enter Harvard Law School. During my second year at law school, a third-year man named Dave Marston (who was in a contest with Attorney General Griffin Bell earlier that year) offered me, through a very conservative white fellow student from Texas, the opportunity to take over his old job as a janitor in one of the apartment buildings in Cambridge. There I had the solitude, and the encouragement, to begin writing seriously. Offering my services in that building was probably the best contract I ever made.

I have not recalled all the above to sing my own praises or to evoke the black American version of the Horatio Alger myth. I have recited these facts as a way of indicating the haphazard nature of events during that ten-year period. I am the product of a contractual process. To put it simply, the 1960s were a crazy time. Opportunities seemed to materialize out of thin air; and if you were lucky, if you were in the right place at the right time, certain contractual benefits just naturally accrued. You were assured of a certain status; you could become a doctor, a lawyer, a dentist, an accountant, an engineer. Achieving these things was easy, if you applied yourself.

But a very hard price was extracted. It seems to me now, from the perspective provided by age and distance, that certain institutional forces, acting impersonally, threw together black peasants and white aristocrats, people who operated on the plane of the intellect and people who valued the perspective of the folk. There were people who were frightened, threatened, and felt inferior; there were light-skinned people who called themselves "black," and there were dark-skinned people who could remember when this term had been used negatively; there were idealists and opportunists, people who seemed to want to be exploited and people who delighted in exploiting them. Old identities were thrown off, of necessity, but there were not many new ones of a positive nature to be assumed. People from backgrounds like my own, those from the South, while content with the new opportunities, found themselves trying to make sense of the growing diversity of friendships, of their increasing familiarity with the various political areas of the country, of the obvious differences between their values and those of their parents. We *were* becoming doctors, lawyers, dentists, engineers; but at the same time our experiences forced us to begin thinking of ourselves in new and different ways. We never wanted to be "white," but we never wanted to be "black" either. And back during that period there was the feeling that we could be whatever we wanted. But, we discovered, unless we joined a group, subscribed to some ideology, accepted some provisional identity, there was no contractual process for defining and stabilizing what it was we wanted to be. We also found that this was an individual problem, and in order to confront it one had to go inside one's self.

Now I want to return to my personal experience, to one of the contracts that took me from segregated Savannah to the Seattle World's Fair. There were many things about my earliest experiences that I liked and wanted to preserve, despite the fact that these things took place in a context of segregation; and there were a great many things I liked about the vision of all those nations interacting at the World's Fair. But the two seemed to belong to separate realities, to represent two different worldviews. Similarly, there were some things I liked about many of the dining-car waiters with whom I worked, and some things I liked about people like Dave Marston whom I met in law school. Some of these people and their values were called "black" and some were called "white," and I learned very quickly that all of us tend to wall ourselves off from experiences different from our own by assigning to these terms greater significance than they should have. Moreover, I found that trying to maintain friendships with, say, a politically conservative white Texan, a liberal-to-radical classmate of Scottish-Italian background, my oldest black friends, and even members of my own family introduced psychological contradictions that became tense and painful as the political climate shifted. There were no contracts covering such friendships and such feelings, and in order to keep the friends and maintain the feelings I had to force myself to find a basis other than race on which contradictory urgings could be synthesized. I discovered that I had to find, first of all, an identity as a writer, and then I had to express what I knew or felt in such a way that I could make something whole out of a necessarily fragmented experience.

While in San Francisco, I saw in the image of the nineteenth-century American locomotive a possible cultural symbol that could represent my folk origins and their values, as well as the values of all the people I had seen at the World's Fair. During that same time, unconsciously, I was also beginning to see that the American language, in its flexibility and variety of idioms, could at least approximate some of the contradictory feelings that had resulted from my experience. Once again, I could not find any contractual guarantee that this would be the most appropriate and rewarding way to hold myself, and my experience, together. I think now there are no such contracts.

I quoted earlier a generalization by Sir Henry Maine to the effect that human society is a matter of movement from status to contract. Actually, I have never read Sir Henry Maine. I lifted his statement from a book by a man named Henry Allen Moe—a great book called *The Power of Freedom*. In that book, in an essay entitled "The Future of Liberal Arts Education," Moe goes on to say that a next step, one that goes beyond contract, is now necessary, but that no one seems to know what that next step should be. Certain trends suggest that it may well be a reversion to status. But if this happens it will be a tragedy of major proportions, because most of the people in the world are waiting for some nation, some people, to provide the model for the next step. And somehow I felt, while writing the last stories in *Elbow Room*, that what the old folks in my hometown wanted in exchange for their censoring was not just status of a conventional kind. I want to think that after having waited so long, after having seen so much, they must have at least expected some new stories that would no longer have to be censored to come out of our experience. I felt that if anything, the long experience of segregation could be looked on as a period of preparation for a next step. Those of us who are black and who have had to defend our humanity should be obliged to continue defending it, on higher and higher levels—not of power, which is a kind of tragic trap, but on higher levels of consciousness.

All of this is being said in retrospect, and I am quite aware that I am rationalizing many complex and contradictory feelings. Nevertheless, I do know that early on, during my second year of law school, I became conscious of a model of identity that might help me transcend, at least in my thinking, a provisional or racial identity. In a class in American constitutional law taught by Paul Freund, I began to play with the idea that the Fourteenth Amendment was not just a legislative instrument devised to give former slaves legal equality with other Americans. Looking at the slow but steady way in which the basic guarantees of the Bill of Rights had, through judicial interpretation, been incorporated into the clauses of that amendment, I began to see the outlines of a new identity.

You will recall that the first line of Section I of the Fourteenth Amendment makes an all-inclusive definition of citizenship: "All persons born or naturalized in the United States, and subject to the jurisdiction thereof, are citizens of the United States. . . ." The rights guaranteed to such a citizen had themselves traveled from the provinces to the World's Fair: from the trial and error of early Anglo-Saxon folk rituals to the rights of freemen established by the Magna Carta, to their slow incorporation into early American colonial charters, and from these charters (especially Virginia's Bill of Rights, written by George Mason) into the U.S. Constitution as its first ten amendments. Indeed, these same rights had served as the basis for the Charter of the United Nations. I saw that through the protean uses made of the Fourteenth Amendment, in the gradual elaboration of basic rights to be protected by federal authority, an outline of something much more complex than "black" and "white" had been begun.

It was many years before I was to go to the Library of Congress and read the brief of the lawyer-novelist Albion W. Tourgee in the famous case *Plessy v. Ferguson*. Argued in 1896 before the United States Supreme Court, Tourgee's brief was the first meaningful attempt to breathe life into the amendment. I will quote here part of his brief, which is a very beautiful piece of literature:

> This provision of Section 1 of the Fourteenth Amendment *creates* a new citizenship of the United States embracing *new* rights, privileges and immunities, derivable in a *new* manner, controlled by *new* authority, having a *new* scope and extent, depending on national authority for its existence and looking to national power for its preservation.

Although Tourgee lost the argument before the Supreme Court, his model of citizenship—and it is not a racial one—is still the most radical idea to come out of American constitutional law. He provided the outline, the clothing, if you will, for a new level of status. What he was proposing in 1896, I think, was that each United States citizen would attempt to approximate the ideals of the nation, be on at least conversant terms with all its diversity, carry the mainstream of the culture inside himself. As an American, by trying to wear these clothes he would be a synthesis of high and low, black and white, city and country, provincial and universal. If he could live with these contradictions, he would be simply a representative American.

This was the model I was aiming for in my book of stories. It can be achieved with or without intermarriage, but it will cost a great many mistakes and a lot of pain. It is, finally, a product of culture and not of race. And achieving it will require that one be conscious of America's culture and the complexity of all its people. As I tried to point out, such a perspective would provide a minefield of delicious ironies. Why, for example, should black Americans raised in southern culture *not* find that some of their responses are geared to country music? How else, except in terms of cultural diversity, am I to account for the white friend in Boston who taught me much of what I know about black American music? Or the white friend in Virginia who, besides developing a homegrown aesthetic he calls "crackertude," knows more about black American folklore than most black people? Or the possibility that many black people in Los Angeles have been just as much influenced by Hollywood's "star system" of the forties and fifties as they have been by society's response to the color of their skins? I wrote about people like these in *Elbow Room* because they interested me, and because they help support my belief that most of us are products of much more complex cultural influences than we suppose.

What I have said above will make little sense until certain contradictions in the nation's background are faced up to, until personal identities are allowed to partake of the complexity of the country's history as well as of its culture. Some years ago, a very imaginative black comedian named Richard Pryor appeared briefly on national television in his own show. He offended a great many people, and his show was canceled after only a few weeks. But I remember one episode that may emphasize my own group's confusion about its historical experience. This was a satiric takeoff on the popular television movie *Roots*, and Pryor played an African tribal historian who was selling trinkets and impromptu history to black American tourists. One tourist, a middle-class man, approached the tribal historian and said, "I want you to tell me who my great-great-granddaddy was." The African handed him a picture. The black American looked at it and said, "But that's a *white* man!" The tribal historian said, "That's right." Then the tourist said, "Well, I want you to tell me where I'm from." The historian looked hard at him and said, "You're from Cleveland, nigger." I think I was trying very hard to say the same thing, but not just to black people.

Today I am not the lawyer my friend in San Francisco thought I should be, but this is the record I wanted to present to him that rainy evening back in 1974. It may illustrate why the terms of my acceptance of society's offer had to be modified. I am now a writer, a person who has to learn to live with contradictions, frustrations, and doubts. Still, I have another quote that sustains me, this one from a book called *The Tragic Sense of Life*, by the Spanish philosopher Miguel de Unamuno. In a chapter called "Don Quixote Today," Unamuno asks, "How is it that among the words the English have borrowed from our language there is to be found this word *desperado*?" And he answers himself: "It is despair, and despair alone, that begets heroic hope, absurd hope, mad hope."

I believe that the United States is complex enough to induce that sort of despair that begets heroic hope. I believe that if one can experience its diversity, touch a variety of its people, laugh at its craziness, distill wisdom from its tragedies, and attempt to synthesize all this inside oneself without going crazy, one will have earned the right to call oneself "citizen of the United States," even though one is not quite a lawyer, doctor, engineer, or accountant. If nothing else, one will have learned a few new stories and, most important, one will have begun on that necessary movement from contract to the next step, from province to the World's Fair, from a hopeless person to a desperado. I wrote about my first uncertain steps in this direction in *Elbow Room* because I have benefited from all the contracts, I have exhausted all the contracts, and at present it is the only new direction I know.

Terry McMillan
(1951–)

TERRY McMILLAN GREW up in Port Huron, Michigan. She received a B.A. in journalism from the University of California at Berkeley. She also attended Columbia University's film school. With the publication of her third novel, *Waiting to Exhale* (1992), Terry McMillan helped create a revolution in the publication of mass market fiction. Her novel about the lives and careers of four African American women became a phenomenal best seller.

She had published two other novels, *Mama* (1987) and *Disappearing Acts* (1989), before *Waiting to Exhale*. Her tireless promotion of her first novels (personally selling them at book readings and hair salons) demonstrates her professionalism and entrepreneurial ambition. *Waiting to Exhale* was eventually produced as a film—directed by the actor Forest Whitaker and featuring the late singer Whitney Houston. McMillan's next novel, *How Stella Got Her Groove Back* (1996), was also a best seller. She has published four other novels—including her latest, *Who Asked You* (2013). She has also edited a collection of fiction by others—*Breaking Ice: An Anthology of Contemporary African-American Fiction* (1990).[15]

McMillan's introduction to the anthology included here tells the story of her own beginnings as a serious reader of literature and, after attending film school, as a writer. She offers young writers some advice: "Do not write to impress. Do not write to prove to a reader how much you know, but instead write in order to *know*."

Introduction to *Breaking Ice* (1990)

As a child, I didn't know that African-American people wrote books. I grew up in a small town in northern Michigan, where the only books I came across were the Bible and required reading for school. I did not read for pleasure, and it wasn't until I was sixteen when I got a job shelving books at the public library that I got lost in a book. It was a biography of Louisa May Alcott. I was excited because I had not really read about poor white folks before; her father was so eccentric and idealistic that at the time I just thought he was crazy. I related to Louisa because she had to help support her family at a young age, which was what I was doing at the library.

Then one day I went to put a book away, and saw James Baldwin's face staring up at me. "Who in the world is this?" I wondered. I remember feeling embarrassed and did not read his book because I was too afraid. I couldn't imagine that he'd have anything better or different to say than Thomas Mann, Henry Thoreau, Ralph Waldo Emerson, Nathaniel Hawthorne, Ernest Hemingway, William Faulkner, etc. and a horde of other mostly white male writers that I'd been introduced to in Literature 101 in high school. I mean, not only had there not been any African-American authors included in any of those textbooks, but I'd never been given a clue that if we did have anything important to say that somebody would actually publish it. Needless to say, I was not just naïve, but had not yet acquired an ounce of black pride. I never once questioned why there were no representative works by us in any of those textbooks. After all, I had never heard of any African-American writers, and no one I knew hardly read *any* books.

And then things changed.

It wasn't until after Malcolm X had been assassinated that I found out who he was. I know I should be embarrassed about this, but I'm not. I read Alex Haley's biography of him and it literally changed my life. First and foremost, I realized that there was no reason to be ashamed of being black, that it was ridiculous. That we had a history, and much to be proud of. I began to notice how we had actually been treated as less than human; began to see our strength as a people whereas I'd only been made aware of our inferiorities. I started thinking about my role in the world and not just on my street. I started *thinking*. Thinking about things I'd never thought about before, and the thinking turned into questions. But I had more questions than answers.

So I went to college. When I looked through the catalog and saw a class called Afro-American Literature, I signed up and couldn't wait for the first day of class. Did *we* really have enough writers to warrant an entire class? I remember the textbook was called *Dark Symphony: Negro Literature in America* because I still have it. I couldn't believe the rush I felt over and over once I discovered Countee Cullen, Langston Hughes, Ann Petry, Zora Neale Hurston, Ralph Ellison, Jean Toomer, Richard Wright, and rediscovered and read James Baldwin, to name a few. I'm surprised I didn't need glasses by the end of the semester. My world opened up. I accumulated and gained a totally new insight about, and perception of, our lives as "black" people, as if I had been an outsider and was finally let in. To discover that our lives held as much significance and importance as our white counterparts was more than gratifying, it was exhilarating. Not only had we lived diverse, interesting, provocative, and relentless lives, but during, through, and as a result of all these painful experiences, some folks had taken the time to write it down.

Not once, throughout my entire four years as an undergraduate, did it occur to me that I might one day *be* a writer. I mean, these folks had genuine knowledge and insight. They also had a fascination with the truth. They had something to write about. Their work was bold, not flamboyant. They learned how to exploit the language so that readers would be affected by what they said and how they said it. And they had talent.

I never considered myself to be in possession of much of the above, and yet when I was twenty years old, the first man I fell in love with broke my heart. I was so devastated and felt so helpless that my reaction manifested itself in a poem. I did not sit down and say, "I'm going to write a poem about this." It was more like magic. I didn't even know I was writing a poem until I had written it. Afterward, I felt lighter, as if something had happened to lessen the pain. And when I read this "thing" I was shocked because I didn't know where the words came from. I was scared, to say the least, about what I had just experienced, because I didn't understand what had happened.

For the next few days, I read that poem over and over in disbelief because *I* had written it. One day, a colleague saw it lying on the kitchen table and read it. I was embarrassed and shocked when he said he liked it, then went on to tell me that he had just started a black literary magazine at the college and he wanted to publish it. Publish it? He was serious and it found its way onto a typeset page.

Seeing my name in print excited me. And from that point on, if a leaf moved on a tree, I wrote a poem about it. If a crack in the sidewalk glistened, surely there was a poem in that. Some of these verbose things actually got published in various campus newspapers that were obviously desperate to fill up space. I did not call myself a poet; I told people I wrote poems.

Years passed.

Those poems started turning into sentences and I started getting nervous. What the hell did I think I was doing? Writing these little go-nowhere vignettes. All these beginnings. And who did I think I was, trying to tell a story? And who cared? Even though I had no idea what I was doing, all I knew was that I was beginning to realize that a lot of things mattered to me, things disturbed me, things that I couldn't change. Writing became an outlet for my dissatisfactions, distaste, and my way of trying to make sense of what I saw happening around me. It was my way of trying to fix what I thought was broken. It later became the only way to explore personally what

I didn't understand. The problem, however, was that I was writing more about ideas than people. Everything was so "large," and eventually I had to find a common denominator. I ended up asking myself what I really cared about: it was people, and particularly African-American people.

The whole idea of taking myself seriously as a writer was terrifying. I didn't know any writers. Didn't know how you knew if you "had" it or not. Didn't know if I was or would ever be good enough. I didn't know how you went about the business of writing, and besides, I sincerely wanted to make a decent living. (I had read the horror stories of how few writers were able to live off of their writing alone, many having lived like bohemians.) At first, I thought being a social worker was the right thing to do, since I was bent on saving the world (I was an idealistic twenty-two years old), but when I found out I couldn't do it that way, I had to figure out another way to make an impact on folks. A positive impact. I ended up majoring in journalism because writing was "easy" for me, but it didn't take long for me to learn that I did not like answering the "who, what, when, where, and why" of anything. I then—upon the urging of my mother and friends who had graduated and gotten "normal" jobs—decided to try something that would still allow me to "express myself" but was relatively safer, though still risky: I went to film school. Of course what was inherent in my quest to find my "spot" in the world was this whole notion of affecting people on some grand scale. Malcolm and Martin caused me to think like this. Writing for me, as it's turned out, is philanthropy. It didn't take years for me to realize the impact that other writers' work had had on me, and if I was going to write, I did not want to write inconsequential, mediocre stories that didn't conjure up or arouse much in a reader. So I had to start by exciting myself and paying special attention to what I cared about, what mattered to me.

Film school didn't work out. Besides, I never could stop writing, which ultimately forced me to stop fighting it. It took even longer to realize that writing was not something you aspired to, it was something you did because you had to.

I did not want this introduction to be a defense, but I must let you know how the whole idea for this anthology came about.

In 1987, I was teaching at the University of Wyoming. In my fiction workshop, since most of the students didn't read too much serious fiction, I wanted to introduce them to what I thought were quality contemporary fiction writers. Since I keep abreast of just about every annual anthology of contemporary writers that's published (from *Pushcart*, to *Editor's Choice, Prize Stories: The O. Henry Awards*, and *The Best American Short Stories*, to name a few), I combed through the last seven years' collections, and it became quite apparent that something was wrong. There was rarely an African-American writer among the "best" of these stories that had supposedly gone through much deliberation and scrutiny. The editors had attested to reading hundreds of stories that had appeared in magazines ranging from *The New Yorker, The Atlantic* on down to the smallest of the literary quarterlies. The few African-American quarterlies (*Callaloo, Catalyst, Sage, Hambone*), and *Essence* magazine, were not among those considered. I was appalled as I snatched every last one of these anthologies off my bookshelf, and could literally count on one hand the number of African-American writers who were in the table of contents.

I sat at my desk and fumed. My heart pounded with anger. How dare they! Then, in the next breath, I found myself standing in front of my "black" shelves, and I pulled out all the recent anthologies of fiction I had: *Black Voices* and *New Black Voices* (both edited by Abraham Chapman), *Black Short Story Anthology* (edited by Woodie King), *19 Necromancers from Now* (edited by Ishmael Reed), and *The Best Short Stories by Negroes* (edited by Langston Hughes). There were others, but most of them had been published prior to the sixties, and they concentrated on fiction, drama, poetry, essays, playwriting, and literary criticism. What became apparent almost immediately was that I couldn't recall any recent anthologies in which contemporary African-American fiction—writers who'd been published from the early seventies to now—had been published. Not sure that I was right, I went to the campus library that afternoon, got a computer printout of everything that fell under the heading of "black . . . fiction, literature, anthology, short story." The list itself was long, mostly because the same books kept reappearing as they were cross-referenced under "black literature." As I continued to go through this list, I realized most of the books were in fact historical, segregated by gender or geography, and I learned quickly that there hadn't been an anthology comprised of fiction in over seventeen years. There were a number of critical (scholarly) texts "about" twentieth century "black" fiction, even an annotated index of "The Afro-American Short Story" compiled by Preston M. Yancy in 1986. By the time I finished going through the computerized tear sheets, I picked up the phone and called a number of knowledgeable folks and asked them: "What's the most recent anthology you know about that has nothing but black fiction writers in it?" Many of them paused, and had to think about it. Some of them couldn't remember at all. Many reported the same few.

Shortly afterward, on a snowy morning I sat in my study and looked out the window. Surely there were enough contemporary African-American fiction writers out there to warrant an anthology. At least thirty of them popped into my mind. Then I thought about all the ones I wasn't aware of. Those who'd probably been trying to get published, but couldn't. Those who'd had one novel or story collection published by a major publisher or small press that went unnoticed in *The New York Times*, by the publisher itself or other critical places. I came to the conclusion that there was a void here, and someone needed to fill it.

Without thinking for a minute of the work that a project like this would entail, I dashed off a letter to my publisher and told them about this "problem," stating my case and backing it up with examples or lack of them. Would they be interested? After several days of "checking into the matter" they agreed with me. There was a void here.

I knew that I wanted an anthology that reflected how our lives have changed on a personal level since the 1960s. Although "protest literature" had its rightful place in time, I knew our work had gone through a series of metamorphoses. It wasn't that race was no longer important, it's just that in much of the work I've read from the seventies to now, race wasn't always the focus. There has been an understanding that many African-American writers write out of our Africaness [*sic*]. To say it differently, our only frame of reference is as African-Americans, so we write about what our experiences mean to us, what concerns us as African-Americans.

However, our visions, voices, outlooks, and even our experiences have changed and/or grown in myriad ways over the last two decades. Much of our work is more intimate, personal, reflects a diversity of styles and approaches to storytelling, and it was this new energy that I hoped to acquire for this anthology. This is exactly what I got.

This is not to say that I for one minute negate the value and significance of writers who made a contribution to African-American literature up through the sixties whose work may have fallen under the heading of "protest" literature. But how much sense would it make in the nineties if folks were still writing "we hate whitey" stories or, say, slave narratives or why we should be proud of our heritage (we've known it for a long time now—our children know it, too). It would be incongruent. And it is for this reason that many of the writers whose work follows on these pages reflect a wide range of experiences that are indicative of the times we live in now. Our backgrounds as African-Americans are not all the same. Neither are our perceptions, values, and morals. The following stories are not filled with anger. Some are warmhearted, some zingy, some have a sting and a bite, some will break your heart, or cause you to laugh out loud, sit back and remember, or think ahead. You may very well see yourself, a member of your family, a loved one, or a friend on these pages, and that is one thing good fiction should do: let you see some aspect of yourself.

Trey Ellis has coined a phrase which he calls "The New Black Aesthetic," a kind of *glasnost*. He believes that all contemporary African-American artists now create art where race is not the only source of conflict. We are a new breed, free to write as we please, in part because of our predecessors, and because of the way life has changed. "For the first time in our history we are producing a critical mass of college graduates who are children of college graduates themselves. Like most artistic booms, the NBA is a post-bourgeois movement; driven by a second generation of [the] middle class. Having scraped their way to relative wealth and, too often, crass materialism, our parents have freed (or compelled) us to bite those hands that fed us and sent us to college. We now feel secure enough to attend art school instead of medical school."

Ellis believes, and I support his position, that "new black artists [are no longer] shocked by racism as were those of the Harlem Renaissance, nor are we preoccupied with it as were those of the Black Arts Movement. For us, racism is a hard and little-changing constant that neither surprises nor enrages."

We now comment on ourselves in our work. We can poke fun, laugh at, and pinpoint ourselves as we see fit. Sometimes there is a price for this. From the production of *For Colored Girls Who Have Considered Suicide When the Rainbow Is Enuf* by Ntozake Shange, and then Alice Walker's *The Color Purple*, on to Gloria Naylor's *The Women of Brewster Place*, members of the African-American community began criticizing these writers because of their negative depiction of African-American men. "We" had no right to "air our dirty laundry" in front of the white world.

In a recent article appearing in *The Washington Post*, staff writer and *Book World* reviewer, David Nicholson's, "Painting It Black: African American Artists, In Search of a New Aesthetic," states: "True artists often travel lonely roads, but black artists are in the unenviable position of having too much company on their journeys—

everybody wants to tell them what to do and how to do it. . . . black literature, films by black filmmakers, black music and black art . . . are expected to carry the weight of politics and sociology. They are subject to the conflicting imperatives—too seldom aesthetic—of various movements and ideologies. They must present a positive image, and they must never, ever reveal unpleasant truths (dissension among blacks, color and caste prejudice) to outside (read 'white') eyes."

Most of the literature by African-Americans appearing from the thirties through the early sixties appeared to be aimed at white audiences. We were telling them who we were and what they'd done wrong. Times have changed. We do not feel the need to create and justify our existence anymore. We are here. We are proud. And most of us no longer feel the need to prove anything to white folks. If anything, we're trying to make sense of ourselves to ourselves.

Needless to say, good fiction is not preaching. If a writer is trying hard to convince you of something, then he or she should stick to nonfiction. These days, our work is often as entertaining as it is informative, thought-provoking as it is uplifting. Some of us would like to think that the experiences of our characters are "universal," and yet sometimes a situation could only happen if the color of your character's skin is black. When a writer sits down to tell a story, staring at a blank page, it amazes me how some people are so naïve as to believe that when we invent a character, that we've got the entire race of African-Americans in mind; that these characters are supposed to be representative of the whole instead of the character we originally had in mind. Let's face it, there are some trifling men and women that some of us have come across, so much so that we *have* to write down the effect they had on us. On the other hand, there are also some kind, loving, tender, gentle, successful, and supportive folks in our lives, who also find their way into our work.

But good fiction is filled with conflict, drama, and tension. If we were to spend our time writing lackluster, adult fairy tales, only to please our readers and critics, I know I would be bored to death. I read enough uneventful stories about dull people who live dull lives, and everything that happens to them is dull. As writers, we have a right to choose our own particular focus.

Without a doubt, writing fiction requires passion and compassion. A sense of urgency. Excitement. Intensity. Stillness. For many of us, writing is our reaction to injustices, absurdities, beauty. It's our way of registering our complaints or affirmations. The best are not didactic. They do not scream out "message," nor are they abstractions. Our stories are our personal response. What we want to specify. What we see. What we feel. Our wide angle lens—our close-up look. And even if the story doesn't quite pinpoint the solution or the answer, it is the exploration itself that is often worth the trip.

It didn't take long to gather a list of potential submissions, and word traveled fast and far about this anthology. I received close to three hundred submissions, and it was hard to narrow it down to the fifty-seven writers who appear here. There are what I have deemed three categories of writers: seasoned, emerging, and unpublished. In order to be democratic, the authors appear alphabetically. There are no stories grouped by themes. These pieces stand on their own. Many are excerpts from novels; there apparently aren't as many short story writers as I thought. Some, however, have been discouraged from writing in that form and were encouraged to write novels if they ever wanted to "make it" or be taken seriously. Of course I disagree with this notion, but it is for this reason that I think we have more novelists than short story writers. How many African-American stories have you ever seen in *The New Yorker*? *The Atlantic Monthly*? *Grand Street*? *Q*? *Redbook*? And even many of the prestigious literary quarterlies?

I've been teaching writing on the university level now for three years, and much to my dismay, rarely have I ever had an African-American student. I wish there were more ways to encourage young people to give writing a shot. Many of them still seem to be intimidated by the English language, and think of writing as "hard"—as in

Composition 101—hard. So many of them are set on "making it" (solely in material terms) that we find many of our students majoring in the "guaranteed" professions: the biological sciences, law, engineering, business, etc. If I can make an appeal to those who will read this anthology, I would like to say this to them: if for whatever reason you do not derive a genuine sense of excitement or satisfaction from your chosen field, if you are majoring in these disciplines because of a parent's insistence, if you are dissatisfied with the world to any extent and find yourself "secretly" jotting it down whenever or wherever you can; if you don't understand why people (yourself included) do the things that they do and it plagues you like an itch—consider taking a fiction writing course. Find out if there are African-American writing groups or *any* workshops that are available in your area. Then write. Read as much "serious" fiction as you can—and not just African-American authors. Then, keep writing. "Push it," says Annie Dillard. "Examine all things intensely and relentlessly. Probe and search . . . do not leave it, do not course over it, as if it were understood, but instead follow it down until you see it in the mystery of its own specificity and strength."

Persist.

Acknowledge your bewilderment.

Remember. Writing is personal. Try to write the kind of stories you'd like to read. Do not write to impress. Do not write to prove to a reader how much you know, but instead write in order *to know.* At the same time, you want to snatch readers' attention, pull them away from what they're doing and keep them right next to your characters. You want them to feel just what your characters feel, experience it with them so the readers are just as concerned about their outcome as the character is. Perhaps, if you do your job well and you're lucky, readers may recognize something until it clicks.

Everyone has a different opinion about what a good story should do and here are a few that I love:

"A story is a war. It is sustained and immediate combat."

"Your character should want something and want it intensely. It need not be melodramatic, earth-shattering or tangible. But it should be important to them whether or not they get it."

"A good story is a power struggle between equal forces. Something keeps getting in the way of the protagonist from achieving whatever they desire."

I like to think of what happens to characters in good novels and stories as knots—things keep knotting up. And by the end of the story—readers see an "unknotting" of sorts. Not what they expect, not the easy answers you get on TV, not wash-and-wear philosophies, but a reproduction of believable emotional experiences. All I want my readers to do is care about what's going to happen to these folks in the story. First, I have to care, and I don't waste my time writing about folks I don't care about. Once I've done this, I hope by delivering an exciting and convincing story with a satisfying ending, I can exhale, and think about what itch I must scratch next. Every story and excerpt in this anthology fits this description.

As for the title, I was living in Wyoming when I was trying to coin a phrase that would suggest what African-American writers have been doing for some time. I was looking out my window at the snow piled up, the thick icicles hanging off the house, and I thought about how hard life is in general, and further, as African-American writers how we have literally been breaking ice not only in getting published, but getting the respect and attention our work deserves. It's often been cold and hard, but we're chipping away, watching it slowly melt.

There is indeed a new generation of African-American writers emerging, and what we have in this collection are a fine group who have strong voices, who have each seen the world from a different stair. Our experiences as African-American women and men are undoubtedly distinctive, and in some cases unconventional. And just like the color of our skin varies in shades of black, so does our vision. The stories here reflect fifty-seven versions of them. If there appear to be omissions of certain authors, it is not out of disrespect, but because their work didn't fall into the time frame that I wanted to capture.

Needless to say, I wish there hadn't been a need to *separate* our work from others, and perhaps, as Dr. Martin Luther King expressed, one day this dream may come true, where all of our work is considered equal, and not measured by its color content, but its literary merit. Notwithstanding, I'm sure there are more of us "out there" just waiting to be discovered. We need as many voices, as many stories as are willing to come forth. And although we are not in the strict sense of the word historians, we are in fact making history. We are capturing and making permanent and indelible, reactions to, and impressions of, our most intimate observations, dreams, and nightmares, experiences and feelings about what it felt like for "us" to be African-Americans from the seventies until now—the nineties.

John Edgar Wideman
(1941–)

AMONG NUMEROUS OTHER accomplishments, John Edgar Wideman is likely the only major American writer who once was an outstanding athlete and a Rhodes Scholar. Born in Washington, D.C., Wideman grew up in the Pittsburgh, Pennsylvania, area, in a neighborhood called Homewood. Homewood is a black neighborhood that Wideman frequently writes about in his novels and memoirs. After graduating from high school as class valedictorian and star basketball player, he received a scholarship to the University of Pennsylvania. While there, he was a stellar student and athlete. He considered pursuing a career in the National Basketball Association (NBA), but he received a Rhodes Scholarship (the second African American to do so, after Alain Locke) and studied at Oxford University.

Wideman returned to the United States in 1966 and enrolled in the University of Iowa's Writers' Workshop. In 1967, he published his first novel, *A Glance Away*. Since his publication debut, Wideman has published a remarkable range of other works—including nine additional novels, five short story collections, and three memoirs. The novels include his *Homewood Trilogy*—*Damballah* (1981), *Hiding Place* (1981), and *Sent for You Yesterday* (1983)—and *Philadelphia Fire* (1990), based on the true story of MOVE, a radical black cult in Philadelphia.[16] His novel *Fanon* (2008) is based on the life and works of Frantz Fanon, the francophone writer and psychotherapist.

His memoirs include *Hoop Roots: Basketball, Race and Love* (2001). Two articles by Wideman are included in this anthology. Given its focus on several issues covered in the anthology, especially African American novelists and their audiences, his preface to

Breaking Ice appears later. In the excerpt from *Brothers and Keepers* (1984) that follows, Wideman candidly discusses his life as a writer in relation to his incarcerated brother.

From *Brothers and Keepers* (1984)

The guard's chest protrudes like there's compressed air instead of flesh inside the gray blouse of his uniform. A square head. Pale skin except on his cheeks, which are bluish and raw from razor burn. His mustache and short curly hair are meticulously groomed, too perfect to be real. The stylized hair of comic-book superheroes. A patch of blue darkness etched with symmetrical accent lines. His eyes avoid mine. He had spoken in a clipped, mechanical tone of voice. Not one man talking to another but a peremptory recital of rules droned at some abstraction in the middle distance where the guard's eyes focus while his lips move. I think, Nazi Gestapo Frankenstein robot motherfucker, but he's something worse. He's what he is and there's no way to get around that or for the moment get around him because he's entrenched in this no-man's land and he is what he is and that's worse than any names I can call him. He's laying down the law and that's it. The law. No matter that all three tables are unoccupied. No matter that I tell him we've sat at them before. No matter that we'll vacate if and when lawyers need them. No matter that I might have a case, make a case that my profession, my status means something outside the walls. No matter, my pride and anger and barely concealed scorn. I move on. We obey because the guard's in power. Will remain in power when I have to leave and go about my business. Then he'll be free to take out on my brother whatever revenge he couldn't exact from me and my smart mouth. So I take low. Shake my head but stroll away (just enough nigger in my walk to tell the guard I know what he thinks of me but that I think infinitely less of him) toward the least crowded space in the row of benches against the wall.

Not much news to relate. Robby cares about family business and likes to keep up with who's doing what, when, how, etc., but he also treats the news objectively, cold-bloodedly. Family affairs have everything and nothing to do with him. He's in exile, powerless to influence what goes on outside the walls, so he maintains a studied detachment; he hears what I say and quickly mulls it over, buries the worrisome parts, grins at good news. When he comments on bad news it's usually a grunt, a nod, or a gesture with his hands that says all there is to say and says, A million words wouldn't make any difference, would they. Learning to isolate himself, to build walls within the walls enclosing him is a matter of survival. If he doesn't insulate himself against those things he can't change, if he can't discipline himself to ignore and forget, to narrow the range of his concerns to what he can immediately, practically affect [sic], he'll go crazy. The one exception is freedom. Beneath whatever else Robby says or does or thinks, the dream of freedom pulses. The worst times, the lowest times are when the pulse seems extinguished. Like in the middle of the night, the hour of the wolf when even the joint is quiet and the earth stops spinning on its axis and he bursts from sleep, the deathly sleep that's the closest thing to mercy prison ever grants, starts from sleep and for a moment hears nothing. In the shadow of that absolute silence he can't imagine himself ever leaving prison alive. For hours, days, weeks the mood of that moment can oppress him. He needs every ounce of willpower he possesses to pick up the pieces of his life, to animate them again with the hope that one day the arbitrary, bitter, little routines he manufactures to sustain himself will make sense because one day he'll be free.

I arrange my pens and yellow pad atop the table. But before we begin working on the book I tell Robby my sawing dream.

I am a man, myself but not myself. The man wakes up and can't see the stars. The smell of death surrounds him. Fifteen hundred other men sleep in the honeycomb of steel that is his home forever. The fitful stirrings, clattering bars, groaning, the sudden outcries of fear, rage, madness, and God knows what else are finally over at this hour of the night or morning as he lies in his cell listening to other men sleep. The monotonous sawing sound reminds him of the funny papers, the little cloud containing saw and log drawn above a character's head so you can see the sound of sleeping. Only the man doesn't see logs floating above the prisoners' heads. As he listens and shuts his eyes and gets as close to praying as he ever does anymore, praying for sleep, for blessed oblivion, the cartoon he imagines behind his closed eyes is himself sawing away the parts of his own body. Doggedly, without passion or haste, drawing a dull saw up and back, up and back through his limbs. Slices drop away on the concrete floor. The man is cutting himself to pieces, there is less of him every time he saws through a section. He is lopping off his own flesh and blood but works methodically, concentrating on the up-and-back motion of the saw. When there's nothing left, he'll be finished. He seems almost bored, almost asleep, ready to snore like the saw's snoring as it chews through his body.

Robby shakes his head and starts to say something but doesn't, and we both leave the dream alone. Pass on to the book, the tasks still to be accomplished.

Robby had said he liked what he'd seen of the first draft. Liked it fine, but something was missing. Trouble was, he hadn't been able to name the missing ingredient. I couldn't either but I knew I had to try and supply it. By the book's conclusion I wanted a whole, rounded portrait of my brother. I'd envisioned a climactic scene in the final section, an epiphany that would reveal Robby's character in a powerful burst of light and truth. As the first draft evolved, I seemed to settle for much less. One early reader had complained of a "sense of frustration . . . By the end of the book I want to know more about Robby than I actually know. I know a lot of facts about his life but most of his inner self escapes me." On target or not, the reaction of this early reader, coupled with Robby's feeling that something crucial was lacking, had destroyed any complacency I had about the book's progress. I reread Robby's letters, returned to the books and articles that had informed my research into prisons and prisoners. I realized no apotheosis of Robby's character could occur in the final section because none had transpired in my dealings with my brother. The first draft had failed because it attempted to impose a dramatic shape on a relationship, on events and people too close to me to see in terms of beginning, middle, and end. My brother was in prison. A thousand books would not reduce his sentence one day. And the only denouement that might make sense of his story would be his release from prison. I'd been hoping to be a catalyst for change in the world upon which the book could conceivably have no effect at all. I'd been waiting to record dramatic, external changes in Robby's circumstances when what I should have been attuned to were the inner changes, his slow, internal adjustment day by day to an unbearable situation. The book was no powerful engine being constructed to set my brother free; it was dream, wish, song.

No, I could not create a man whose qualities were self-evident cause for returning him to the world of free people. Prison had changed my brother, not broken him, and therein lay the story. The changes were subtle, incremental; bit by bit he had been piecing himself together. He had not become a model human being with a cure for cancer at his fingertips if only the parole board would just give him a chance, turn him loose again on the streets of Home-wood. The character traits that landed Robby in prison are the same ones that have allowed him to survive with dignity, and pain and a sense of himself as infinitely better than the soulless drone prison demands he become. Robby knows his core is intact; his optimism, his intelligence, his capacity for love, his pride, his dream of making it big, becoming somebody special. And though these same qualities helped get him in trouble and could derail him again, I'm happy they are still there. I rejoice with him.

The problem with the first draft was my fear. I didn't let Robby speak for himself enough. I didn't have enough confidence in his words, his vision, his insights. I wanted to clean him up. Manufacture compelling before-and-after images. Which meant I made the bad too bad and the good too good. I knew what I wanted; so, for fear

I might not get what I needed, I didn't listen carefully, probe deeply enough. As I tried his story again I began to recognize patterns, a certain consistency in his responses, a basic impetuous honesty that made him see himself and his world with unflinching clarity. He never stopped asking questions. He never allowed answers to stop him. The worst things he did followed from the same impulse as the best. He could be unbelievably dumb, corrupt, selfish, and destructive but those qualities could keep him down no more than his hope, optimism, his refusal to accept a dull, inferior portion could buoy him above the hell that engulfed black boys in the Homewood streets. . . .

I let Robby know I've rewritten the book, virtually from start to finish. Plenty of blurred, gray space, lots of unfilled gaps and unanswered questions and people to interview, but the overall design is clearer now. I'm trying to explain to Robby how I feel released rather than constrained by the new pattern beginning to emerge. The breakthrough came when I started to hear what was constant, persistent beneath the changes in his life. The book will work if the reader participates, begins to grasp what I have. I hadn't been listening closely enough, so I missed the story announcing itself. When I caught on, there I was, my listening, waiting self, part of the story, listening, waiting for me.

Yet I remained apprehensive about the prison section of the book. Robby wouldn't be able to help me as much in this last section as he had with the others. The method we'd evolved was this: Robby would tell his stories. I'd listen, take notes, reconstruct the episodes after I'd allowed them time to sink in, then check my version with Rob to determine if it sounded right to him. Letters and talk about what I'd written would continue until we were both satisfied. We'd had lots of practice performing that operation and I was beginning to feel a measure of confidence in the results it eventually produced. "Doing Time" was a different matter. The book would end with this section. Since I was writing the book, one way or another I'd be on center stage. Not only would the prison section have to pull together many loose ends, but new material had to surface and be resolved.

Aside from logical and aesthetic considerations, finishing the book as object, completing the performance, there was the business of both rendering and closing down the special relationship between my brother and myself that writing the book had precipitated. All the questions I'd decided to finesse or sidestep or just shrug off in order to get on with writing would now return, some in the form of issues to be addressed in concluding the book, some as practical dilemmas in the world outside the book, the world that had continued to chug along while I wrote.

Robby was still a prisoner. He was inside and I was outside. Success, fame, ten million readers wouldn't change that. The book, whether it flopped or became a best-seller, would belong to the world beyond the prison walls. Ironically, it would validate the power of the walls, confirm the distance between what transpired inside and outside. Robby's story would be "out there," but he'd still be locked up. Despite my attempts to identify with my brother, to reach him and share his troubles, the fact was, I remained on the outside. With the book. Though I never intended to steal his story, to appropriate it or exploit, in a sense that's what would happen once the book was published.

His story would be out there in a world that ignored his existence. It could be put to whatever uses people chose. Of course I was hoping Robby would benefit from a book written about him, but the possible benefits did not alter the fact that imprisonment profoundly alienated him from the finished product of our collaboration.

Simple things like sharing financial profits could be handled; but how could I insure a return on the emotional investment my brother had made? Once I'd gotten the book I'd come for, would I be able to sustain the bond that had grown between us? Would I continue to listen with the same attention to his stories? Would he still possess a story? Much of what he'd entrusted to me had nothing to do with putting a book together. Had I identified with him because I discovered that was the best way to write the book? Would the identification I'd achieved become a burden, too intense, too pressurized to survive once the book was completed? Was the whole thing between us about a book or had something finer, truer been created? And even if a finer, truer thing had come into being, would it be shattered by the noisy explosion (or dull thud) of the book's appearance in the world beyond the prison walls?

Some of these questions could be asked outright. Others were too intimidating, too close to the bone to raise with my brother. Yet we had to deal with all of them. In the world and in the prison section. The book, if there was to be a book, must end, must become in some senses an artifact. I wanted to finish it but I didn't want to let it go. I might be losing much more than a book.

The fears I could put into words I tried to share with Robby. He nodded, clenched and unclenched his big hands, smiled at the funny parts, the blackly comic pratfalls and cul de sacs neither of us nor anybody in the world can avoid. Yeah, shit's gon hit the fan. Yeah, sounds like it might get rough . . . but then again . . . what can you do but do? Many of my worries clearly were not his. I was the writer, that was *my* kitchen, *my* heat. He'd thought about some of the stuff worrying me but I could tell he hadn't spent lots of time fretting over it. And wouldn't. Many of the troubles I anticipated were too far down the line to tease out Robby's concern. In prison he had learned to walk a very fine line. On one side of the line was the minute-by-minute, day-by-day struggle for survival to which he must devote his undivided attention. On the other side his vision of something better, a life outside the walls, an existence he could conceive only if he allowed himself the luxury of imagination, of formulating plans in a future divorced from his present circumstances. The line was thin, was perilous because any energy he squandered on envisioning the future was time away, a lapse in the eternal vigilance he must maintain to stay alive in his cage. Yet the struggle to survive, the heightened awareness he must sustain to get through each moment, each day made no sense unless his efforts were buying something other than more chunks of prison routine. And plans for the future were pipe dreams unless he could convince himself he possessed the stamina and determination to make it step by step through the withering prison regimen. These options, realities, consequences defined the straight and narrow path Robby was forced to tread. Like Orpheus ascending from Hades or Ulysses chained to the mast or a runaway slave abandoning his family and fleeing toward the North Star, my brother knew the only way he might get what he desperately wanted was to turn his back on it, pretend it didn't exist.

Walking the line, leaning neither too far to the left nor too far to the right, balancing, always balancing the pulls of heart and head in one direction against the tugs wrenching him in the other—that was Robby's unbearable burden, made more unbearable because to escape it all he had to do was surrender, tilt one way or the other, and let the weight on his shoulders drag him down.

The source of my brother's strength was a mystery to me. When I put myself in his shoes, tried to imagine how I'd cope if I were sentenced to life imprisonment, I couldn't conceive of any place inside myself from which I could draw the courage and dignity he displayed. In prison Robby had achieved an inner calm, a degree of self-sufficiency and self-reliance never apparent when he was running the streets. I didn't know many people, inside or out, who carried themselves the way he did now. Like my mother, he'd grown accustomed to what was unbearable, had named it, tamed it. He'd fallen, but he'd found the strength to rise again. Inch by inch, hand over hand, he'd pulled himself up on a vine he'd never known was there, a vine still invisible to me. I knew the vine was real because I'd watched my brother grasp it, because I could feel its absence in the untested air when I thought of myself in his situation. To discover the source of my brother's strength I found myself comparing what I'd accomplished outside the walls with what he'd managed inside. The comparison made me uncomfortable.

I didn't envy my brother. I'd learned enough about the hell of prison life not to mistake what I was feeling for envy. No, I wouldn't trade my problems for his. I'd take my chances on the outside. Yet something like envy was stirring. Worse than envy. The ancient insatiability of ego kicking up. Why hadn't I ever been able to acknowledge a talent, success, or capacity in another person without feeling that person's accomplishment either diminished me or pointed to some crucial deficiency in my constitution? What compound of greed, insecurity, and anger forced me always to compare, compete? Why couldn't I just leave myself out of it and celebrate Robby's willpower, his grace under pressure? Why couldn't I simply applaud and be grateful for whatever transformation of self he'd performed? Were my visits to prison about freeing him or freeing myself from the doubt that perhaps, after all, in spite of it all, maybe my brother has done more with his life than I've done with mine. Maybe he's the better man and maybe the only way I can face that truth about him, about myself, is to demystify the secret of his survival. Maybe I'm inside West Pen to warm myself by his fire, to steal it. Perhaps in my heart of hearts or, better, my ego of egos, I don't really want to tear down the walls, but tear my brother down, bring him back to my level, to the soft, uncertain ground where my feet are planted.

If somebody has sung the praises of a book or movie, I go in looking for flaws, weaknesses. No matter how good these books or movies, my pleasure is never unalloyed because I'm searching for the bad parts, groping for them even when they're not there; so I usually come away satisfied by my dissatisfaction. I'm stuck with a belief that nothing can stand too close an examination. The times when I experience the world as joy, as song, some part of me insists even in the midst of the joy, the song, that these moments will pass and nothing, nothing promises they will ever come again. My world is fallen. It's best to be suspicious, not to trust anything, anyone too far. Including myself. Especially the treacherous, layered reality of being whatever I think I am at a given moment. It's a fallen world. My brother is rising from the ashes but because he is my brother, another fall is as certain as this rising and my particular burden is to see both always. I can't help it.

Does what he's achieved in the narrow confines of a cell mock the cage I call freedom? What would I do in his place? How would I act? Are the walls between us permanent? Do we need them, want them? Is there a better place without barred windows and steel doors and locked cells where there's room for both of us, all of us?

What it comes down to is saying yes. Yes to the blood making us brothers. Blood bonding us, constraining us to the unspoken faith that I'm trying to do my best and he's trying to do his best but nothing we do can insure the worst won't happen so we keep at it, as best we can, doing the book and hoping it will turn out okay.

He's been thinking a lot about the time on the road, the three months as a fugitive when he and his partners crisscrossed the country, playing hide and seek with the law. He's tried to write some of it down but he's been too busy. Too much's been happening. School. He'll graduate in January. A little ceremony for the few guys who made it all the way through the program. An associate degree in engineering technology and three certificates. Rough. Real rough. The math he'd never had in high school. The slow grind of study. Hours relearning to be a student. Learning to take the whole business seriously while you hear the madness of the prison constantly boiling outside your cell. But I'm gon get it, Bruh. Few more weeks. These last exams kicking my ass but I'm gon get it. Most of the fellows dropped out. Only three of us completed the program. It'll look good on my record, too. But I ain't had time to do nothing else. Them books you sent. I really enjoy reading them but lately I ain't been doing nothing but studying.

PART TWO

On Aesthetics, Craft, and Publication

W. E. B. Du Bois
(1868–1963)

WILLIAM EDWARD BURGHARDT Du Bois was born in Great Barrington, Massachusetts. Starting in the late 1890s until just before his death in Accra, Ghana, in 1963, Du Bois published an impressive range of works. In 1895, he was the first African American to receive a Ph.D. from Harvard. His dissertation, "The Suppression of the African Slave Trade, 1638–1870," was published the following year. He was a pioneering sociologist who wrote *The Philadelphia Negro* (1899), partly based on qualitative interviews he conducted with African Americans in Philadelphia.[17] He was the principal organizer of the Atlanta University Studies of the Negro Problem. He published *Black Reconstruction* (1936), a provocative work of historical scholarship that challenged the prevailing ideas about the Reconstruction period as largely a failure. Du Bois was also an editor, most notably of *Crisis*, the NAACP's official magazine to which he frequently contributed articles, reviews, and editorials. Du Bois wrote three autobiographies, in which he recounts his boyhood days in Great Barrington. His final autobiography, *The Autobiography of W. E. B. Du Bois* (1968), was published posthumously. Since the late 1960s, his most influential book, *The Souls of Black Folk* (1903), has been widely taught in colleges and universities. Numerous students and scholars have alluded to or quoted the passage describing the Negro's "double-consciousness"—"two souls, two thoughts, two unreconciled strivings." Others, at least until the end of the twentieth century, frequently quoted his assertion that "the problem of the twentieth century is the problem of the color line."

Du Bois' remarkable work as a historian and sociologist as well as social activist and prototypical public intellectual has overshadowed his creative writing. But he wrote poetry, including "A Litany at Atlanta." He also published five novels: *The Quest of the Silver Fleece* (1911), *Dark Princess: A Romance* (1928), and the Black Flame trilogy: *The Ordeal of Mansart* (1957), *Mansart Builds a School* (1959), and *Worlds of Color* (1961).

Du Bois was a Communist. After being hounded by the U.S. government for years, he left the United States in 1961 and moved to Ghana. He became a Ghanaian citizen and died in Accra in 1963.

"Criteria of Negro Art" (1926), included here, shows Du Bois weighing in on the art-versus-propaganda question. When Du Bois refers to art, he certainly includes the art of fiction, especially the novel. But his essay—published around the time of similar essays by Langston Hughes, James Weldon Johnson, and Alain Locke—is comprehensive in scope. He is also referring to music and painting.[18]

Criteria of Negro Art (1926)

I do not doubt but there are some in this audience who are a little disturbed at the subject of this meeting, and particularly at the subject I have chosen. Such people are thinking something like this: "How is it that an organization like this, a group of radicals trying to bring new things into the world, a fighting organization which has come up out of the blood and dust of battle, struggling for the right of black men to be ordinary human beings—how is it that an organization of this kind can turn aside to talk about Art? After all, what have we who are slaves and black to do with Art?"

Or perhaps there are others who feel a certain relief and are saying, "After all it is rather satisfactory after all this talk about rights and fighting to sit and dream of something which leaves a nice taste in the mouth."

Let me tell you that neither of these groups is right. The thing we are talking about tonight is part of the great fight we are carrying on and it represents a forward and an upward look—a pushing onward.

You and I have been breasting hills; we have been climbing upward; there has been progress and we can see it day by day looking back along blood-filled paths. But as you go through the valleys and over the foothills, so long as you are climbing, the direction,—north, south, east or west,—is of less importance. But when gradually the vista widens and you begin to see the world at your feet and the far horizon, then it is time to know more precisely whither you are going and what you really want.

What do we want? What is the thing we are after? As it was phrased last night it had a certain truth: We want to be Americans, full-fledged Americans, with all the rights of other American citizens. But is that all? Do we want simply to be Americans? Once in a while through all of us there flashes some clairvoyance, some clear idea, of what America really is. We who are dark can see America in a way that white Americans can not. And seeing our country thus, are we satisfied with its present goals and ideals?

In the high school where I studied we learned most of Scott's "Lady of the Lake" by heart. In after life once it was my privilege to see the lake. It was Sunday. It was quiet. You could glimpse the deer wandering in unbroken forests; you could hear the soft ripple of romance on the waters. Around me fell the cadence of that poetry of my youth. I fell asleep full of the enchantment of the Scottish border. A new day broke and with it came a sudden rush of excursionists. They were mostly Americans and they were loud and strident. They poured upon the little pleasure boat,—men with their hats a little on one side and drooping cigars in the wet corners of their mouths; women who shared their conversation with the world. They all tried to get everywhere first. They pushed other people out of the way. They made all sorts of incoherent noises and gestures so that the quiet home folk and the visitors from other lands silently and half-wonderingly gave way before them. They struck a note not evil but wrong. They carried, perhaps, a sense of strength and accomplishment, but their hearts had no conception of the beauty which pervaded this holy place.

If you tonight suddenly should become full-fledged Americans; if your color faded, or the color line here in Chicago was miraculously forgotten; suppose, too, you became at the same time rich and powerful;—what is it that you would want? What would you immediately seek? Would you buy the most powerful of motor cars and outrace Cook County? Would you buy the most elaborate estate on the North Shore? Would you be a Rotarian or a Lion or a What-not of the very last degree? Would you wear the most striking clothes, give the richest dinners and buy the longest press notices?

Even as you visualize such ideals you know in your hearts that these are not the things you really want. You realize this sooner than the average white American because, pushed aside as we have been in America, there has come to us not only a certain distaste for the tawdry and flamboyant but a vision of what the world could be if it were really a beautiful world; if we had the true spirit; if we had the Seeing Eye, the Cunning Hand, the Feeling Heart; if we had, to be sure, not perfect happiness, but plenty of good hard work, the inevitable suffering that always comes with life; sacrifice and waiting, all that—but, nevertheless, lived in a world where men know, where men create, where they realize themselves and where they enjoy life. It is that sort of a world we want to create for ourselves and for all America.

After all, who shall describe Beauty? What is it? I remember tonight four beautiful things: The Cathedral at Cologne, a forest in stone, set in light and changing shadow, echoing with sunlight and solemn song; a village of the Veys in West Africa, a little thing of mauve and purple, quiet, lying content and shining in the sun; a black and velvet room where on a throne rests, in old and yellowing marble, the broken curves of the Venus of Milo; a single phrase of music in the Southern South—utter melody, haunting and appealing, suddenly arising out of night and eternity, beneath the moon.

Such is Beauty. Its variety is infinite, its possibility is endless. In normal life all may have it and have it yet again. The world is full of it; and yet today the mass of human beings are choked away from it, and their lives distorted and made ugly. This is not only wrong, it is silly. Who shall right this well-nigh universal failing? Who shall let this world be beautiful? Who shall restore to men the glory of sunsets and the peace of quiet sleep?

We black folk may help for we have within us as a race new stirrings; stirrings of the beginning of a new appreciation of joy, of a new desire to create, of a new will to be; as though in this morning of group life we had awakened from some sleep that at once dimly mourns the past and dreams a splendid future; and there has come the conviction that the Youth that is here today, the Negro Youth, is a different kind of Youth, because in some new way it bears this mighty prophecy on its breast, with a new realization of itself, with new determination for all mankind.

What has this Beauty to do with the world? What has Beauty to do with Truth and Goodness—with the facts of the world and the right actions of men? "Nothing," the artists rush to answer. They may be right. I am but an humble disciple of art and cannot presume to say. I am one who tells the truth and exposes evil and seeks with Beauty and for Beauty to set the world right. That somehow, somewhere eternal and perfect Beauty sits above Truth and Right I can conceive, but here and now and in the world in which I work they are for me unseparated and inseparable.

This is brought to us peculiarly when as artists we face our own past as a people. There has come to us—and it has come especially through the man we are going to honor tonight [Carter G. Woodson, 12th Spingarn medallist]—a realization of that past, of which for long years we have been ashamed, for which we have apologized. We thought nothing could come out of that past which we wanted to remember; which we wanted to hand down to our children. Suddenly, this same past is taking on form, color and reality, and in a half shamefaced way we are beginning to be proud of it. We are remembering that the romance of the world did not die and lie forgotten in the Middle Age; that if you want romance to deal with you must have it here and now and in your own hands.

I once knew a man and woman. They had two children, a daughter who was white and a daughter who was brown; the daughter who was white married a white man; and when her wedding was preparing the daughter who was brown prepared to go and celebrate. But the mother said, "No!" and the brown daughter went into her room and turned on the gas and died. Do you want Greek tragedy swifter than that?

Or again, here is a little Southern town and you are in the public square. On one side of the square is the office of a colored lawyer and on all the other sides are men who do not like colored lawyers. A white woman goes into the black man's office and points to the white-filled square and says, "I want five hundred dollars now and if I do not get it I am going to scream."

Have you heard the story of the conquest of German East Africa? Listen to the untold tale: There were 40,000 black men and 4,000 white men who talked German. There were 20,000 black men and 12,000 white men who talked English. There were 10,000 black men and 400 white men who talked French. In Africa then where the Mountains of the Moon raised their white and snowcapped heads into the mouth of the tropic sun, where Nile and Congo rise and the Great Lakes swim, these men fought; they struggled on mountain, hill and valley, in river, lake and swamp, until in masses they sickened, crawled and died; until the 4,000 white Germans had become mostly bleached bones; until nearly all the 12,000 white Englishmen had returned to South Africa, and the 400 Frenchmen to Belgium and Heaven; all except a mere handful of the white men died; but thousands of black men from East, West and South Africa, from Nigeria and the Valley of the Nile, and from the West Indies still struggled, fought and died. For four years they fought and won and lost German East Africa; and all you hear about it is that England and Belgium conquered German Africa for the allies!

Such is the true and stirring stuff of which Romance is born and from this stuff come the stirrings of men who are beginning to remember that this kind of material is theirs; and this vital life of their own kind is beckoning them on.

The question comes next as to the interpretation of these new stirrings, of this new spirit: Of what is the colored artist capable? We have had on the part of both colored and white people singular unanimity of judgment in the past. Colored people have said: "This work must be inferior because it comes from colored people." White people have said: "It is inferior because it is done by colored people." But today there is coming to both the realization that the work of the black man is not always inferior. Interesting stories come to us. A professor in the University of Chicago read to a class that had studied literature a passage of poetry and asked them to guess the author. They guessed a goodly company from Shelley and Robert Browning down to Tennyson and Masefield. The author was Countée Cullen. Or again the English critic John Drinkwater went down to a Southern seminary, one of the sort which "finishes" young white women of the South. The students sat with their wooden faces while he tried to get some response out of them. Finally he said, "Name me some of your Southern poets." They hesitated. He said finally, "I'll start out with your best: Paul Laurence Dunbar!"

With the growing recognition of Negro artists in spite of the severe handicaps, one comforting thing is occurring to both white and black. They are whispering, "Here is a way out. Here is the real solution of the color problem. The recognition accorded Cullen, Hughes, Fauset, White and others shows there is no real color line. Keep quiet! Don't complain! Work! All will be well!"

I will not say that already this chorus amounts to a conspiracy. Perhaps I am naturally too suspicious. But I will say that there are today a surprising number of white people who are getting great satisfaction out of these younger Negro writers because they think it is going to stop agitation of the Negro question. They say, "What is the use of your fighting and complaining; do the great thing and the reward is there." And many colored people are all too eager to follow this advice; especially those who are weary of the eternal struggle along the color line, who are afraid to fight and to whom the money of philanthropists and the alluring publicity are subtle and deadly bribes. They say, "What is the use of fighting? Why not show simply what we deserve and let the reward come to us?"

And it is right here that the National Association for the Advancement of Colored People comes upon the field, comes with its great call to a new battle, a new fight and new things to fight before the old things are wholly won; and to say that the Beauty of Truth and Freedom which shall some day be our heritage and the heritage of all civilized men is not in our hands yet and that we ourselves must not fail to realize.

There is in New York tonight a black woman molding clay by herself in a little bare room, because there is not a single school of sculpture in New York where she is welcome. Surely there are doors she might burst through, but when God makes a sculptor He does not always make the pushing sort of person who beats his way through doors thrust in his face. This girl is working her hands off to get out of this country so that she can get some sort of training.

There was Richard Brown. If he had been white he would have been alive today instead of dead of neglect. Many helped him when he asked but he was not the kind of boy that always asks. He was simply one who made colors sing.

There is a colored woman in Chicago who is a great musician. She thought she would like to study at Fontainebleau this summer where Walter Damrosch and a score of leaders of Art have an American school of music. But the application blank of this school says: "I am a white American and I apply for admission to the school."

We can go on the stage; we can be just as funny as white Americans wish us to be; we can play all the sordid parts that America likes to assign to Negroes; but for any thing else there is still small place for us.

And so I might go on. But let me sum up with this: Suppose the only Negro who survived some centuries hence was the Negro painted by white Americans in the novels and essays they have written. What would people in a hundred years say of black Americans? Now turn it around. Suppose you were to write a story and put in it the kind of people you know and like and imagine. You might get it published and you might not. And the "might not" is still far bigger than the "might." The white publishers catering to white folk would say, "It is not interesting"—to white folk, naturally not. They want Uncle Toms, Topsies, good "darkies" and clowns. I have in my office a story with all the earmarks of truth. A young man says that he started out to write and had his stories accepted. Then he began to write about the things he knew best about, that is, about his own people. He submitted a story to a magazine which said, "We are sorry, but we cannot take it." "I sat down and revised my story, changing the color of the characters and the locale and sent it under an assumed name with a change of address and it was accepted by the same magazine that had refused it, the editor promising to take anything else I might send in providing it was good enough."

We have, to be sure, a few recognized and successful Negro artists; but they are not all those fit to survive or even a good minority. They are but the remnants of that ability and genius among us whom the accidents of education and opportunity have raised on the tidal waves of chance. We black folk are not altogether peculiar in this. After all, in the world at large, it is only the accident, the remnant, that gets the chance to make the most of itself; but if this is true of the white world it is infinitely more true of the colored world. It is not simply the great clear tenor of Roland Hayes that opened the ears of America. We have had many voices of all kinds as fine as his and America was and is as deaf as she was for years to him. Then a foreign land heard Hayes and put its imprint on him and immediately America with all its imitative snobbery woke up. We approved Hayes because London, Paris and Berlin approved him and not simply because he was a great singer.

Thus it is the bounden duty of black America to begin this great work of the creation of Beauty, of the preservation of Beauty, of the realization of Beauty, and we must use in this work all the methods that men have used before. And what have been the tools of the artist in times gone by? First of all, he has used the Truth—not for the sake of truth, not as a scientist seeking truth, but as one upon whom Truth eternally thrusts itself as the highest handmaid of imagination, as the one great vehicle of universal understanding. Again artists have used Goodness—goodness in all its aspects of justice, honor and right—not for sake of an ethical sanction but as the one true method of gaining sympathy and human interest.

The apostle of Beauty thus becomes the apostle of Truth and Right not by choice but by inner and outer compulsion. Free he is but his freedom is ever bounded by Truth and Justice; and slavery only dogs him when he is denied the right to tell the Truth or recognize an ideal of Justice.

Thus all Art is propaganda and ever must be, despite the wailing of the purists. I stand in utter shamelessness and say that whatever art I have for writing has been used always for propaganda for gaining the right of black folk to love and enjoy. I do not care a damn for any art that is not used for propaganda. But I do care when propaganda is confined to one side while the other is stripped and silent.

In New York we have two plays: "White Cargo" and "Congo." In "White Cargo" there is a fallen woman. She is black. In "Congo" the fallen woman is white. In "White Cargo" the black woman goes down further and further and in "Congo" the white woman begins with degradation but in the end is one of the angels of the Lord. You know the current magazine story: A young white man goes down to Central America and the most beautiful colored woman there falls in love with him. She crawls across the whole isthmus to get to him. The white man says nobly, "No." He goes back to his white sweetheart in New York.

In such cases, it is not the positive propaganda of people who believe white blood divine, infallible and holy to which I object. It is the denial of a similar right of propaganda to those who believe black blood human, lovable and inspired with new ideals for the world. White artists themselves suffer from this narrowing of their field. They cry for freedom in dealing with Negroes because they have so little freedom in dealing with whites. DuBose Heywood writes "Porgy" and writes beautifully of the black Charleston underworld. But why does he do this? Because he cannot do a similar thing for the white people of Charleston, or they would drum him out of town. The only chance he had to tell the truth of pitiful human degradation was to tell it of colored people. I should not be surprised if Octavius Roy Cohen had approached the *Saturday Evening Post* and asked permission to write about a different kind of colored folk than the monstrosities he has created; but if he has, the *Post* has implied, "No. You are getting paid to write about the kind of colored people you are writing about."

In other words, the white public today demands from its artists, literary and pictorial, racial prejudgment which deliberately distorts Truth and Justice, as far as colored races are concerned, and it will pay for no other.

On the other hand, the young and slowly growing black public still wants its prophets almost equally unfree. We are bound by all sorts of customs that have come down as secondhand soul clothes of white patrons. We are ashamed of sex and we lower our eyes when people will talk of it. Our religion holds us in superstition. Our worst side has been so shamelessly emphasized that we are denying we have or ever had a worst side. In all sorts of ways we are hemmed in and our new young artists have got to fight their way to freedom.

The ultimate judge has got to be you and you have got to build yourselves up into that wide judgment, that catholicity of temper which is going to enable the artist to have his widest chance for freedom. We can afford the Truth. White folk today cannot. As it is now we are handing everything over to a white jury. If a colored man wants to publish a book, he has got to get a white publisher and a white newspaper to say it is great; and then you and I say so. We must come to the place where the work of art when it appears is reviewed and acclaimed by our own free and unfettered judgment.

And we are going to have a real and valuable and eternal judgment only as we make ourselves free of mind, proud of body and just of soul to all men.

And then do you know what will be said? It is already saying. Just as soon as true Art emerges; just as soon as the black artist appears, someone touches the race on the shoulder and says, "He did that because he was an American, not because he was a Negro; he was born here; he was trained here; he is not a Negro—what is a Negro anyhow? He is just human; it is the kind of thing you ought to expect."

I do not doubt that the ultimate art coming from black folk is going to be just as beautiful, and beautiful largely in the same ways, as the art that comes from white folk, or yellow, or red; but the point today is that until the art of the black folk compells recognition they will not be rated as human. And when through art they will compell recognition then let the world discover if it will that their art is as new as it is old and as old as new.

I had a classmate once who did three beautiful things and died. One of them was a story of a folk who found fire and then went wandering in the gloom of night seeking again the stars they had once known and lost; suddenly out of blackness they looked up and there loomed the heavens; and what was it that they said? They raised a mighty cry: "It is the stars, it is the ancient stars, it is the young and everlasting stars!"

Langston Hughes

IN "The Negro Artist and the Racial Mountain" (1926), Hughes spells out what he believes is the unique contribution all African American artists, including novelists, can make. He says, "Without going outside his race, . . . there is sufficient matter to furnish a black artist with a lifetime of creative work. And when he chooses to touch on the relations between Negroes and whites, . . . especially literature and the drama, there is an inexhaustible supply of themes at hand."

The Negro Artist and the Racial Mountain (1926)

One of the most promising of the young Negro poets said to me once, "I want to be a poet—not a Negro poet," meaning, I believe, "I want to write like a white poet"; meaning, subconsciously, "I would like to be a white poet"; meaning behind that, "I would like to be white." And I was sorry the young man said that, for no great poet has ever been afraid of being himself. And I doubted then that, with his desire to run away spiritually from his race, this boy would ever be a great poet. But this is the mountain standing in the way of any true Negro art in America—this urge within the race toward whiteness, the desire to pour racial individuality into the mold of American standardization, and to be as little Negro and as much American as possible.

But let us look at the immediate background of this young poet. His family is of what I suppose one would call the Negro middle class: people who are by no means rich, yet never uncomfortable nor hungry—smug, contented, respectable folk, members of the

Baptist church. The father goes to work every morning. He is a chief steward at a large white club. The mother sometimes does fancy sewing or supervises parties for the rich families of the town. The children go to a mixed school. In the home they read white papers and magazines. And the mother often says, "Don't be like niggers" when the children are bad. A frequent phrase from the father is, "Look how well a white man does things." And so the word white comes to be unconsciously a symbol of all the virtues. It holds for the children beauty, morality and money. The whisper of "I want to be white" runs silently through their minds. This young poet's home is, I believe, a fairly typical home of the colored middle class. One sees immediately how difficult it would be for an artist born in such a home to interest himself in interpreting the beauty of his own people. He is never taught to see that beauty. He is taught rather not to see it, or if he does, to be ashamed of it when it is not according to Caucasian patterns.

For racial culture the home of a self-styled "high-class" Negro has nothing better to offer. Instead there will perhaps be more aping of things white than in a less cultured or less wealthy home. The father is perhaps a doctor, lawyer, landowner, or politician. The mother may be a social worker, or a teacher, or she may do nothing and have a maid. Father is often dark but he has usually married the lightest woman he could find. The family attends a fashionable church where few really colored faces are to be found. And they themselves draw a color line. In the North they go to white theaters and white movies. And in the South they have at least two cars and a house "like white folks." Nordic manners, Nordic faces, Nordic hair, Nordic art (if any), and an Episcopal heaven. A very high mountain indeed for the would-be racial artist to climb in order to discover himself and his people.

But then there are the low-down folks, the so-called common element, and they are the majority—may the Lord be praised! The people who have their nip of gin on Saturday nights and are not too important to themselves or the community, or too well fed, or too learned to watch the lazy world go round. They live on Seventh Street in Washington or State Street in Chicago and they do not particularly care whether they are like white folks or anybody else. Their joy runs, bang! into ecstasy. Their religion soars to a shout. Work maybe a little today, rest a little tomorrow. Play awhile. Sing awhile. O, let's dance! These common people are not afraid of spirituals, as for a long time their more intellectual brethren were, and jazz is their child. They furnish a wealth of colorful, distinctive material for any artist because they still hold their own individuality in the face of American standardizations. And perhaps these common people will give to the world its truly great Negro artist, the one who is not afraid to be himself. Whereas the better-class Negro would tell the artist what to do, the people at least let him alone when he does appear. And they are not ashamed of him—if they know he exists at all. And they accept what beauty is their own without question.

Certainly there is, for the American Negro artist who can escape the restrictions the more advanced among his own group would put upon him, a great field of unused material ready for his art. Without going outside his race, and even among the better classes with their "white" culture and conscious American manners, but still Negro enough to be different, there is sufficient matter to furnish a black artist with a lifetime of creative work. And when he chooses to touch on the relations between Negroes and whites in this country, with their innumerable overtones and undertones, surely, and especially for literature and the drama, there is an inexhaustible supply of themes at hand. To these the Negro artist can give his racial individuality, his heritage of rhythm and warmth, and his incongruous humor that so often, as in the Blues, becomes ironic laughter mixed with tears. But let us look again at the mountain.

A prominent Negro clubwoman in Philadelphia paid eleven dollars to hear Raquel Meller sing Andalusian popular songs. But she told me a few weeks before she would not think of going to hear "that woman," Clara Smith, a great black artist, sing Negro folksongs. And many an upper-class Negro church, even now, would not dream of employing a spiritual in its services. The drab melodies in white folks' hymnbooks are much to be preferred. "We want to worship the Lord correctly and quietly. We don't believe in 'shouting.' Let's be dull like the Nordics," they say, in effect.

The road for the serious black artist, then, who would produce a racial art is most certainly rocky and the mountain is high. Until recently he received almost no encouragement for his work from either white or colored people. The fine novels of Chesnutt go out of print with neither race noticing their passing. The quaint charm and humor of Dunbar's dialect verse brought to him, in his day, largely the same kind of encouragement one would give a sideshow freak (A colored man writing poetry! How odd!) or a clown (How amusing!).

The present vogue in things Negro, although it may do as much harm as good for the budding colored artist, has at least done this: it has brought him forcibly to the attention of his own people among whom for so long, unless the other race had noticed him beforehand, he was a prophet with little honor. I understand that Charles Gilpin acted for years in Negro theaters without any special acclaim from his own, but when Broadway gave him eight curtain calls, Negroes, too, began to beat a tin pan in his honor. I know a young colored writer, a manual worker by day, who had been writing well for the colored magazines for some years, but it was not until he recently broke into the white publications and his first book was accepted by a prominent New York publisher that the "best" Negroes in his city took the trouble to discover that he lived there. Then almost immediately they decided to give a grand dinner for him. But the society ladies were careful to whisper to his mother that perhaps she'd better not come. They were not sure she would have an evening gown.

The Negro artist works against an undertow of sharp criticism and misunderstanding from his own group and unintentional bribes from the whites. "O, be respectable, write about nice people, show how good we are," say the Negroes. "Be stereotyped, don't go too far, don't shatter our illusions about you, don't amuse us too seri-

ously. We will pay you," say the whites. Both would have told Jean
Toomer not to write *Cane*. The colored people did not praise it. The
white people did not buy it. Most of the colored people who did
read *Cane* hate it. They are afraid of it. Although the critics gave
it good reviews the public remained indifferent. Yet (excepting the
work of DuBois) *Cane* contains the finest prose written by a Negro
in America. And like the singing of Robeson it is truly racial.

But in spite of the Nordicized Negro intelligentsia and the desires
of some white editors we have an honest American Negro literature
already with us. Now I await the rise of the Negro theater. Our folk
music, having achieved world-wide fame, offers itself to the genius
of the great individual American Negro composer who is to come.
And within the next decade I expect to see the work of a growing
school of colored artists who paint and model the beauty of dark
faces and create with new technique the expressions of their own
soul-world. And the Negro dancers who will dance like flame and the
singers who will continue to carry our songs to all who listen—they
will be with us in even greater numbers tomorrow.

Most of my own poems are racial in theme and treatment, derived
from the life I know. In many of them I try to grasp and hold some
of the meanings and rhythms of jazz. I am sincere as I know how to
be in these poems and yet after every reading I answer questions like
these from my own people: "Do you think Negroes should always
write about Negroes? I wish you wouldn't read some of your poems
to white folks. How do you find anything interesting in a place like
a cabaret? Why do you write about black people? You aren't black.
What makes you do so many jazz poems?"

But jazz to me is one of the inherent expressions of Negro life in
America: the eternal tom-tom beating in the Negro soul—the tom-
tom of revolt against weariness in a white world, a world of subway
trains and work, work, work; the tom-tom of joy and laughter,
and pain swallowed in a smile. Yet the Philadelphia clubwoman is
ashamed to say that her race created it and she does not like me to
write about it. The old subconscious "white is best" runs through

her mind. Years of study under white teachers, a lifetime of white books, pictures, and papers, and white manners, morals, and Puritan standards made her dislike the spirituals. And now she turns up her nose at jazz and all its manifestations—likewise almost everything else distinctly racial. She doesn't care for the Winold Reiss portraits of Negroes because they are "too Negro." She does not want a true picture of herself from anybody. She wants the artist to flatter her, to make the white world believe that all Negroes are as smug and as near white in soul as she wants to be. But, to my mind, it is the duty of the younger Negro artist, if he accepts any duties at all from outsiders, to change through the force of his art that old whispering, "I want to be white," hidden in the aspirations of his people, to "Why should I want to be white? I am a Negro—and beautiful!"

So I am ashamed for the black poet who says, "I want to be a poet, not a Negro poet," as though his own racial world were not as interesting as any other world. I am ashamed, too, for the colored artist who runs from the painting of Negro faces to the painting of sunsets after the manner of the academicians because he fears the strange un-whiteness of his own features. An artist must be free to choose what he does, certainly, but he must also never be afraid to do what he might choose.

Let the blare of Negro jazz bands and the bellowing voice of Bessie Smith singing Blues penetrate the closed ears of the colored near-intellectuals until they listen and perhaps understand. Let Paul Robeson singing "Water Boy," and Rudolph Fisher writing about the streets of Harlem, and Jean Toomer holding the heart of Georgia in his hands, and Aaron Douglas drawing strange black fantasies cause the smug Negro middle class to turn from their white, respectable, ordinary books and papers to catch a glimmer of their own beauty. We younger Negro artists who create now intend to express our individual dark-skinned selves without fear or shame. If white people are pleased we are glad. If they are not, it doesn't matter. We know we are beautiful. And ugly too. The tom-tom cries and the tom-tom laughs. If colored people are pleased we are glad. If they are not, their displeasure doesn't matter either. We build our temples for tomorrow, strong as we know how, and we stand on top of the mountain, free within ourselves.

Gayl Jones
(1949–)

BORN IN LEXINGTON, Kentucky, in 1949, Gayl Jones attended
Connecticut College. She majored in English and started writing
fiction. After graduating, she enrolled in Brown University's graduate creative writing program. She was awarded both a master's
and doctorate in creative arts. During her time at Brown, she was
mentored by the poet Michael Harper.

Jones' first two novels—*Corregidora* (1975) and *Eva's Man*
(1976)—and *White Rat* (1977), a collection of short stories, were
published in swift succession. Toni Morrison, then a senior editor at Random House, served as Jones' editor. Given her creative
promise, Jones was hired as an assistant professor at the University
of Michigan at Ann Arbor in 1976. While in Ann Arbor, Jones met
and eventually married Robert Higgins, an ideologue and activist.
During the early 1980s, Higgins was arrested and charged with
felonious assault. Thereafter, Jones' life and literary career took a
dramatic turn.

Before his trial, Higgins and Jones fled the United States and
eventually settled in Paris. They remained there for five years and
then returned to the United States. Jones went home to Lexington to
live with her ailing mother. The couple led a relatively quiet life until
after her mother's death. Just before the publication of *The Healing*, her third novel, in 1998, Jones' mother died. Higgins blamed
the hospital for his mother-in-law's death and began a public and
vitriolic campaign against the hospital and the local police. The
police eventually traced a bomb threat that arrived at their office
to Higgins. When they surrounded Jones' mother's residence, Jones

and Higgins threatened to commit suicide. As the police stormed the home, Higgins killed himself. Jones was rescued.

During her unusual literary career, Jones also published several poetry collections and a play. In 1991, Harvard University Press published Jones' *Liberating Voices: Oral Tradition in African American Literature*, a book of literary criticism. After her husband's sensational death, Jones became a recluse and still resides in her mother's home. In her tribute to Robert Higgins, she wrote: "The world denied his light, his Pure Spirit, but I saw it and I see it still."[19]

In "About My Work" (1988), Jones discusses "problematic characters."

About My Work (1988)

". . . I am interested in human relationships, but I do not make moral judgments or political judgments or political judgments of my characters."

I am interested principally in the psychology of characters—and the way(s) in which they order their stories—their myths, dreams, nightmares, secret worlds, ambiguities, contradictions, ambivalences, memories, imaginations, their "puzzles." For this reason I cannot claim "political compulsions" nor "moral compulsions" if by either of these one means certain kinds of restrictions on "imaginative territory" or if one means maintaining a "literary decorum." I am interested in human relationships, but I do not make moral judgments or political judgments of my characters. Sometimes I will allow certain characters to make moral judgments of other characters. I will allow certain characters to be didactic—mostly when I do not share their views. I am not a didactic writer. Characters and readers have the freedom of moral judgment. For instance, my disapproval of Eva's action/choice (in *Eva's Man*) does not enter the work at all.

She simply tells her story. I allow her to tell it, as much as she will tell. I wish I had broken more out of the "realistic" mode, done more to suggest the psychological changes and strategies, through modes of expressionism, surrealism, more fragments of experiences, and so forth in getting at the "truth" of that *particular* character. Eva Canada stands for no one but Eva Canada.

To deal with such a character as Eva becomes problematic in the way that "Trueblood" becomes problematic in *Invisible Man*. It raises the questions of possibility. Should a Black writer ignore such characters, refuse to enter "such territory" because of the "negative image" and because such characters can be misused politically by others, or should one try to reclaim such complex, contradictory characters as well as try to reclaim the idea of the "heroic image"? I am interested in the idea of the "heroic image" and the "ideal of heroism"—but only when such characterizations are complex, multidimensional, and sometimes even "problematic" themselves, in the sense of their acknowledged "wholeness." Some of the things I am writing now try to deal with the question of heroism and the heroic image, but at the same time I do not want to avoid the Truebloods or to refuse to see that complicated territory. In fact, one can see Trueblood also as heroic in his acceptance of the moral responsibility.

I do not have a political "stance," but I am interested sometimes in the relationship between history, society, morality, and personality. I believe that all literatures can have political uses and misuses. Sometimes politics can enhance, sometimes it can get in the way of imaginative literature. Sometimes politics or political strategies, like any kind of strategy and system, can be useful in the organization and structuring of one's own work, the selecting of character, of event, the choosing of ideas, but it can also tell you what you cannot do, tell you what you must avoid, tell you that there's a certain territory politics won't allow you to enter, certain questions politics won't allow you to ask—in order to be "politically correct." I think sometimes you just have to be "wrong"; there's a lot of imaginative territory that you have to be "wrong" in order to enter. I'm not sure one can be a creative writer and a politician—not a "good" politician.

In terms of personal/private relationships I suppose I'm more besieged as a woman. In terms of public/social relationships I suppose I'm more besieged as a Black. Being both, it's hard to sometimes distinguish the occasion for being "besieged."

The individuals who have influenced my work are my mother, Lucille Jones; my creative writing teachers, Michael Harper and William Meredith, and my high school Spanish teacher, Anna Dodd. Because of their own persons, their own writing, their encouragement. I began to seriously write when I was seven, because I saw my mother writing, and because she would read stories to my brother and me, stories that she had written.

I like the idea of Kentucky in my work, though I don't always place my stories there. But it's like a "magic word." Often in works that take place somewhere else I'll make references to Kentucky, or have some of the characters be from there, even if they travel to other places—except for my historical novels that take place in Brazil in the seventeenth and eighteenth centuries. After a while, I probably won't place my characters in the "past" anymore; I'd like to work more with the contemporary or "modern" world whether in Kentucky or elsewhere. But I think there'll always be references to Kentucky as place/as home even when the characters are somewhere else. (I probably don't deal enough with place in terms of landscape.)

I notice people more than landscape. I notice voices.

I think people more than events affect/impact on my creativity.

I don't know who I am really. I like surprises. I don't go about "searching for an identity." I guess I like to explore in terms of my imagination. I like to write about imaginary people—become their "voices."

I don't think there's a role or a special niche for anyone. People can make them. I think "all letters" belong in "all letters"/world letters.

I work anytime that I have time and inclination. Sometimes I work when I don't have time or inclination. Sometimes I work early in the mornings, sometimes during the day, sometimes at night, sometimes but rarely in the middle of the night. But I can generally work anytime. I usually write in longhand, revise in longhand, and then type it out.

Teaching full time makes it so that I don't write as much as I did when I was in the doctor of arts graduate school program in creative writing at Brown. But teaching other writers can make you think more about certain themes, literary techniques, and strategies, which I think can be helpful, though it can sometimes make you self-conscious about these matters too. I'm teaching a course entitled *Introduction to the Short Story and the Novel* and even though I didn't initially intend it, works I particularly enjoyed have assumed a pattern that appears to include the "self-invented" or "self-created" hero or what Robert Stepto calls the "self-imagined" hero. We're reading such writers such as Kate Chopin, Zora Neale Hurston, James Joyce, Ralph Ellison, Jean Toomer, Carlos Fuentes, Toni Morrison, Miguel de Cervantes. And like Don Quixote all the characters are trying to "invent" themselves: some do, some don't, some are left with the dilemma, the question, some leave the reader with that. So such things make you think consciously about something you might not think about just writing or just reading and not having to "teach" the books. I prefer writing to teaching, though. And I prefer teaching literature to teaching writing. I like "teaching" individuals to "teaching" groups.

I consider my material "material." Or I call it "work."

I think I have an unfortunate public image, because of the published work. People imagine you're the person you've imagined.

I think I'm trying some new stylistic modes, some new themes.

Sometimes I write as a woman, sometimes as a man, sometimes as a person; by that I mean in terms of narrative "voice." But I mostly prefer writing about women and having women tell the stories to using a man as the storyteller. I should probably try that with a novel—just to try it—to see how the man would order his world, events, and character.

I am very much interested in form and structure. I am as interested in *how* things are said as I am in what is said. Toomer's *Cane* or Cervantes' *Don Quixote* wouldn't be the same if they didn't say what they say the way they say it. They are marvelous. Also, when dealing with the psychology of character, you choose what characters say and how they say it.

James Weldon Johnson
(1871–1938)

JAMES WELDON JOHNSON grew up in Jacksonville, Florida, and graduated from Atlanta University. During the late 1890s, he was the first African American to pass the Florida bar exam. Over the years, he was a teacher, poet, lyricist, journalist, editor, attorney, and diplomat. He also served as field secretary of the NAACP. Since he was one of the major contributors to the Harlem Renaissance, it is appropriate to call him a Renaissance man.

By any measure, he is an outstanding man of letters. He edited *The Book of American Negro Poetry* (1922) and *The Book of American Negro Spirituals* (1925). African Americans who sing "Lift Ev'ry Voice and Sing," known as the "Negro National Anthem," may be unaware that Johnson wrote the inspirational lyrics. The music was composed by his brother, J. Rosamond Johnson. Older African Americans may have read or recited "The Creation," Johnson's famous poem about God's creation of the earth. The poem is included in Johnson's collection *God's Trombones* (1926).[20] The volume includes seven folk sermons frequently preached by black ministers in the rural South. Johnson abbreviated and rewrote the sermons in poetic stanzas. He attempted to capture the black preachers' magisterial use of language. Some of the preachers, though uneducated, could make parables from the King James Bible, such as "The Prodigal Son," spring vividly to life.

Johnson published (at first anonymously) one novel, *The Autobiography of an Ex–Colored Man* (1912)—a novel that explores the consequences of an African American musician's decision to pass for white. The book is still widely taught in colleges and universities. Johnson was a fine prose writer. He published an autobiography,

Along This Way (1933). His book *Black Manhattan* (1934) received the W. E. B. Du Bois Prize as "the best book of prose written by an African American during a three year period."[21]

In "Negro Authors and White Publishers" (1929), Johnson, like Langston Hughes and African American writers decades later, addresses the promises and challenges African American writers face when they deal with the publishing industry.

Negro Authors and White Publishers (1929)

Negro writers, like all writing folks, have many things to complain about. Writers always have felt and many of them have plainly said that the world did not fully appreciate their work. This attitude has seldom been justified. The great or good writers who have not been acknowledged as such by the generation in which they lived are rare. And where such acknowledgment has not been accorded by the generations which touched an author's life, posterity has hardly ever revoked the unfavorable judgment.

Nevertheless, writers have many good reasons for complaining; for their lot is a hard one. And it may be that Negro writers have some special good reasons for complaining; I am not sure that at the present time this is so. However that may be, there is one complaint that some younger Negro writers are uttering with greater and greater insistence which I do not think is based on the facts and which reacts to the injury of the writers uttering it. This complaint is: that the leading white publishers have set a standard which Negro writers must conform to or go unpublished; that this standard calls only for books depicting the Negro in a manner which tends to degrade him in the eyes of the world; that only books about the so-called lower types of Negroes and lower phases of Negro life find consideration and acceptance.

Now, in the first place, there is a certain snobbishness in terming the less literate and less sophisticated, the more simple and more primitive classes of Negroes as "lower." At least as literary material, they are higher. They have greater dramatic and artistic potentialities for the writer than the so-called higher classes, who so closely resemble the bourgeois white classes. The vicious and criminal elements—and we must admit that even in our own race there are such elements—are rightly termed "lower," but even they have more accessible dramatic values than the ordinary, respectable middle-class element. It takes nothing less than supreme genius to make middle-class society, black or white, interesting—to say nothing of making it dramatic.

But I am jotting down this brief essay with the prime purpose of pointing out the dangers, especially to young writers, in complaining that publishers refuse to consider their work because it portrays Negro life on too high a level. When a writer begins to say and then believe that the reason why he cannot get published is because his work is *too good* he is in a bad way. This is the way that leads to making a fetish of failure. It is a too easy explanation of the lack of accomplishment. It is this "superior work—sordid publishers—low brow public" complex that gives rise to the numerous small coteries of unsuccessful writers, white as well as colored; the chief function of the members of these coteries being the mutual admiration of each other's unpublished manuscripts. This attitude brings its adherents to a position of pathetic futility or ludicrous superiority.

Within these seven or eight years of literary florescence I doubt that any first class publisher has turned down first rate work by any Negro writer on the ground that it was *not on a low enough level.* Now, suppose we look at the actual facts as shown by the books published in these recent years by leading publishers. Let us first take fiction and list the books depicting Negro life on the "upper" levels or shedding a favorable light on the race that have been published:

There Is Confusion.. Jessie Fauset
Fire in the Flint.. Walter White
Flight .... Walter White
The Prince of Washington Square .... Harry F. Liscomb

Quicksand.. Nella Larsen

Dark Princess... W. E. B. Du Bois

Plum Bun.. Jessie Fauset

Now, those depicting Negro life on the "lower" levels:

Cane...Jean Toomer

Tropic Death.. Eric Walrond

Home to Harlem...Claude McKay

Walls of Jericho...Rudolph Fisher

The Blacker the Berry..Wallace Thurman

Banjo...Claude McKay

The score is eight to six—with "Tropic Death," "Walls of Jericho" and "Cane" on the border line. In non fiction the "upper level" literature scores still higher. In that class we have:

A Social History of the American Negro...................Benjamin Brawley

Negro Folk Rhymes...Thomas W. Talley

The Book of American Negro Poetry...........Ed. James Weldon Johnson

The New Negro.. Ed. Alain Locke

The Book of American Negro Spirituals......Ed. James Weldon Johnson

The Second Book of American Negro Spirituals.........Ed. James Weldon
Johnson

Color ....Countée Cullen

Caroling Dusk...Ed. Countée Cullen

Darkwater..W. E. B. Du Bois

Gift of Black Folk..W. E. B. Du Bois

Plays of Negro Life...Ed. Locke and Gregory

God's Trombones...James Weldon Johnson

Copper Sun...Countée Cullen

Negro Labor in the United States .... Charles H. Wesley

A Bibliography of the Negro in Africa and America....Monroe N. Work

What the Negro Thinks..R. R. Moton

Rope and Faggot..Walter White

An Autumn Love Cycle..............................Georgia Douglas Johnson

In the other column, in non fiction, we have only:

The Weary Blues...Langston Hughes
Fine Clothes to the Jew...Langston Hughes

And it must be said that although Mr. Hughes shows a predilection for singing the "lower" and "humbler" classes of Negroes, these two volumes contain many poems that are highly inspirational.

In non fiction the score is nineteen to two. I do not see how any one who looks at these figures can fail to see that the complaint against the publishers is not in consonance with the facts. I believe that Negro writers who have something worthwhile to say and the power and skill to say it have as fair a chance today of being published as any other writers.

Zora Neale Hurston
(1891–1960)

ALTHOUGH HER NOVELS were published in the 1930s, Zora Neale Hurston is known as a prominent figure of the Harlem Renaissance. Born in Eatonville, Florida, an all-black township, Hurston eventually met a white actress who was in a traveling theater show. Hurston was her assistant for several years. However, after traveling with her to Washington, D.C., Hurston settled there, where she eventually met Alain Locke. With Locke's encouragement, she moved to New York City in 1925 and got to know, among others, Georgia Douglas Johnson, Langston Hughes, and Wallace Thurman. Thurman included a character modeled on Hurston in his novel *Infants of the Spring*. While in New York, Hurston eventually met the novelist Fannie Hurst and became her personal secretary. Hurst encouraged her to enroll in Barnard College. While at Barnard, she studied with noted anthropologist Franz Boas.[22] Her interest in anthropology revived her childhood interest in folktales.

Hurston published her first novel, *Jonah's Gourd Vine*, in 1934. In 1937, she published her second novel, *Their Eyes Were Watching God*. Upon publication, this novel was praised by some and criticized by, among others, Richard Wright. For several decades thereafter, little notice was given to her novel. However, during the late 1960s and early 1970s, a group of black women critics began to discuss the novel as one of the major novels of the Harlem Renaissance. Feminist critics began to read it as a prototypical feminist text. Various critical debates followed. Numerous critical articles have been written on *Their Eyes Were Watching God*. Hurston's novel has been widely taught in a range of college courses. She published two other novels during her lifetime—*Moses, Man of the Mountain*

(1939) and *Seraph on the Suwanee* (1948). These novels have not received the critical acclaim of *Their Eyes Were Watching God*.

Hurston became a controversial figure later in her life and returned to Florida, where she lived in relative obscurity until her death in 1960. She was buried in an unmarked grave. Alice Walker wrote an essay, "Looking for Zora," in which she recounts going to find Hurston's grave in a rural Florida cemetery. In 1973, Walker erected a tombstone in Hurston's honor near the writer's grave site.

In "What White Publishers Won't Print" (1950), Hurston discusses certain misconceptions and discriminatory practices of the publishing industry.

What White Publishers Won't Print (1950)

I have been amazed by the Anglo-Saxon's lack of curiosity about the internal lives and emotions of the Negroes, and for that matter, any non-Anglo-Saxon peoples within our borders, above the class of unskilled labor.

This lack of interest is much more important than it seems at first glance. It is even more important at this time than it was in the past. The internal affairs of the nation have bearings on the international stress and strain, and this gap in the national literature now has tremendous weight in world affairs. National coherence and solidarity is implicit in a thorough understanding of the various groups within a nation, and this lack of knowledge about the internal emotions and behavior of the minorities cannot fail to bar our understanding. Man, like all the other animals fears and is repelled by that which he does not understand, and mere difference is apt to connote something malign.

The fact that there is no demand for incisive and full-dress stories around Negroes above the servant class is indicative of something of vast importance to this nation. This blank is NOT filled by the fiction built around upper-class Negroes exploiting the race problem. Rather, it tends to point it up. A college-bred Negro still is not a person like other folks, but an interesting problem, more or less. It calls to mind a story of slavery time. In this story, a master with more intellectual curiosity than usual, set out to see how much he could teach a particularly bright slave of his. When he had gotten him up to higher mathematics and to be a fluent reader of Latin, he called in a neighbor to show off his brilliant slave, and to argue that Negroes had brains just like the slave-owners had, and given the same opportunities, would turn out the same.

The visiting master of slaves looked and listened, tried to trap the literate slave in Algebra and Latin, and failing to do so in both, turned to his neighbor and said:

"Yes, he certainly knows his higher mathematics, and he can read Latin better than many white men I know, but I cannot bring myself to believe that he understands a thing that he is doing. It is all an aping of our culture. All on the outside. You are crazy if you think that it has changed him inside in the least. Turn him loose, and he will revert at once to the jungle. He is still a savage, and no amount of translating Virgil and Ovid is going to change him. In fact, all you have done is to turn a useful savage into a dangerous beast."

That was in slavery time, yes, and we have come a long, long way since then, but the troubling thing is that there are still too many who refuse to believe in the ingestion and digestion of western culture as yet. Hence the lack of literature about the higher emotions and love life of upperclass Negroes and the minorities in general.

Publishers and producers are cool to the idea. Now, do not leap to the conclusion that editors and producers constitute a special class of unbelievers. That is far from true. Publishing houses and theatrical promoters are in business to make money. They will sponsor anything that they believe will sell. They shy away from romantic stories about Negroes and Jews because they feel that they know the public indifference to such works, unless the story or play involves racial tension. It can then be offered as a study in Sociology, with the romantic side subdued. They know the skepticism in general about the complicated emotions in the minorities. The average American just cannot conceive of it, and would be apt to reject the notion, and publishers and producers take the stand that they are not in business to educate, but to make money. Sympathetic as they might be, they cannot afford to be crusaders.

In proof of this, you can note various publishers and producers edging forward a little, and ready to go even further when the trial balloons show that the public is ready for it. This public lack of interest is the nut of the matter.

The question naturally arises as to the why of this indifference, not to say skepticism, to the internal life of educated minorities.

The answer lies in what we may call THE AMERICAN MU-SEUM OF UNNATURAL HISTORY. This is an intangible built on folk belief. It is assumed that all non-Anglo-Saxons are uncom-plicated stereotypes. Everybody knows all about them. They are lay figures mounted in the museum where all may take them in at a glance. They are made of bent wires without insides at all. So how could anybody write a book about the nonexistent?

The American Indian is a contraption of copper wires in an eter-nal warbonnet, with no equipment for laughter, expressionless face and that says "How" when spoken to. His only activity is treachery leading to massacres. Who is so dumb as not to know all about Indians, even if they have never seen one, nor talked with anyone who ever knew one?

The American Negro exhibit is a group of two. Both of these mechanical toys are built so that their feet eternally shuffle, and their eyes pop and roll. Shuffling feet and those popping, rolling eyes denote the Negro, and no characterization is genuine without this monotony. One is seated on a stump picking away on his banjo and singing and laughing. The other is a most amoral character before a sharecropper's shack mumbling about injustice. Doing this makes him out to be a Negro "intellectual." It is as simple as all that.

The whole museum is dedicated to the convenient "typical." In there is the "typical" Oriental, Jew, Yankee, Westerner, Southerner,

Latin, and even out-of-favor Nordics like the German. The English-man "I say old chappie," and the gesticulating Frenchman. The least observant American can know them all at a glance. However, the public willingly accepts the untypical in Nordics, but feels cheated if the untypical is portrayed in others. The author of *Scarlet Sister Mary* complained to me that her neighbors objected to her book on the grounds that she had the characters thinking, "and everybody know that Nigras don't think."

But for the national welfare, it is urgent to realize that the mi-norities do think, and think about something other than the race problem. That they are very human and internally, according to natural endowment, are just like everybody else. So long as this is not conceived, there must remain that feeling of unsurmountable difference, and difference to the average man means something bad. If people were made right, they would be just like him.

The trouble with the purely problem arguments is that they leave too much unknown. Argue all you will or may about injustice, but as long as the majority cannot conceive of a Negro or a Jew feeling and reacting inside just as they do, the majority will keep right on believing that people who do not look like them cannot possibly feel as they do, and conform to the established pattern. It is well known that there must be a body of waived matter, let us say, things accepted and taken for granted by all in a community before there can be that commonality of feeling. The usual phrase is having things in common. Until this is thoroughly established in respect to Negroes in America, as well as of other minorities, it will remain impossible for the majority to conceive of a Negro experiencing a deep and abiding love and not just the passion of sex. That a great mass of Negroes can be stirred by the pageants of Spring and Fall; the extravaganza of summer, and the majesty of winter. That they can and do experience discovery of the numerous subtle faces as a foundation for a great and selfless love, and the diverse nuances that go to destroy that love as with others. As it is now, this capacity, this evidence of high and complicated emotions, is ruled out. Hence the lack of interest in a romance uncomplicated by the race struggle has so little appeal.

This insistence on defeat in a story where upperclass Negroes are portrayed, perhaps says something from the subconscious of the majority. Involved in western culture, the hero or the heroine, or both, must appear frustrated and go down to defeat, somehow. Our literature reeks with it. Is it the same as saying, "You can translate Virgil, and fumble with the differential calculus, but can you really comprehend it? Can you cope with our subtleties?"

That brings us to the folklore of "reversion to type." This curious doctrine has such wide acceptance that it is tragic. One has only to examine the huge literature on it to be convinced. No matter how high we may *seem* to climb, put us under strain and we revert to type, that is, to the bush. Under a superficial layer of western culture, the jungle drums throb in our veins.

This ridiculous notion makes it possible for that majority who accept it to conceive of even a man like the suave and scholarly Dr. Charles S. Johnson to hide a black cat's bone on his person, and indulge in a midnight voodoo ceremony, complete with leopard skin and drums if threatened with the loss of the presidency of Fisk University, or the love of his wife. "Under the skin . . . better to deal with them in business, etc., but otherwise keep them at a safe distance and under control. I tell you, Carl Van Vechten, think as you like, but they are just not like us."

The extent and extravagance of this notion reaches the ultimate in nonsense in the widespread belief that the Chinese have bizarre genitals, because of that eye-fold that makes their eyes seem to slant. In spite of the fact that no biology has ever mentioned any such difference in reproductive organs makes no matter. Millions of people believe it. "Did you know that a Chinese has. . . ." Consequently, their quiet contemplative manner is interpreted as a sign of slyness and a treacherous inclination.

But the opening wedge for better understanding has been thrust into the crack. Though many Negroes denounced Carl Van Vechten's *Nigger Heaven* because of the title, and without ever reading it, the book, written in the deepest sincerity, revealed Negroes of wealth and culture to the white public. It created curiosity even when it aroused skepticism. It made folks want to know. Worth Tuttle Hedden's *The Other Room* has definitely widened the opening. Neither of these well-written works takes a romance of upperclass Negro life as the central theme, but the atmosphere and the background is there. These works should be followed up by some incisive and intimate stories from the inside.

The realistic story around a Negro insurance official, dentist, general practitioner, undertaker and the like would be most revealing. Thinly disguised fiction around the well known Negro names is not the answer, either. The "exceptional" as well as the Ol' Man Rivers has been exploited all out of context already. Everybody is already resigned to the "exceptional" Negro, and willing to be entertained by the "quaint." To grasp the penetration of western civilization in a minority, it is necessary to know how the average behaves and lives. Books that deal with people like in Sinclair Lewis' *Main Street* is the necessary métier. For various reasons, the average, struggling, nonmorbid Negro is the best-kept secret in America. His revelation to the public is the thing needed to do away with that feeling of difference which inspires fear, and which ever expresses itself in dislike.

It is inevitable that this knowledge will destroy many illusions and romantic traditions which America probably likes to have around. But then, we have no record of anybody sinking into a lingering death on finding out that there was no Santa Claus. The old world will take it in its stride. The realization that Negroes are no better nor no worse, and at times just as boring as everybody else, will hardly kill off the population of the nation.

Outside of racial attitudes, there is still another reason why this literature should exist. Literature and other arts are supposed to hold up the mirror to nature. With only the fractional "exceptional" and the "quaint" portrayed, a true picture of Negro life in America cannot be. A great principle of national art has been violated.

These are the things that publishers and producers, as the accredited representatives of the American people, have not yet taken into consideration sufficiently. Let there be light!

John Edgar Wideman

IN HIS PREFACE to the anthology *Breaking Ice* (1990), edited by Terry McMillan, John Edgar Wideman expresses significant concerns about the publishing industry. Given the expectations of major publishing houses, Wideman wonders about the true nature of a black novelist's artistic freedom: "Is there any difference between sitting in at an all-white lunch counter and a minority writer composing a story in English? What's the fate of a black story in a white world of white stories?. . . How do we break out of the circle of majority controlled publishing houses, distributors, critics, editors, readers?"

Preface to *Breaking Ice* (1990)

Dear Terry,

Congratulations. It's time we had a new anthology of African-American fiction. I don't know what you've gathered, but I'm sure your sample will be enjoyable and instructive. The notes that follow are wishes, cautions, play with the issues and ideas that could/should, in my view, surface in a collection of contemporary Afro-American writing.

The African artist allows wide scope to his fantasy in the mask. . . . With colors, feathers, and horns he accomplishes some astonishingly lively effects. In a slow creative process he brings to life a work which constitutes a new unit, a new being. If the sculpture proves to be a success, a helpful medium, the tribe adheres to this form and passes it on from generation to generation. . . . Thus we have a style, a firmly established formal canon, which may not be lightly discarded. . . . For this reason a style retains its specific character for decades, even centuries. It stands and falls with the faith to which it is linked.

—*The Art of Black Africa*, Elsy Leuzinger

Since we're seen as marginal politically, economically, and culturally, African-American writers have a special, vexing stake in reforming, revitalizing the American imagination. History is a cage, a conundrum we must escape or resolve before our art can go freely about its business. As has always been the case, in order to break into print we must be prepared to deal with the extra-literary forces that have conspired to keep us silent, or our stories, novels, and poems will continue to be treated as marginally as our lives, unhinged, unattached to the everyday reality of "mainstream," majority readers. Magazine editors know that their jobs depend upon purveying images the public recognizes and approves, so they seldom include our fictions, and almost never choose those which transcend stereotypes and threaten to expose the fantasies of superiority, the bedrock lies and brute force that sustain the majority's power over the *other*. Framed in foreign, inimical contexts, minority stories appear at best as exotic slices of life and local color, at worst as ghettoized irrelevancies.

However, as the assumptions of the mono-culture are challenged, overrun, defrock themselves daily in full view of the shameless media, more and more of the best fiction gravitates toward the category of "minority." The truth that each of us starts out alone, a minority of one, each in a slightly different place (no place), resides somewhere in the lower frequencies of our communal consciousness. New worlds, alternative versions of reality are burgeoning. In spite of enormous, overwhelming societal pressures to conform, to standardize the shape and meaning of individual lives, voices like Ralph Ellison's reach us, impelling us to attend to the *chaos which lives within the pattern* of our certainties.

Good stories transport us to these extraordinarily diverse regions where individual lives are enacted. For a few minutes we can climb inside another's skin. Mysteriously, the dissolution of ego also sharpens the sense of self, reinforces independence and relativity of point of view. People's lives resist a simple telling, cannot be understood safely, reductively from some static still point, some universally acknowledged center around which all other lives orbit. Narrative is a reciprocal process, regressive and progressive, dynamic. When a culture hardens into heliocentricity, fancies itself the star of creation, when otherness is imagined as a great darkness except for what the star illuminates, it's only a matter of time until the center collapses in upon itself, imploding with sigh and whimper.

Minority writers hold certain peculiar advantages in circumstances of cultural breakdown, reorientation, transition. We've accumulated centuries of experience dealing with problems of marginality, problems that are suddenly on center stage for the whole society: inadequacy of language, failure of institutions, a disintegrating metropolitan vision that denies us or swallows us, that attracts and repels, that promises salvation and extinction. We've always been outsiders, orphans, bastard children, hard-pressed to make our claims heard. In order to endure slavery and oppression it's been necessary to cultivate the double-consciousness of seer, artist, mother. Beaten down by countless assertions of the inadequacy, the repugnance of our own skin, we've been forced to enter the skins of others, to see, as a condition of survival, the world and ourselves through the eyes of others. Our stories can place us back at the center, at the controls; they can offer alternative realities, access to the sanctuary we carry around inside our skulls. The African-American imagination has evolved as discipline, defense, coping mechanism, counterweight to the galling facts of life. We've learned to confer upon ourselves the power of making up our lives, changing them as we go along.

Marginality has also refined our awareness, our proficiency in nonliterary modes of storytelling. Folk culture preserves and expresses an identity, a history, a self-evaluation apart from those destructive, incarcerating images proliferated by the mainline culture. Consciously and unconsciously we've integrated these resources of folk culture into our writing. Our songs, dreams, dances, styles of walk and talk, dressing, cooking, sport, our heroes and heroines provide a record of how a particular group has lived in the world, in it, but not of it. A record so distinctive and abiding that its origins in culture have been misconstrued as rooted in biology. A long-tested view of history is incorporated in the art of African-American people, and our history can be derived from careful study of forms and influences that enter our cultural performances and rituals. In spite of and because of marginal status, a powerful, indigenous vernacular tradition has survived, not unbroken, but unbowed, a magnet, a focused energy, something with its own logic, rules, and integrity connecting current developments to the past. An articulate, syncretizing force our best artists have drawn upon, a force sustaining both individual talent and tradition. Though minstrel shows were popularized as a parody of black life, these musical reviews were also a vehicle for preserving authentic African-derived elements of black American culture. Today rap, for all its excesses and commercialization, reasserts the African core of black music: polyrhythmic dance beat, improvisational spontaneity, incantatory use of the word to name, blame, shame, and summon power, the obligation of ritual to instruct and enthuse. It's no coincidence that rap exploded as the big business of music was luring many black artists into "crossing over." Huge sums were paid to black recording artists; then a kind of lobotomy was performed on their work, homogenizing, commodifying, pacifying it by removing large portions of what made the music think and be. Like angry ancestral spirits, the imperatives of tradition rose up, reanimated themselves, mounted the corner chanters and hip hoppers. As soul diminished to a category on the pop charts, the beat from the street said no-no-no, you're too sweet.

Try some of this instead. Stomp your feet. Don't admit defeat. Put your hands together. Hit it. Hit. Boom. Crank up the volume. Bare bones percussion and chant holler scream. Our loud selves, our angry selves. Our flying feet and words and raunchy dreams. Instruments not possessed mimicked by our voices. Electronics appropriated. Recording tricknology explored and deconstructed, techniques reversed, foregrounded, parodied. Chaboom. Boom. Sounds of city, of machines of inner space and outer space merge. Boom boxes. Doom boxes. Call the roll of the ancestors. Every god from Jah, Isis, Jehovah, Allah, and Shango to James Brown and the Famous Flames. Say the names. Let them strut the earth again. Get right, children. Rap burst forth precisely where it did, when it did because that's where the long, long night of poverty and discrimination, of violent marginality remained a hurting truth nobody else was telling. That's where the creative energies of a subject people were being choked and channeled into self-destruction.

When an aesthetic tradition remembers its roots, the social conditions (slavery, oppression, marginality) and the expressive resources it employed to cope with these conditions, the counter version of these conditions it elaborated through art, when it doesn't allow itself to be distracted, that is, keeps telling the truth which brought it into being—the necessity of remaining human, defining human in its own terms, resisting those destructive definitions in the Master's tongue, attitudes and art—then that tradition remains alive, a referent, a repository of value, money we can take to the bank. Afro-American traditions contain the memory of a hard, unclean break. This partially accounts for key postures that are subversive, disruptive, disjunctive. To the brutality that once ripped us away and now tries to rip us apart, we turn a stylized mask of indifference, of malleability, a core of iron, silent refusal. Boom. Chaboom. Boom. While our feet, feet, feet, dance to another beat.

I look for, cherish this in our fiction.

On the other hand—or should I say other face, since the shield I'm raising has two sides and one cannot be lifted without the other—

what about the future? Is there any difference between sitting in at an all-white lunch counter and a minority writer composing a story in English? What's the fate of a black story in a white world of white stories? What can we accomplish with our *colors, feathers, and horns*, how can we fruitfully extend our tradition? How do we break out of the circle of majority-controlled publishing houses, distributors, critics, editors, readers? Vernacular language is not enough. Integration is not enough, unless one views mathematical, proportional representation as a goal instead of a step. If what a writer wants is freedom of expression, then somehow that larger goal must be addressed implicitly/explicitly in our fictions. A story should somehow contain clues that align it with tradition and critique tradition, establish the new space it requires, demands, appropriates, hint at how it may bring forth other things like itself, where these others have, will, and are coming from. This does not mean defining criteria for admitting stories into some ideologically sound, privileged category, but seeking conditions, mining territory that maximizes the possibility of free, original expression. We must continue inventing our stories, sustaining, not sacrificing, the double consciousness that is a necessity for any writing with the ambition of forging its own place.

Black music again illuminates glories and pitfalls, the possibility of integrity, how artists nourished by shared cultural roots can prove again and again that, even though they are moving through raindrops, they don't have to get soaked. Their art signifies they are in the storm but not of it. Black music is a movable feast, fluid in time, space, modality, exhibiting in theme and variations multiple relationships with the politically, socially, aesthetically dominant order, the fullest possible range of relationships, including the power and independence to change places, reverse the hierarchy, *be* the dominant order.

What lessons are transferable to the realm of literature? Is musical language freer, less inscribed with the historical baggage of European hegemony, exploitation, racism? Is it practical within the forms and frequencies of this instrument (written English) to roll back history, those negative accretions, those iron bars and "White Only" signs that steal one's voice, one's breath away?

Are there ways fiction can express the dialectic, the tension, the conversation, the warfare of competing versions of reality English contains? One crucial first step may be recognizing that black/white, either/or perceptions of the tensions within language are woefully inadequate. Start by taking nothing for granted, giving nothing away. Study the language. The way we've begun to comb the past. Rehistoricize. Contest. Contest. Return junk mail to sender. Call into question the language's complacencies about itself. At the level of spelling, grammar, how it's taught, but also deeper, its sounds, their mamas, its coded pretensions to legitimacy, gentility, exclusivity, seniority, logic. Unveil chaos within the patterns of certainty. Restate issues and paradigms so they are not simply the old race problem relexified. Whose language is it, anyway?

Martin Bernal in *Black Athena* has traced the link between European theories of race and language. How nineteenth-century theories of language development parallel, buttress, and reinforce hierarchical concepts of race and culture. How social "sciences," the soft core posing as the hard core of academic humanities curricula, were tainted at their inception by racist assumptions and agendas. How romantic linguistic theory was used as a tool to prove the superiority of the West. How uncritical absorption of certain hallowed tenets of Western thought is like participating in your own lynching. Be prepared to critique any call for "back to basics" in light of the research Bernal gathers and summarizes. The great lie that systems of thought are pure, universal, uncontaminated by cultural bias is once more being gussied up for public consumption. Whose Great Books in whose interest must be read? Whose stories should be told? By whom? To what ends?

How does language grow, change? What are the dynamics that allow individual speakers to learn a language, adapt it to the infinite geography of their inner imaginative worlds, the outer social play, the constant intercourse of both? Can the writer love language and also keep it at arm's length as material, a medium, foregrounding its arbitrariness, its treacherousness, never calling it his/her own, never completely identifying with it but making intimate claims by exploring what it can do, what it could do if the writer has patience, luck, skill, and practices, practices, practices?

In it, but not of it. And that stance produces bodies of enabling legislation, a grammar of nuanced tensions, incompatibilities, doors and windows that not only dramatize the stance itself but implicate the medium. A reciprocal unraveling below whose surface is always the unquiet recognition that this language we're using constantly pulls many directions at once and unless we keep alert, keep fighting the undertow, acknowledge the currents going our way and every other damned way, we drown. We are not alone but not separate either; any voice we accomplish is really many voices, and the most powerful voices are always steeped in unutterable silences. A story is a formula for extracting meaning from chaos, a handful of water we scoop up to recall an ocean. Nothing really stands still for this reduction, this abstraction. We need readers who are willing to be coconspirators. It's at this level of primal encounter that we must operate in order to reclaim the language for our expressive purposes. The hidden subject remains: what is our situation with respect to this language? Where does it come from? Where do I come from? Where do we meet and how shall I name this meeting place? What is *food*? What is *eating*? Why do people go to lunch counters? Black music offers a counter integrative model because it poses this species of question about music and fills us with the thrill of knowing yes, yes, the answers, if there are any, and it probably doesn't matter whether there are or not, yay or nay, the answers and the questions are still up for grabs.

Martha Southgate
(1960–)

BORN IN CLEVELAND, Ohio, Martha Southgate attended Smith College and graduated in 1982. She later received an M.F.A. from Goddard College. For years, Southgate worked as a journalist for the *New York Daily News*, *Essence*, and other periodicals. She has published four novels. Southgate's latest novel, *The Taste of Salt*, was considered one of the best novels published in 2011 by the *San Francisco Chronicle* and the *Boston Globe*. The novel tells the story of Josie Henderson, a marine biologist. She is a rare bird in a white world; but she does not care to go home again to the black neighborhood in Cleveland. She is afraid of drowning in alcohol and dysfunction, like her father and brother.

Southgate published three earlier novels: *Another Way to Dance* (1997), *The Fall of Rome* (2002), and *Third Girl from the Left* (2005). Southgate has taught creative writing at Vermont College of the Fine Arts and Sarah Lawrence College. In addition to her novels, Southgate has published essays in *Essence*, *O* magazine, and the *New York Times Book Review*—where "Writers Like Me" first appeared.[23] She discusses African American writers and the publishing industry.

Writers Like Me (2007)

I am a 46-year-old writer of "literary" fiction. I've had three novels published—the first for young people, the last two for adults. All have won minor prizes, been respectfully reviewed and sold modestly. I've been awarded a few fairly competitive fellowships and grants. The business is full of fiction writers like me. With one difference: I'm black, born and raised in the United States. At the parties and conferences I attend, and in the book reviews I read, I rarely encounter other African-American "literary" writers, particularly in my age bracket. There just don't seem to be that many of us out there, and that's something I've come to wonder about a great deal. And so I got on the phone with some editors and some African-American writers to talk about it.

For many writers, middle age is when they hit their stride. Robert Gottlieb of Knopf, who has been Toni Morrison's editor for many years, said, "Many very fine writers take time to get there." Looking at the white American fiction writers who have the most cultural prominence, one quickly sees a large group in their 40s or 50s (Michael Chabon, Jonathan Franzen, Rick Moody, Jane Smiley, Michael Cunningham et al.) who have generally had four or more major works of fiction published. Gottlieb points out that Morrison's first two books sold adequately, but it wasn't until her third novel, *Song of Solomon*, published the year she turned 46, that she had a commercial breakthrough. "It was larger and more ambitious, demonstrating a new power and authority, and the world noticed," he said. "Some careers start with a bang—*Invisible Man, Catch-22*. Others take time to find a significant readership—Anne Tyler, Toni. And sometimes I feel that those are the healthiest ones."

But when you look at the careers of African-American writers, you don't always see that healthy arc. Ralph Ellison, for example, seemed to lose his way completely after *Invisible Man*. These days, there are only a few names of black authors born in the United States, beyond Morrison's, that the average reader of serious fiction might easily drop—Colson Whitehead, ZZ Packer, Edward P. Jones. Of these three, only Jones is over 40.

In some ways, the American literary scene is more racially and culturally diverse than ever. A few examples: Of the 21 writers on *Granta*'s recent Best of Young American Novelists list, six (including Packer and Uzodinma Iweala) are people of color (many colors:

black, South and East Asian, Hispanic), and seven were born or raised outside the United States. Indian writers born or educated here, like Jhumpa Lahiri, Vikram Chandra and Kiran Desai, win critical acclaim and big sales. "Girlfriend," "urban-lit" and other branches of commercial genre fiction by African-Americans have continued to enjoy a boom since the door-busting success of Terry McMillan's *Waiting to Exhale* in 1992. But black authors writing in an ambitious, thoughtful way about American subjects are harder to find—even when they do get published. Malaika Adero, a senior editor at Atria Books, said: "Literary African-American writers have difficulty getting publicity. The retailers then don't order great quantities of the books. Readers don't know what books are available and therefore don't ask for them. It's a vicious cycle."

Though the publishing industry remains overwhelmingly white, editors say they are always looking for good, marketable work by writers of any background. Morgan Entrekin, publisher of Grove/Atlantic, which recently published Michael Thomas's first novel, *Man Gone Down*—one of the few novels by an African-American to grace the cover of this publication of late—said: "I don't tend to approach the black writers we publish as African-American. I see them as writers first."

But there's colorblindness, and then there's blindness. Christopher Jackson, executive editor at Spiegel & Grau, a division of Random House, tells a story about being mistaken for Iweala at the launch party for *Granta*'s Best of Young American Novelists issue—even though Iweala is more than 10 years Jackson's junior, had just left the stage as an honoree and, frankly, doesn't look much like Jackson. Let's face it, something like that is awfully unlikely to happen to a white editor or writer. It's hard to say whether this obtuseness translates into a lack of interest in African-American work, but some black writers think it might. The novelist Tayari Jones, author of *The Untelling*, said: "I know that there are very few black authors who publish the fourth novel. Hardly any of us are considered prestige authors, so no one is going to sign us up for our names alone." Calvin

Reid, a senior news editor at *Publishers Weekly*, who often covers African-American publishing, agrees that black writers stuck in the midlist face an uphill battle, but he sees it as a business reality, not a racial thing: "If you have two or three books out and you've never sold more than 3,000 copies, people make decisions based on that."

Things are tough all over, but arguably tougher for some. For many black writers, a writing life very rarely unfolds the way it does for so many white writers you could name: know you want to be a writer from the age of 10, get your first book published at 26, go on to produce slowly but steadily over a lengthy career. Even Morrison didn't follow that timeline: her first novel wasn't published until she was nearly 40 and had worked for a number of years as a teacher and then an editor at Random House. And she didn't quit that day job until urged to do so by Gottlieb in the mid-1970s, after *Sula* was published.

So what's holding us up? Sometimes it's just the ordinary difficulty of juggling family, writing and earning a living. But African-American writers also speak of a larger problem of what I'd call internal or cultural permission. It's just plain harder to decide to be a writer if you don't have a financial cushion or a long cultural tradition of people going out on that bohemian limb. Consider the case of Edward P. Jones. He published his first book, *Lost in the City*, in 1992 (he was 41 at the time) to much critical acclaim and a number of significant honors, if not huge sales. He returned to his day job at *Tax Notes* magazine, where he remained until he was laid off 10 years later. He then wrote *The Known World* in about six months—though he told me he'd been thinking about it nearly those whole 10 years. The novel won the Pulitzer Prize.

When asked why he didn't make the leap to full-time writing sooner, Jones spoke firmly: "If you're born poor or you're born working-class, a job is important. People who are born with silver spoons in their mouths never have to worry. They know someone will take care of them. Worrying about not having a job would have put a damper on any creativity that I would have had. So I'm glad I had that job."

The problem isn't just money, says Randall Kenan, a 1994 Whiting Award winner who published two critically acclaimed books of fiction in 1989 and 1992, and two nonfiction books since 1999: "I think among middle-class black folk, it's still a struggle to validate literature as a worthy way to spend your time." ZZ Packer, the author of the story collection *Drinking Coffee Elsewhere*, who is currently at work on a novel, said the situation is somewhat different for those who are younger. (She is 34.) "People who came half a generation before us were the first ones to begin to go to elite colleges in larger numbers," she said. "They were beholden to a lot of their parents' expectations, namely, that if you go to a prestigious school, you're going to become a doctor or a lawyer, you're not going to 'waste your time' writing. People who are around my age have seen blacks in the Northeastern establishment for a while. . . . They don't always feel the same obligation to ditch their dream for something more practical."

It saddens me to think of the dreams that have been ditched, the stories that haven't been told because of racism, because of fear and economic insecurity, because that first novel didn't move enough copies. I hope to see the day when there are more of us at the party (and the parties), when the work of African-Americans who tell our part of the American story well receives the celebration, and the sales, it deserves.

Charles Johnson
(1948–)

CHARLES JOHNSON HAS praised his mother for getting him started as a writer. When he was twelve, she gave him a blank book and told him to keep a journal. He took her advice. He says, "[O]nce I started writing on those pages about my feelings, about my friends and relatives, once I saw how I was free to say *any*thing that came into my head about them, I was addicted. . . . Since that day, I've filled up probably a hundred diaries, journals, and writers' notebooks."[24]

Johnson grew up in Evanston, Illinois, and attended Southern Illinois University. He majored in philosophy and journalism. At first, Johnson was interested in drawing and wanted to become a cartoonist. In 1970, he published *Black Humor*, a collection of his cartoons. He also started writing fiction while still in college. He quickly wrote several "apprentice novels."

A Buddhist, Johnson's interest in philosophy comes through in his first published novel, *Faith and the Good Thing* (1974). His second novel, *The Oxherding Tale* (1974), is written in the form of a slave narrative. It prepared him for writing his third novel, *Middle Passage*, for which he won the 1990 National Book Award for fiction. In 1998, Johnson published *Dreamer*, a novel partly based on the life of Dr. Martin Luther King, Jr.

Johnson has written a range of essays. One of his nonfiction collections is titled *Turning the Wheel: Essays on Buddhism and Writing* (2003). The brief selection included here is taken from *I Call Myself an Artist: Writings by and about Charles Johnson* (1999), edited by Rudolph P. Byrd. The selection is a partial outline for *Middle Passage* (1990).

The Writer's Notebook:
A Note on Working Methods (1999)

I started keeping a diary when I was about 12; my mother suggested the idea. In college the diary transformed into a journal in which I wrote poetry, brief essays to myself, and (as with a diary) tried to make sense of daily events. When I started writing fiction, the journal moved more in the direction of being a writing tool. I use cheap, spiral notebooks. Into them go notes on everything I experience; I jot down images, phrases used by my friends, fragments of thoughts ... (I now keep an entirely separate journal for recording personal matters.) These writing notebooks sit on my desk 15-inches deep, along with notebooks I kept from college classes (I save everything, it's shameless) ...

When I write, I sit down and let a first draft flow out for as long as inspiration stays with me. I let that first draft be chaotic, if need be: a rush of everything I can feel, imagine, or dredge up. Then I go over it and weed out the junk. Somewhere around the third draft, I begin going through my notebooks hunting for thoughts, images I've had, or ideas about characters (usually observations I make of people around me). Although it takes at least six hours to go back through all these notebooks, I can count on finding some sentence, phrase, or idea I had, say, 20 years ago that is currently useful. I don't carry any of the journals with me—I can't afford to lose them. Instead, I jot notes on whatever is available—hotel stationery, the margins of an old newspaper—and slip it into the notebooks when I get back home.

Characters

Crew of Republic	New Orleans	Makanda, Ill.
Rutherford Calhoun	Isadora Bailey	Jackson Calhoun
Capt. Ebenezer Falcon+	Madame Toulouse	Peleg Chandler
Peter Cringle, mate	Papa Zeringue	
Josiah Squibb, cook	Santos	
Tommy, cabin-boy		
Rev. Meadows		
Matthew McIntosh, boatswain+		
Lighthands (boys)+		
Ngonyama		

Extras
Squibb's parrot
Unga-galant

Bangalang	Aquarius
Owen Bogha	El
Ahman-de-bellah	The King

Number of locations = 5
Total characters (Named) = 19
Number of major characters: 10
+ = died during mutiny

Chapter Outline

Chap. One ——— The bargain.

Chap. Two ——— Calhoun meets Capt. Falcon and
learns that Zeringue has financed
this voyage. He learns life at sea,
the horror and hardship, and the
crew. He tells story of his brother.

Chap. Three ——— Allmuseri slaves are taken on
board. The revolt. Calhoun is
captain by default.

Chap. Four ——— The wandering. He learns of
Allmuseri culture. Supplies get low.
Slaves die of disease. The ghost ship is
following them. They sight land.

Chap. Five ——— Journey to the Dystopia } A world
Chap. Six ——— Escape from the Dystopia. } without blacks.

Chap. Seven ——— Back at sea, wandering in space
and time. } A world
Chap. Eight ——— Journey to Dystopia. } without whites.
A few of the Allmuseri stay here.

Chap. Nine ——— At sea again, storms and
violent weather, etc.

Chap. Ten ——— Rutherford boards the Ghost ship.
Sees Capt. Falcon and the dead crew
and himself. The magical ship returns
him to New Orleans.

Walter Mosley
(1952–)

WALTER MOSLEY IS a unique figure among contemporary African American novelists. He writes mystery novels and crime novels with a difference. His exploration of such themes has met with both financial success and critical acclaim. He grew up in South Central Los Angeles and eventually attended Johnson State College in Vermont. His famous character, Easy Rawlins, first appeared in *Devil in a Blue Dress* (1990), which was a best seller and was later produced as a Hollywood movie starring Denzel Washington.

Easy Rawlins, whose background is similar to Mosley's father's, has appeared in several of Mosley's other novels. Using Easy Rawlins as a character, Mosley creates a practical yet deeply reflective character who must determine how to resolve moral complexities and ethical choices, both as a detective and as a black man.

Mosley is a prolific writer who has written a series of books, including the Easy Rawlins mysteries, the Leonid McGill series, and other novels. He has also published several books of nonfiction, including *This Year You Write Your Novel* (2007).[25] In a chapter titled "The General Disciplines That Every Writer Needs," Mosley says, "[T]he first thing you have to know about writing is that it is something you must do every day—every morning or every night, whatever time it is that you have. Ideally, the time you decide on is also the time when you do your best work." Mosley elaborates in the following article (2001).

For Authors, Fragile Ideas Need Loving Every Day (2001)

If you want to be a writer, you have to write every day. The consistency, the monotony, the certainty, all vagaries and passions are covered by this daily reoccurrence.

You don't go to a well once but daily. You don't skip a child's breakfast or forget to wake up in the morning. Sleep comes to you each day, and so does the muse.

She comes softly and quietly, behind your left ear or in a corner of the next room. Her words are whispers, her ideas shifting renditions of possibilities that have not been resolved, though they have occurred and reoccurred a thousand times in your mind. She, or it, is a collection of memories not exactly your own.

These reminiscences surface in dreams or out of abstract notions brought on by tastes and excitations, failures and hopes that you experience continually. These ideas have no physical form. They are smoky concepts liable to disappear at the slightest disturbance. An alarm clock or a ringing telephone will dispel a new character; answering the call will erase a chapter from the world.

Our most precious ability, the knack of creation, is also our most fleeting resource. What might be fades in the world of necessity.

How can I create when I have to go to work, cook my dinner, remember what I did wrong to the people who have stopped calling? And even if I do find a moment here and there—a weekend away in the mountains, say—how can I say everything I need to say before the world comes crashing back with all of its sirens and shouts and television shows?

"I know I have a novel in me," I often hear people say. "But how can I get it out?"

The answer is, always is, every day.

The dream of the writer, of any artist, is a fickle and amorphous thing. One evening you're remembering a homeless man, dressed in clothes that smelled like cheese rinds, who you once stood next to on a street corner in New York. Your memory becomes a reverie, and in this daydream you ask him where he's from. With a thick accent he tells you that he was born in Hungary, that he was a freedom fighter, but that now, here in America, his freedom has deteriorated into the poverty of the streets.

You write down a few sentences in your journal and sigh. This exhalation is not exhaustion but anticipation at the prospect of the wonderful tale exposing a notion that you still only partly understand.

A day goes by. Another passes. At the end of the next week you find yourself in the same chair, at the same hour when you wrote about the homeless man previously. You open the journal to see what you'd written. You remember everything perfectly, but the life has somehow drained out of it. The words have no art to them; you no longer remember the smell. The idea seems weak, it has dissipated, like smoke.

This is the first important lesson that the writer must learn. Writing a novel is gathering smoke. It's an excursion into the ether of ideas. There's no time to waste. You must work with that idea as well as you can, jotting down notes and dialogue.

The first day the dream you gathered will linger, but it won't last long. The next day you have to return to tend to your flimsy vapors. You have to brush them, reshape them, breathe into them and gather more.

It doesn't matter what time of day you work, but you have to work every day because creation, like life, is always slipping away from you. You must write every day, but there's no time limit on how long you have to write.

One day you might read over what you've done and think about it. You pick up the pencil or turn on the computer, but no new words come. That's fine. Sometimes you can't go further. Correct a misspelling, reread a perplexing paragraph, and then let it go. You have reentered the dream of the work, and that's enough to keep the story alive for another twenty-four hours.

The next day you might write for hours; there's no way to tell. The goal is not a number of words or hours spent writing. All you need is to keep your heart and mind open to the work.

Nothing we create is art at first. It's simply a collection of notions that may never be understood. Returning every day thickens the atmosphere. Images appear. Connections are made. But even these clearer notions will fade if you stay away more than a day.

Reality fights against your dreams, it tries to deny creation and change. The world wants you to be someone known, someone with solid ideas, not blowing smoke. Given a day, reality will begin to scatter your notions; given two days, it will drive them off.

The act of writing is a kind of guerrilla warfare; there is no vacation, no leave, no relief. In actuality there is very little chance of victory. You are, you fear, like that homeless man, likely to be defeated by your fondest dreams.

But then the next day comes, and the words are waiting. You pick up where you left off, in the cool and shifting mists of morning.

PART THREE

On Writing
Major Novels

Richard Wright

IN THE FOLLOWING EXCERPT taken from Richard Wright's introduction to *Native Son*, "How 'Bigger' Was Born" (1940), Wright describes the joyous feeling of existing for hours on end in a creative zone of new ideas and emotions: "That was the deep fun of the job: to feel within my body that I was pushing out to new areas of feeling, strange landmarks of emotion, tramping upon foreign soil, compounding new relationships of perceptions, making new and—until that very split second of time!—unheard-of and unfelt effects with words. . . . That is writing as I feel it, a kind of significant living."

From "How 'Bigger' Was Born" (1940)

Now, for the writing. During the years in which I had met all of those Bigger Thomases, those varieties of Bigger Thomases, I had not consciously gathered material to write of them; I had not kept a notebook record of their sayings and doings. Their actions had simply made impressions upon my sensibilities as I lived from day to day, impressions which crystallized and coagulated into clusters and configurations of memory, attitudes, moods, ideas. And these subjective states, in turn, were automatically stored away somewhere in me. I was not even aware of the process. But, excited over the book which I had set myself to write, under the stress of the emotion, these things came surging up, tangled, fused, knotted, entertaining me by the sheer variety and potency of their meaning and suggestiveness.

With the whole theme in mind, in an attitude almost akin to prayer, I gave myself up to the story. In an effort to capture some phase of Bigger's life that would not come to me readily, I'd jot down as much of it as I could. Then I'd read it over and over, adding each time a word, a phrase, a sentence until I felt that I had caught all the shadings of reality I felt dimly were there. With each of these rereadings and rewritings it seemed that I'd gather in facts and facets that tried to run away. It was an act of concentration, of trying to hold within one's center of attention all of that bewildering array of facts which science, politics, experience, memory, and imagination were urging upon me. And then, while writing, a new and thrilling relationship would spring up under the drive of emotion, coalescing and telescoping alien facts into a known and felt truth. That was the deep fun of the job: to feel within my body that I was pushing out to new areas of feeling, strange landmarks of emotion, tramping upon foreign soil, compounding new relationships of perceptions, making new and—until that very split second of time!—unheard-of and unfelt effects with words. It had a buoying and tonic impact upon me; my senses would strain and seek for more and more of such relationships; my temperature would rise as I worked. That is writing as I feel it, a kind of significant living.

The first draft of the novel was written in four months, straight through, and ran to some 576 pages. Just as a man rises in the mornings to dig ditches for his bread, so I'd work daily. I'd think of some abstract principle of Bigger's conduct and at once my mind would turn it into some act I'd seen Bigger perform, some act which I hoped would be familiar enough to the American reader to gain his credence. But in the writing of scene after scene I was guided by but one criterion: to tell the truth as I saw it and felt it. That is, to objectify in words some insight derived from my living in the form of action, scene, and dialogue. If a scene seemed improbable to me, I'd not tear it up, but ask myself: "Does it reveal enough of what I feel to stand in spite of its unreality?" If I felt it did, it stood. If I felt that it did not, I ripped it out. The degree of morality in my writing depended upon the degree of felt life and truth I could put down upon the printed page. For example, there is a scene in *Native*

Son where Bigger stands in a cell with a Negro preacher, Jan, Max, the State's Attorney, Mr. Dalton, Mrs. Dalton, Bigger's mother, his brother, his sister, Al, Gus, and Jack. While writing that scene, I knew that it was unlikely that so many people would ever be allowed to come into a murderer's cell. But I wanted those people in that cell to elicit a certain important emotional response from Bigger. And so the scene stood. I felt that what I wanted that scene to say to the reader was *more important than its surface reality or plausibility.*

Always, as I wrote, I was both reader and writer, both the conceiver of the action and the appreciator of it. I tried to write so that, in the same instant of time, the objective and subjective aspects of Bigger's life would be caught in a focus of prose. And always I tried to *render, depict,* not merely to tell the story. If a thing was cold, I tried to make the reader *feel* cold, and not just tell about it. In writing in this fashion, sometimes I'd find it necessary to use a stream of consciousness technique, then rise to an interior monologue, descend to a direct rendering of a dream state, then to a matter-of-fact depiction of what Bigger was saying, doing, and feeling. Then I'd find it impossible to say what I wanted to say without stepping in and speaking outright on my own; but when doing this I always made an effort to retain the mood of the story, explaining everything only in terms of Bigger's life and, if possible, in the rhythms of Bigger's thought (even though the words would be mine). Again, at other times, in the guise of the lawyer's speech and the newspaper items, or in terms of what Bigger would overhear or see from afar, I'd give what others were saying and thinking of him. But always, from the start to the finish, it was Bigger's story, Bigger's fear, Bigger's flight, and Bigger's fate that I tried to depict. I wrote with the conviction in mind (I don't know if this is right or wrong; I only know that I'm temperamentally inclined to feel this way) that the main burden of all serious fiction consists almost wholly of character-destiny and the items, social, political, and personal, of that character-destiny.

As I wrote I followed, almost unconsciously, many principles of the novel which my reading of the novels of other writers had made me feel were necessary for the building of a well-constructed book. For the most part the novel is rendered in the present; I wanted the reader to feel that Bigger's story was happening *now*, like a play upon the stage or a movie unfolding upon the screen. Action follows action, as in a prize fight. Wherever possible, I told of Bigger's life in close-up, slow-motion, giving the feel of the grain in the passing of time. I had long had the feeling that this was the best way to "enclose" the reader's mind in a new world, to blot out all reality except that which I was giving him.

Then again, as much as I could, I restricted the novel to what Bigger saw and felt, to the limits of his feeling and thoughts, even when I was conveying *more* than that to the reader. I had the notion that such a manner of rendering made for a sharper effect, a more pointed sense of the character, his peculiar type of being and consciousness. Throughout there is but one point of view: Bigger's. This, too, I felt, made for a richer illusion of reality.

I kept out of the story as much as possible, for I wanted the reader to feel that there was nothing between him and Bigger; that the story was a special *première* given in his own private theater.

I kept the scenes long, made as much happen within a short space of time as possible; all of which, I felt, made for greater density and richness of effect.

In a like manner I tried to keep a unified sense of background throughout the story; the background would change, of course, but I tried to keep before the eyes of the reader at all times the forces and elements against which Bigger was striving.

And, because I had limited myself to rendering only what Bigger saw and felt, I gave no more reality to the other characters than that which Bigger himself saw.

This, honestly, is all I can account for in the book. If I attempted to account for scenes and characters, to tell why certain scenes were written in certain ways, I'd be stretching facts in order to be pleasantly intelligible. All else in the book came from my feelings reacting upon the material, and any honest reader knows as much about the rest of what is in the book as I do; that is, if, as he reads, he is willing to let his emotions and imagination become as influenced by the materials as I did. As I wrote, for some reason or other, one image, symbol, character, scene, mood, feeling evoked its opposite, its parallel, its complementary, and its ironic counterpart. Why? I don't know. My emotions and imagination just like to work that way. One can account for just so much of life, and then no more. At least, not yet.

With the first draft down, I found that I could not end the book satisfactorily. In the first draft I had Bigger going smack to the electric chair; but I felt that two murders were enough for one novel. I cut the final scene and went back to worry about the beginning. I had no luck. The book was one-half finished, with the opening and closing scenes unwritten. Then, one night, in desperation—I hope that I'm not disclosing the hidden secrets of my craft!—I sneaked out and got a bottle. With the help of it, I began to remember many things which I could not remember before. One of them was that Chicago was overrun with rats. I recalled that I'd seen many rats on the streets, that I'd heard and read of Negro children being bitten by rats in their beds. At first I rejected the idea of Bigger battling a rat in his room; I was afraid that the rat would "hog" the scene. But the rat would not leave me; he presented himself in many attractive guises. So, cautioning myself to allow the rat scene to disclose *only* Bigger, his family, their little room, and their relationships, I let the rat walk in, and he did his stuff.

Many of the scenes were torn out as I reworked the book. The mere rereading of what I'd written made me think of the possibility of developing themes which had been only hinted at in the first draft. For example, the entire guilt theme that runs through *Native Son* was woven in *after* the first draft was written.

At last I found out how to end the book; I ended it just as I had begun it, showing Bigger living dangerously, taking his life into his hands, accepting what life had made him. The lawyer, Max, was placed in Bigger's cell at the end of the novel to register the moral—or what *I* felt was the moral—horror of Negro life in the United States.

The writing of *Native Son* was to me an exciting, enthralling, and even a romantic experience. With what I've learned in the writing of this book, with all of its blemishes, imperfections, with all of its unrealized potentialities, I am launching out upon another novel, this time about the status of women in modern American society. This book, too, goes back to my childhood just as Bigger went, for, while I was storing away impressions of Bigger, I was storing away impressions of many other things that made me think and wonder. Some experience will ignite somewhere deep down in me the smoldering embers of new fires and I'll be off again to write yet another novel. It is good to live when one feels that such as that will happen to one. Life becomes sufficient unto life; the rewards of living are found in living.

I don't know if *Native Son* is a good book or a bad book. And I don't know if the book I'm working on now will be a good book or a bad book. And I really don't care. The mere writing of it will be more fun and a deeper satisfaction than any praise or blame from anybody.

I feel that I'm lucky to be alive to write novels today, when the whole world is caught in the pangs of war and change. Early American writers, Henry James and Nathaniel Hawthorne, complained bitterly about the bleakness and flatness of the American scene. But I think that if they were alive, they'd feel at home in modern America. True, we have no great church in America; our national traditions are still of such a sort that we are not wont to brag of them; and we have no army that's above the level of mercenary fighters; we have no group acceptable to the whole of our country upholding certain humane values; we have no rich symbols, no colorful rituals. We only have a money-grubbing, industrial civilization. But we do have in the Negro the embodiment of a past tragic enough to appease the spiritual hunger of even a James; and we have in the oppression of the Negro a shadow athwart our national life dense and heavy enough to satisfy even the gloomy broodings of a Hawthorne. And if Poe were alive, he would not have to invent horror; horror would invent him.

Ralph Ellison
(1913–1994)

BORN IN OKLAHOMA CITY, Ralph Waldo Ellison graduated from Frederick Douglass School. He was a good trumpet player. Having heard of the African American composer William Dawson, who taught at Tuskegee Institute, Ellison enrolled there to study music and become a classical composer. While at Tuskegee, he read T. S. Eliot's *The Wasteland* and became deeply interested in literature. During the summer of his junior year, he worked in New York City. He never returned to Tuskegee. Shortly after his arrival in New York, he met Langston Hughes. Hughes introduced him to Richard Wright, who suggested that Ellison write a book review for *New Challenge*. The assignment got him started as a writer.

In 1952, Ralph Ellison published *Invisible Man*, the only novel he completed during his celebrated literary career. His novel was awarded the National Book Award for fiction in 1953. In 1965, when *Book Week* conducted a poll of prominent writers, critics, and editors, they chose Ellison's novel as "the most distinguished American novel written since World War II." The novelist received other important accolades—including the Medal of Freedom, the highest civilian honor, awarded to him by President Lyndon Johnson.

Ellison published two collections of essays—*Shadow and Act* (1964) and *Going to the Territory* (1984)—all included in *The Collected Essays of Ralph Ellison* (1995).[26] Ellison covers a range of topics in his essays. In "Hidden Name and Complex Fate," he discusses his boyhood in Oklahoma City as a rich source for his imagination and fiction. He, after Alain Locke, writes some of the first essays on jazz as an indigenous American musical genre. His essays feature prominent Oklahoma jazzmen, such as Charlie Christian and Jimmy Rushing as well as more famous jazz musicians—Louis Armstrong, Duke Ellington, and Charlie Parker. He also includes essays on other significant figures such as Mahalia Jackson, the gospel singer; Lyndon B. Johnson; and his friend, the artist Romare Bearden. Ellison's essays, like *Invisible Man*, often highlight the ironies and contradictions of American culture.[27] In "What America Would Be Like Without Blacks," he describes the "deceptive metamorphoses" and "blending of identities" frequently found in all areas of American history and culture. He concludes that most whites are "part Negro without even knowing it."

After the publication of *Invisible Man*, Ellison worked on another novel for the rest of his life. Excerpts from that forthcoming novel appeared in various journals during his lifetime. A version of his novel-in-progress was published posthumously. *Juneteenth*—edited by John Callahan, literary critic and executor of Ellison's estate—was published in 1999. And *Three Days Before the Shooting* (a compendium of varying drafts and sections of the novel)—edited by John Callahan and Adam Bradley—was published in 2010.[28]

In his "Introduction to the Thirtieth Anniversary Edition of *Invisible Man*," an autobiographical essay that captures the seven-year period of his novel's composition, Ellison takes us to the settings where he wrote, from a barn in Waitsfield, Vermont, to his ground-floor apartment on St. Nicholas Avenue in Harlem, to the eighth floor of the glamorous Fifth Avenue address of a friend.

The excerpt included here is the last section of his introduction (1981). While writing in a Vermont barn in 1947, he hears an ironic voice inside his head, the voice of the nameless protagonist of *Invisible Man*.

From "Introduction to the Thirtieth Anniversary Edition of *Invisible Man*" (1981)

Shortly before the spokesman for invisibility intruded, I had seen in a nearby Vermont village a poster announcing the performance of a "Tom Show," that forgotten term for blackface minstrel versions of Mrs. Stowe's *Uncle Tom's Cabin*. I had thought such entertainment a thing of the past, but there in a quiet northern village it was alive and kicking, with Eliza, frantically slipping and sliding on the ice, still trying—and this during World War II!—to escape the slavering hounds. . . . *Oh, I went to the hills / To hide my face / The hills cried out, No hiding place / There's no hiding place / Up here!*

No, because what is commonly assumed to be past history is actually as much a part of the living present as William Faulkner insisted. Furtive, implacable and tricky, it inspirits both the observer and the scene observed, artifacts, manners and atmosphere, and it speaks even when no one wills to listen.

So as I listened, things once obscure began falling into place. Odd things, unexpected things. Such as the poster that reminded me of the tenacity which a nation's moral evasions can take on when given the trappings of racial stereotypes, and the ease with which its deepest experience of tragedy could be converted into blackface farce. Even information picked up about the backgrounds of friends and acquaintances fell into the slowly emerging pattern of implication. The wife of the racially mixed couple who were our hosts was the granddaughter of a Vermonter who had been a general in the Civil War, adding new dimensions to the poster's presence. Details of old photographs, rhymes, riddles, children's games, church services, college ceremonies, practical jokes and political activities observed during my prewar days in Harlem—all fell into place. I had reported the riot of 1943 for the *New York Post*, had agitated earlier for the release of Angelo Herndon and the Scottsboro Boys, had marched behind Adam Clayton Powell, Jr., in his effort to desegregate the stores along 125th Street, and had been part of a throng which blocked off Fifth Avenue in protest of the role being played by Germany and Italy in the Spanish Civil War. Everything and anything appeared as grist for my fictional mill, some speaking up clearly, saying, "Use me right here," while others were disturbingly mysterious.

Like my sudden recall of an incident from my college days when, opening a vat of Plasticine donated to an invalid sculptor friend by some Northern studio, I found enfolded within the oily mass a frieze of figures modeled after those depicted on Saint-Gaudens's monument to Colonel Robert Gould Shaw and his 54th Massachusetts Negro Regiment, a memorial which stands on the Boston Common. I had no idea why it should surface, but perhaps it was to remind me that since I was writing fiction and seeking vaguely for images of black and white fraternity I would do well to recall that Henry James's brother Wilky had fought as an officer with those Negro soldiers, and that Colonel Shaw's body had been thrown into a ditch with those of his men. Perhaps it was also to remind me that war could, with art, be transformed into something deeper and more meaningful than its surface violence.

At any rate, it now appeared that the voice of invisibility issued from deep within our complex American underground. So how crazy-logical that I should finally locate its owner living—and oh, so garrulously—in an abandoned cellar. Of course the process was far more disjointed than I make it sound, but such was the inner-outer, subjective-objective process of the developing fiction, its pied rind and surreal heart.

Even so, I was still inclined to close my ears and get on with my interrupted novel, but like many writers atoss in what Conrad described as the "destructive element," I had floundered into a state of hyper-receptivity, a desperate condition in which a fiction writer finds it difficult to ignore even the most nebulous idea-emotion that might arise in the process of creation. For he soon learns that such amorphous projections might well be unexpected gifts from his daydreaming muse that might, when properly perceived, provide exactly the materials needed to keep afloat in the turbulent tides of composition. On the other hand, they might wreck him, drown him in the quicksands of indecision. I was already having enough difficulty trying to avoid writing what might turn out to be nothing more than another novel of racial protest instead of the dramatic study in comparative humanity which I felt any worthwhile novel should be, and the voice appeared to be leading me precisely in that direction. But then as I listened to its taunting laughter and speculated on what kind of individual would speak in such accents, I decided that it would be one who had been forged in the underground of American experience and yet managed to emerge less angry than ironic. That he would be a blues-toned laugher-at-wounds who included himself in his indictment of the human condition. I liked the idea, and as I tried to visualize the speaker I came to relate him to those ongoing conflicts, tragic and comic, that had claimed my group's energies since the abandonment of the Reconstruction. And after coaxing him into revealing a bit more about himself, I concluded that he was without question a "character," and this in the dual meaning of the term. I saw that he was young, powerless (reflecting the difficulties of Negro leaders of the period) and ambitious for a role of leadership—a role at which he was doomed to fail. Having nothing to lose, and by way of providing myself with the widest field for success or failure, I associated him, ever so distantly, with the narrator of Dostoevsky's *Notes from Underground*. With that *I* began to structure the movement of my plot, while *he* began to merge with my more specialized concerns with fictional form and with certain problems arising out of the pluralistic literary tradition from which I spring.

Among these was the question of why most protagonists of Afro-American fiction (not to mention the black characters in fiction written by whites) were without intellectual depth. Too often they were figures caught up in the most intense forms of social struggle, subject to the most extreme forms of the human predicament, yet seldom able to articulate the issues which tortured them. Not that many worthy individuals aren't in fact inarticulate, but that there were, and are, enough exceptions in real life to provide the perceptive novelist with models. And even if they did not exist it would be necessary, both in the interest of fictional expressiveness and as examples of human possibility, to invent them. Henry James had taught us much with his hyperconscious, "Super subtle fry," characters who embodied in their own cultured, upper-class way the American virtues of conscience and consciousness. Such ideal creatures were unlikely to turn up in the world I inhabited, but one never knew because so much in this society is unnoticed and unrecorded. On the other hand, I felt that one of the ever-present challenges facing the American novelist was that of endowing his inarticulate characters, scenes and social processes with eloquence. For it is by such attempts that he fulfills his social responsibility as an American artist.

Here it would seem that the interests of art and democracy converge, with the development of conscious, articulate citizens an established goal of this democratic society, and the creation of conscious, articulate characters indispensable to the creation of resonant compositional centers through which an organic consistency can be achieved in the fashioning of fictional forms. By way of imposing meaning upon our disparate American experience the novelist seeks to create forms in which acts, scenes and characters speak for more than their immediate selves, and in this enterprise the very nature of language is on his side. For by a trick of fate (our racial problems notwithstanding) the human imagination is integrative—and the same is true of the centrifugal force that inspirits the democratic process. And while fiction is but a form of symbolic action, a mere game of "as if," therein lies its true function and its potential for effecting change. For at its most serious, just as is true of politics at its best, it is a thrust toward a human ideal. And it approaches that ideal by a subtle process of negating the world of things as given in favor of a complex of man-made positives.

So if the ideal of achieving a true political equality eludes us in reality—as it continues to do—there is still available that fictional *vision* of an ideal democracy in which the actual combines with the ideal and gives us representations of a state of things in which the highly placed and the lowly, the black and the white, the Northerner and the Southerner, the native-born and the immigrant combine to tell us of transcendent truths and possibilities such as those discovered when Mark Twain set Huck and Jim afloat on the raft.

Which suggested to me that a novel could be fashioned as a raft of hope, perception and entertainment that might help keep us afloat as we tried to negotiate the snags and whirlpools that mark our nation's vascillating course toward and away from the democratic ideal.

There are, of course, other goals for fiction. Yet I recalled that during the early, more optimistic days of this republic it was assumed that each individual citizen could become (and should prepare to become) President. For democracy was considered not only a collectivity of individuals, as was defined by W. H. Auden, but a collectivity of politically astute citizens who, by virtue of our vaunted system of universal education and our freedom of opportunity, would be prepared to govern. As things turned out it was an unlikely possibility—but not entirely, as attested by the recent examples of the peanut farmer and the motion-picture actor.

Even for Afro-Americans there was the brief hope that had been encouraged by the presence of black congressmen in Washington during the Reconstruction. Nor could I see any reason for allowing our more chastened view of political possibility (not long before I began this novel A. Phillip Randolph had to threaten our beloved F.D.R. with a march on Washington before our war industries were opened to Negroes) to impose undue restrictions upon my novelist's freedom to manipulate imaginatively those possibilities that existed both in Afro-American personality and in the restricted structure of American society. My task was to transcend those restrictions. As an example, Mark Twain had demonstrated that the novel *could* serve as a comic antidote to the ailments of politics, and since in 1945, as well as now, Afro-Americans were usually defeated in their bouts with circumstance, there was no reason why they, like Brer

Rabbit and his more literary cousins, the great heroes of tragedy and comedy, shouldn't be allowed to snatch the victory of conscious perception from the forces that overwhelmed them. Therefore I would have to create a narrator who could think as well as act, and I saw a capacity for conscious self-assertion as basic to his blundering quest for freedom.

So my task was one of revealing the human universals hidden within the plight of one who was both black and American, and not only as a means of conveying my personal vision of possibility, but as a way of dealing with the sheer rhetorical challenge involved in communicating across our barriers of race and religion, class, color and region—barriers which consist of the many strategies of division that were designed, and still function, to prevent what would otherwise have been a more or less natural recognition of the reality of black and white fraternity. And to defeat this national tendency to deny the common humanity shared by my character and those who might happen to read of his experience, I would have to provide him with something of a world view, give him a consciousness in which serious philosophical questions could be raised, provide him with a range of diction that could play upon the richness of our readily shared vernacular speech, and construct a plot that would bring him in contact with a variety of American types as they operated on various levels of society. Most of all, I would have to approach racial stereotypes as a given fact of the social process and proceed, while gambling with the reader's capacity for fictional truth, to reveal the human complexity which stereotypes are intended to conceal.

It would be misleading, however, to leave the impression that all the process of writing this book was so solemn, for in fact there was a great deal of fun along the way. I knew that I was composing a work of fiction, a work of literary art and one that would allow me to take advantage of the novel's capacity for telling the truth while actually telling a "lie," which is the Afro-American folk term for an improvised story. Having worked in barbershops where that form of oral art flourished, I knew that I could draw upon the rich culture of the folk tale as well as that of the novel, and that uncertain of my skill, I would have to improvise upon my materials in the manner of a jazz musician putting a musical theme through a wild star-burst of metamorphosis. By the time I realized that the words of the Prologue contained the germ of the ending as well as that of the beginning, I was free to enjoy the surprises of incident and character as they popped into view.

And there were surprises. Five years before the book was completed, Frank Taylor, who had given me my first book contract, showed a section to Cyril Connolly, the editor of the English magazine *Horizon*, and it was published in an issue devoted to art in America. This marked the initial publication of the first chapter, which appeared in America shortly afterward in the 1948 volume of the now defunct *Magazine of the Year*—a circumstance which accounts for the 1947 and 1948 copyright dates that have caused confusion for scholars. The actual publication date of the complete volume was 1952.

These surprises were both encouraging and intimidating because after savoring that bit of success I became afraid that this single section, which contained the "Battle Royal" scene, might well be the novel's only incident of interest. But I persisted and finally arrived at the moment when it became meaningful to work with my editor, Albert Erskine. The rest, as the saying goes, is history. My highest hope for the novel was that it would sell enough copies to prevent my publishers from losing their investment and my editor from having wasted his time. But as I said in the beginning, this has always been a most willful, most self-generating novel, and the proof of this statement is witnessed by the fact that here, thirty astounding years later, it has me writing about it again.

Margaret Walker
(1915–1998)

MARGARET WALKER ALEXANDER was born in Birmingham, Alabama, and graduated from Northwestern University. During her years in Chicago, she met Richard Wright and helped him do significant research while he was writing *Native Son*. Given her interest in writing poetry, she attended the University of Iowa's Writers' Workshop. While at Iowa, she completed *For My People* (1942), her first volume of poems. She received the Yale University Younger Poets Award for the collection. She subsequently published other poems, including "Prophets for a New Day" (1970).[29]

Walker also wrote *Richard Wright: Daemonic Genius*, an intellectual biography about his early life and its influence on his work. Describing Wright, Walker says, "One day as Wright and I walked together to the elevator station [in Chicago], he turned to me and said, 'Margaret, if a voice speaks within you, you can live.' And the voice spoke. A daemonic spirit within him found literary expression."[30] *Jubilee* (1966) is the only novel Margaret Walker ever published. She worked on the novel for many years. The excerpt included here is taken from Walker's "How I Wrote *Jubilee*."

From "How I Wrote *Jubilee*" (1972)

I went to the University of Iowa and studied at the Writers' Workshop there. I wanted my master's thesis to be the Civil War story of my family, but once again my poetry was chosen. Nevertheless, it was at Iowa that I began the long period of research for *Jubilee*. I enrolled in a course on American civilization and was instructed to do three things: (1) Compile and read a long list of books about the South, the Negro during slavery, and the slave codes in Georgia (such books include Ulrich B. Phillips, *American Negro Slavery*; William E. Dodd, *The Cotton Kingdom*; Clement Eaton, *A History of the Old South*; Frederick Law Olmstead, *Journey in the Seaboard Slave States*; and Francis A. Kemble, *Journal of a Residence on a Georgian Plantation in 1838–1839*); (2) Make a thorough study of a Negro woman of the antebellum period; and (3) Learn how to find and use primary sources and documents.

I set myself immediately to the first task, reading Civil War stories and history books. These history books were divided into three classes, according to their viewpoints: (1) history from the southern white point of view, (2) history from the northern white viewpoint, and (3) history from the Negro viewpoint. I was trained as a child in the South to read books at school from the southern viewpoint and books at home from the Negro viewpoint. Once I was out of the South I read more and more from the northern viewpoint. It was amazing to discover how widely these history books differed.

For instance, southern historians claimed slavery was a beneficial system with benign masters; northerners did not oppose slavery as long as it was "contained" in the South and did not spread into the territories; while Negro historians regarded slavery as a cruel, inhuman system. White southerners claimed they fought a war between the states for independence; white northerners claimed it was a rebellion of the southerners against the Union, and Negroes said it was a war of liberation. White southerners claimed Reconstruction was the darkest page in history and a tragic era with Negro rule, while northerners blamed the troubles of that period on the death of Lincoln, on Andrew Johnson, and on ignorant Negroes and Congress. On the other hand, Negroes claimed it was an age of progress, with universal suffrage, land reform, and the first public school system. Then the Ku Klux Klan intimidated and disfranchised Negroes in the counterrevolution to reestablish white home rule. As for Negro rule, my authors reminded me that Negroes were never majority office holders in any state. Faced with these three conflicting viewpoints, a novelist in the role of social historian finds it difficult to maintain an "objective" point of view. Obviously she must choose one or the other—or create her own.

Three years passed before I could get beyond the first historical task assigned to me at Iowa, for I left the university in 1940 with my master's degree and my thesis, the poems, *For My People*. Then in 1942, when *For My People* was published, I visited the New York Public Library's Schomburg Collection of Negro history, on 135th Street in Harlem, for the first time. I found Lawrence Reddick serving as curator of that collection and we renewed a family friendship that dated from his days as professor of history at Dillard University in New Orleans. With his doctorate in history he proved an able teacher of southern history, and gave me excellent leads to Georgia's laws on Negroes. Our friendship and association continue to this day.

In 1944 I received a Rosenwald Fellowship to begin serious research on *Jubilee*. (This came just as I was expecting my first child, so my work was delayed and somewhat handicapped.) At that time I was seeking information about free Negroes in Georgia as well as about my antebellum slave woman. Carter G. Woodson had written a book on *The Heads of Free Negro Families in 1830*, and among those listed was a family named Ware—the name of my maternal great-grandmother. I found that this family might have originated on the Atlantic Coast, in Virginia or the Carolinas. At least they had made early appearances there and may have emigrated to America from the West Indies. Then, as I was reading materials from the congressional investigations of the Ku Klux Klan, I found that one of the victims was an artisan named Ware, who was living in a county adjacent to my story's location. I could not swear that Randall Ware was a member of our family, but one could make a good, educated guess that he was.

Actually I had only recently pinpointed the place for the setting of my novel, for it was not until late in my grandmother's life that I had learned of her birthplace. I said to her one day, rather skeptically, "Oh, Grandma, you don't even know where you were born." And she answered, with the usual indignation that came whenever her story was questioned, "Yes, I do. I was born in Dawson, Terrell County, Georgia."

In 1947, in the course of a speaking engagement in Albany, Georgia, I discovered that I was in the vicinity of Dawson and could make the trip and return to Albany the same day. My grandmother had been dead three years, and I knew no one in Dawson. I went into the colored community and began inquiring about my great-grandparents. I found a man who remembered my great-grandfather, Randall Ware. He said he had lived into his nineties, and had died about 1925. If I wished, the man said, he would show me Ware's smithy, his grist mill, and his homeplace. All this was completely astonishing to me, since I had never known much about Randall Ware except my grandmother's remarks that he was a freeman from birth, that he was a smith who owned his own smithy, that he could read and write, and that he was a rich man. Now I was thrilled to see the smithy with his anvil, his grist mill, and his gingerbread house. I had a camera and tried to take pictures of this anvil on which my great-grandfather had forged a hundred years before, but it was a very gray day and my photography was not expert, so my pictures did not turn out well.

In 1948 I blocked out the story according to its three major periods. (I was living with my husband and two children in High Point, North Carolina, and was idle except for my desultory housekeeping.) For the first time I clearly envisioned the development of a folk novel, and prepared an outline of incidents and general chapter headings. I knew that the center of my story was Vyry and that the book should end with Randall Ware's return. Many of the titles in the book belong to this outline of 1948, such as "Death is a mystery that only the squinch owl knows" and "Freedom is a secret word I dare not say." I anticipated about two hundred fifty such incidents and then reduced them to about one hundred. In essence, I never deviated from that outline. I was beginning to see the story in terms of its own organic growth and wholeness, and I was anxious to put down many of the folk sayings verbatim. Many of these chapter headings are exact repetitions of my grandmother's words.

So, when I say that I have been writing *Jubilee* all my life, that is literally true. It has been a consuming ambition, driving me relentlessly. Whenever I took a job, whether in Chicago in the thirties, in West Virginia and North Carolina between 1942 and 1945, or in Jackson, Mississippi, where I began teaching in 1949, I would hound the librarians to help me find books and materials relating to my story. After I had combed books that I found through card catalogs and reference materials, I sent the librarians on further hunts for obscure items and for bits of information I had picked up here and there. In the course of these searches one of my greatest disappointments came in 1950, when I learned of an excellent collection of books on Georgia and the Negro being offered for sale and was unable to purchase them. There were at least two hundred fifty books and other items, but I lacked the two hundred dollars required. I considered borrowing the money, but it seemed unfeasible in view of family finances, so I had to forget that.

In addition to history books, I was also interested in Civil War novels and any items relating to the period. Although I read most of the prominent Civil War novels of the thirties and a majority of those listed in Robert Lively's *Fiction Fights the Civil War*, these were either from the southern white or northern white point of view. As Lively noted, there was little or no attention paid to the Negro in such works.

Two of my most rewarding experiences came after I received a Ford Fellowship, in 1953, to complete the research on *Jubilee*. In August of that year my husband, our three children, and I were returning from my father's funeral in New Orleans when we decided to make the journey to Greenville, Alabama, and then trace my family's path from there back to Dawson, Georgia. In Greenville, I found my grandmother's youngest, and last-surviving, sister, who gave me a picture of my great-grandmother, corroborated my grandmother's account, and let me see the family Bible and the chest my great-grandmother had carried from the plantation. Later, as we traveled through the Georgia environs of what was my lost plantation, we found an antebellum home near Bainbridge, Georgia, with the square pillars and the separated kitchen-house as described in the story. The lady of the house was kind enough to let me come in and look through her place. . . .

* * *

But the end of the first draft is not by any means the end of the writing. I believe that writing is nine-tenths rewriting. Since I write almost nil in longhand, and since my fingers on the typewriter never go as fast as my thoughts, I always write too much and too easily and therefore I must always cut, cut, cut and revise many times. A first draft is only the beginning.

A writer is fortunate if he has an editor to do the first big scissors-and-paste job for him. I do not know how many times through the years the first part of the novel had been revised. The final version bears very little resemblance to my first draft, except that it began as always with Hetta dying when Vyry was two years old, and the manuscript always repeated the same incidents of the flogging through Randall Ware's return to take Jim away. One major revision entailed reorganization for me, cutting out all the heavy expository and purely historical passages. This freed the story of unnecessary burdens. Another revision tackled only language and dialect, in which every word of dialect had to be changed for spelling and modernization. In these two respects the thesis copy in the University of Iowa Library bears no resemblance to the printed copy. The final polishing of *Jubilee* was for me the least satisfactory of all jobs, since it was done in a hurry. Such a revision usually involves tying in all the transitions, straightening sentences, cutting out clichés, and "taking out the whiches." I hope I'll write other books, and next time I'll try to do better. I really think I can.

People ask me how I find time to write, with a family and a

teaching job. I don't. That is one reason I was so long with *Jubilee*. A writer needs time to write a certain number of hours every day. This is particularly true with prose fiction and absolutely necessary with the novel. Writing poetry may be different, but the novel demands long hours every day at a steady pace until the thing is done. It is humanly impossible for a woman who is a wife and mother to work on a regular teaching job and write. Weekends and nights and vacations are all right for reading, but not enough for writing. This is a fulltime job, but for me, such full attention has only been possible during the three Depression years I was on the Writers' Project and during that one school year in which I finished *Jubilee*. I enjoyed the luxury.

How much of *Jubilee* is fiction and how much fact? When you have lived with a story as long as I have with this one, it is difficult sometimes to separate the two, but let us say that the basic skeleton of the story is factually true and authentic. Imagination has worked with this factual material, however, for a very long time. The entire story follows a plot line of historical incidents from the first chapter until the last: the journeys, the Big Road, the violence, the battles, the places Vyry and Innis lived and the reasons they moved.

Ernest J. Gaines
(1933–)

ERNEST J. GAINES ACHIEVED literary fame after publishing *The Autobiography of Miss Jane Pittman* (1971). Since his novel tells the story of Miss Jane's life—from her childhood as a slave through the beginning of the civil rights movement—the book has frequently been mistaken for a true autobiography. The novel was also released as a TV movie in 1974. Cicely Tyson played Miss Jane Pittman, winning two Emmy Awards for her performance.

Born in Oscar, Louisiana, on January 15, 1933, Gaines had a childhood that profoundly influenced his short stories and novels. His early life was spent in a rural, racially segregated and Catholic parish (Pointe Coupee Parish) inhabited by black farmworkers and white bosses. He and his siblings were raised by his aunt, Augusteen Jefferson. Since his aunt could not walk, her home and front porch became a local gathering place where relatives and neighbors visited and exchanged stories and gossip.

During his teenage years, Gaines moved to Vallejo, California. He eventually enrolled in junior college, where he started writing short stories and reading widely. After spending two years in the U.S. Army, he enrolled in San Francisco State University and graduated in 1957. He kept writing short stories and was soon sufficiently impressive to be awarded a Wallace Stegner Fellowship to study creative writing with Stegner and others at Stanford. The honing of his craft at Stanford and the mentoring he received there led to the publication of his first novel, *Catherine Carmier* (1964). To date, he has published four other novels: *In My Father's House* (1978), *A Gathering of Old Men* (1983), and *A Lesson Before Dying* (1993).

Gaines has also published two early collections of short stories—*Of Love and Dust* (1967) and *Bloodline* (1968).

In 2005, Gaines published *Mozart and Leadbelly: Stories and Essays*.[31] His books have been nominated for various prestigious prizes and won a number of them. *A Lesson Before Dying*, for example, was given the National Book Critics Circle Award for Fiction in 1993. His own major awards include being chosen as a MacArthur Fellow. In 2012, President Barack Obama presented Gaines with the National Medal of the Arts for his distinguished literary career.

In "Miss Jane and I," Gaines discusses his early life and the genesis of his writing career.

Miss Jane and I (1978)

I shall try to say a little about myself, about my writing, and about Miss Jane Pittman and how she and I came to meet. Since the publication of *The Autobiography of Miss Jane Pittman*, I've read reviews in which critics have called Miss Jane a real person. A representative of *Newsweek* asked me to send the editors of the magazine a picture of Miss Jane Pittman to be used with a review of the novel. I had to inform her that I could not, since Miss Jane is a creation of my imagination. The lady who called me was both shocked and embarrassed—"Oh, my God! Oh, my God! Oh, my God!" she said. The actress Ruby Dee, when reviewing the novel for *Freedomways*, also mistook Miss Jane for a real person. Several newspapers made the same mistake. One lady accused me of using a tape recorder, then calling the interview a novel after I had cut out all the inconsequential material. A good friend of mine who writes for one of the leading newspapers in San Francisco felt that *Miss Jane* is definitely a novel, but he also felt that I must have, at some time in the past, interviewed my grandmother or my aunt who raised me when I lived in the South. Bob Cromie on *Bookbeat* out of Chicago also thought I had interviewed my grandmother.

But *The Autobiography of Miss Jane Pittman* is absolute fiction. By that I mean I created Miss Jane, and if I did not create all the events she mentions in her narrative, I definitely created all the situations that she is personally involved in.

It is written somewhere that when Gertrude Stein was dying, Alice B. Toklas leaned over her and asked, "Gertrude, Gertrude, what is the answer?" Gertrude Stein raised up on her dying bed and said, "Dear Alice, but what is the question?"

Who is Miss Jane Pittman? But first, who is Ernest J. Gaines? Because to get part of the answer to the former question we must go back, back, back—not to 1968, when I started writing the novel, but to 1948, when I had to leave the South.

Until I was fifteen years old, I had been raised by an aunt, a lady who had never walked a day in her life, but who crawled over the floor as a six-month-old child might. Some people have said that she had been dropped on the floor by another child when she was small; others have said that she was born with that affliction. To this day I do not know which story is true—but I've never met anyone who ever saw her walk.

When I say that my aunt raised me, I mean she did more than just look after me, my brothers, and my sister. I can remember us children bringing the potatoes, rice, meat, flour, and water to her sitting on her bench by the stove so that she could cook for us. I can remember the loaves of bread, cookies, and cakes she used to bake for us in the oven of the woodstove. I can remember seeing her sitting on her bench and leaning over a washboard, washing our clothes in a tin tub. Once this was done, and after she had taken her afternoon nap, she wanted to do more. She wanted to go into her garden then and chop grass from between the rows of beans, cabbages, and tomatoes. She had a small hoe, about half the size of the regular hoe. After sharpening it well with her file, she would let it down on the ground, and then in some way, but with true dignity, she would slide from step to step until she had reached the ground—then she would go into her garden. Other times she would go into the backyard with her little rice sack and gather pecans under the trees. No pecan, not even the smallest one, could hide itself in the bull grass from her eyes forever. They would try hard, the little pecans, but eventually they would give up the ghost just like all the rest. These are just a few of the things I can remember about my aunt, but there is much, much more.

Then there were the people who used to come to our house, because she was crippled and could not go to theirs. In summer they would sit out on the porch, the gallery—"the Garry," we called it—and they would talk for hours. There was no television then, and only a few people had radios, so people would talk. Sometimes there would be only one other person besides my aunt; other times, maybe a half dozen. Sometimes they would sew on quilts and mattresses while they talked; other times they would shell peas and beans while they talked. Sometimes they would just sit there smoking pipes, chewing pompee, or drinking coffee while they talked. I, being the oldest child, was made to stay close by and serve them coffee or water or whatever else they needed. In winter, they moved from the porch and sat beside the fireplace and drank coffee—and sometimes a little homemade brew—while they talked. But regardless of what time of year it was, under whatever conditions, they would find something to talk about. I did not know then that twenty or twenty-five years later I would try to put some of their talk in a book that I would title *The Autobiography of Miss Jane Pittman*.

This all took place before 1948. In 1948, I had to leave my aunt and the South to go West to my mother and stepfather to finish my education. I probably—I definitely—would have stayed in the South if I could have received the education that they thought I rightly deserved. But since there was no junior high or senior high school near me, and since I would have to go away to school anyhow, my mother and stepfather thought I should come to California, where they were. I remember the day I left. It was Sunday. It took me all day to pack, unpack, and repack the old brown leather suitcase. I didn't have many clothes, I can assure you, but for some reason

I could not get it done. Maybe it was the bag of oranges, or the shoebox of fried chicken and bread, or the tea cakes and pralines wrapped in brown paper, or the bag of unshelled pecans—maybe it was one of these or all of these that kept me opening and shutting the suitcase. But, finally, I got it done and came out onto the porch. Everybody was there: the old people on the porch talking to my aunt and the children in the yard waiting for me to come down the steps so they could follow me to the road. I went to each one of the old people, shook their hands, and listened to their advice on how to live "up North." Then I went to my aunt. She sat on the floor—just inside the door. "I'm going, Aunty," I said. I did not lean over to kiss her—though I loved her more than I have loved anyone else in my life. I did not take her hand, as I had taken the other people's hands, because that would have been the most inappropriate thing in the world to do. I simply said, "I'm going, Aunty." She looked up at me from the floor. I saw the tears in her eyes. She nodded her head and looked down again. When I came out into the road, I looked back at her. I waved and smiled; she waved back. The old people were silent all this time—but I'm sure that before I reached the highway to catch the bus, they were talking again.

I went to Vallejo, California, a seaport town, because my stepfather was in the merchant marine. I had gone there in summer, and I had nothing much to do during the day but play with other children. We lived in the government projects at the time, and my friends were a complete mixture of races: Chinese, Japanese, Filipinos, Mexicans, Puerto Ricans, whites, and Indians. I made friends quite easily, and most of the time, especially during the day, I was very happy. But at night, when my new friends had gone, I sat alone in a room and thought about home. Many times I wished that my aunt would write my mother and tell her to send me back—or that some wise man would come up and tell me how futile an education was when I had to sacrifice so much for it.

A few months after I had gone to Vallejo, my parents moved out of the projects into another part of town. I did not have nearly as many friends there, and my stepfather warned me against those young people I did meet. They were a rough bunch, and he felt that they would all end up in jail before they graduated from high school. I took his advice about staying away from them, and that's how I found myself in the public library.

I soon found out that all I needed was a library card and then I could take out as many books as I could carry in my arms. At first I took books indiscriminately—I would choose one simply because I liked its dust jacket. But soon, because of the schoolwork, or maybe because of the weight of the books, I began to select only those that I would definitely read. Number one, they had to be about the South, and two, they had to be fiction.

So I read many novels, many short stories, plays—all written by white writers—because there was such a limited number of works at the time by black writers in a place like Vallejo. I found most of the work that I read untrue and unreal to my own experience, yet because I hungered for some kind of connection between myself and the South, I read them anyhow. But I did not care for the language of this writing. I found it too oratorical, and the dialects, especially that of blacks, quite untrue. (Twain and Faulkner can be put into or left out of this category, depending on your taste.) I did not care for the way black characters were drawn. (Twain and Faulkner can be accepted or not accepted here—again, depending on your taste.) Whenever a black person was mentioned in these novels, either she was a mammy, or he was a Tom; and if he was young, he was a potential Tom, a good nigger; or he was not a potential Tom, a bad nigger. When a black woman character was young, she was either a potential mammy or a nigger wench. For most of these writers, choosing something between was unheard of.

Despite their descriptions of blacks, I often found something in their writing that I could appreciate. Sometimes they accurately captured sounds that I knew well: a dog barking in the heat of hunting, a train moving in the distance, a worker calling to another across the road or field. Pasternak once said that Southern writers wrote well about the earth and the sun. These writers, who so poorly described blacks, did well with the odor of grass and trees after a summer rain; they were especially adept at describing the sweat odor in the clothes of men coming in from the fields; you could see, better than if you were actually there, the red dust in Georgia or the black mud of Mississippi.

I read all of the Southern writers I could find in the Vallejo library; then I began to read any writer who wrote about nature or about people who worked the land. So I discovered John Steinbeck and the Salinas Valley; and Willa Cather and her Nebraska—anyone who would say something about dirt and trees, clear streams, and open sky.

Eventually, I would discover the great European writers. My favorite at this time was the Frenchman Guy de Maupassant—de Maupassant because he wrote so beautifully about the young, and besides that he told good stories, used the simplest language, and most times made the stories quite short. So for a long time it was de Maupassant. Then I must have read somewhere that the Russian Anton Chekhov was as good as or better than de Maupassant, so I went to Chekhov. From Chekhov to Tolstoy, then to the rest of the Russians—among them Pushkin, Gogol, and Turgenev, especially Turgenev's *A Sportsman's Sketches* and his *Fathers and Sons*. The nineteenth-century Russian writers became my favorites, and to this day as a group of writers of any one country, they still are. I felt that they wrote truly about peasantry, or, put another way, truer than any other group of writers of any other country. Their peasants were not caricatures or clowns. They did not make fun of them. They were people—they were good, they were bad. They could be as brutal as any man, they could be as kind. The American writers in general, the Southern writer in particular, never saw peasantry, especially black peasantry, in this way; blacks were either caricatures of human beings or they were problems. They needed to be saved or they were saviors. They were either children or they were seers. But they were very seldom what the average being was. There were exceptions, of course, but I'm talking about a total body of writers, the conscience of a people.

Though I found the nineteenth-century Russian writers superior for their interest in the peasants, they, too, could not give me the satisfaction that I was looking for. Their four- and five-syllable names were foreign to me. Their greetings were not the same as greetings were at home. Our religious worship was not the same; icons were foreign to me. I had eaten steamed cabbage, boiled cabbage, but not cabbage soup. I had drunk clabber, but never kvass. I had never slept on a stove, and I still don't know how anyone can. I knew the distance of a mile—never have I learned the distance of a verst. The Russian steppes sounded interesting, but they were not the swamps of Louisiana; Siberia could be as cruel, but it was not Angola State Prison. So even those who I thought were nearest to the way I felt still were not close enough.

I wanted to smell that Louisiana earth, feel that Louisiana sun, sit under the shade of one of those Louisiana oaks, search for pecans in that Louisiana grass in one of those Louisiana yards next to one of those Louisiana bayous, not far from a Louisiana river. I wanted to see on paper those Louisiana black children walking to school on cold days while yellow Louisiana buses passed them by. I wanted to see on paper those black parents going to work before the sun came up and coming back home to look after their children after the sun went down. I wanted to see on paper the true reason why those black fathers left home—not because they were trifling or shiftless, but because they were tired of putting up with certain conditions. I wanted to see on paper the small country churches (schools during the week), and I wanted to hear those simple religious songs, those simple prayers—that true devotion. (It was Faulkner, I think, who said that if God were to stay alive in the country, the blacks would have to keep Him so.) And I wanted to hear that Louisiana dialect—that combination of English, Creole, Cajun, black. For me there's no more beautiful sound anywhere—unless, of course, you take exceptional pride in "proper" French or "proper" English. I wanted to read about the true relationship between whites and blacks—about the people that I had known.

When I first started writing—it was about when I was sixteen or seventeen—my intentions were not to write polemics or anything controversial. At that time I had not read much writing by black writers, so I did not know what especially a black youth trying to write his first novel was supposed to write about. (I still don't know what a black writer is supposed to write about unless it is the same thing that a Frenchman writes about—and that is what he feels deeply enough inside of him to write about.) No, when I first started writing, I wanted to write a simple little novel about people at home. I think the first title I gave it was *A Little Stream*, because it dealt with two families, one very fair, one dark—separated from each other by a stream of water. But I gave the novel at least a dozen different titles before I was finished with it. Whenever the plot took a sudden change—a direction beyond my control—I erased the original title and gave the manuscript one that was more fitting.

The book I started in 1949 or 1950 was finally published in a completely different version in 1964 under the title *Catherine Carmier*. I had changed the title many times in those fifteen years. When it came time for publication the book was simply called *Catherine*. My editor wrote me a letter saying, "Listen, you ought to give it another title." I said, "*Catherine* sounds all right to me." Once I had been in love with a girl named Catherine, and, too, I had just finished reading Hemingway's novel *A Farewell to Arms*, whose heroine's name is Catherine. I figured what was good enough for Hemingway was good enough for Ernie Gaines. So I said, "What's wrong with *Catherine?*" My editor said he thought something else ought to go with it. I said, "All right, her last name is Carmier, call her that. Call her anything—as long as I don't have to think up another title. Because then I'd have to write a new book—and I'm tired." So in 1964, it was called *Catherine Carmier*. It was published in Germany, and they called it *It Was the Nightingale*. And that came after they had even left out one of the main chapters in the book.

But let's go back to '49 ('49 or '50), when I first started writing. I wrote the manuscript out on sheets of paper about half the size of regular notebook paper. Where I got paper that size I've forgotten. Whether I typed the manuscript in single or double space I can't recall either. I do know that it was not typed well, because I had rented a typewriter for that single project without knowing where the letters *A* and *B* were located. I worked twelve hours a day at times, typing with two fingers until I got tired. Then I would lean on one hand and type with the index finger of the other. Finally, it was done—it had taken me all summer to do it. (I should mention here that before trying to type the novel, I had written the novel out in longhand. So it took me that entire summer to type it up and send it out.) After sending the manuscript to New York, I expected any day to receive a telegram telling me that I had written a masterpiece, and I thought a check of several thousand dollars would soon follow. But nothing of the sort happened. I supposed after the editors had shaken the little package, which was about half the size of what a manuscript ought to be, and found that it was not a bomb, and after they had smelled it and found that it was not a fruitcake, they quite possibly played football with it a few weeks when they had nothing else to do. Then they sent it back to me in the original brown paper, tied with its original broken and knotted strings. Only by now the paper and strings were a little dirtier than they were when I sent the manuscript out. I broke the strings and paper loose, found the blue or pink or yellow rejection slip, and took the rejection slip and manuscript out to the incinerator. Of course I felt the great letdown all beginning writers do. I had envisioned thousands of dollars, a nice place to live, a car, clothes of all kinds, and money to send back to my younger brothers, my sister, and my aunt. I was let down when it did not go that way. But between the time that I sent the manuscript out and the time it came back—a couple of months, at least—I had decided no matter what happened I would continue to write. So when the manuscript came back in its original wrapper, tied with its original string, yes, I felt let down, but I was determined to go on. I had only lost the first battle; I had not lost the war—yet.

From then on, school and working in summers kept me from writing another book, so I did not try again until I went into the army. I tried to write one in my off-duty hours, but I found that I liked shooting pool, playing pinochle, and playing softball too much to stick to the pencil. All I got accomplished was a short story that was good enough to take second place on the island of Guam, where I was stationed. The story was sent to our command headquarters in Japan to compete with all the other short stories by GIs in the Far East. There it got honorable mention. So I made fifteen dollars for second prize on Guam and ten dollars for honorable mention in Japan. I cashed the ten-dollar check as soon as I received it, but the fifteen-dollar check is at the house in a little glass bank that belonged to my aunt, who died in 1953. After her death, the bank was given to me to remember her by.

I was discharged from the army in 1955, and I enrolled at San Francisco State College. When I told my adviser that I wanted to be a writer, he asked me what else I wanted to be. I told him nothing else. He broke down the percentage of those who made their living writing. It was frightening. Then he told me the percentage of blacks who made their living writing. This was ten times as frightening. I told him I didn't care how hard it would be, I could not think of anything else I wanted to do. He saw that I was not going to change my mind, and he said, "You can't study writing here because you cannot get a degree in writing." (I should note here that you could take writing classes at San Francisco State at the time, but you could not major in writing. You can do either now.) He said, "You can't study writing here because you can't get a degree in writing. And in order to stay in college you must study toward a degree. So there." "All right," I said. "What is the closest thing to writing that I can study here?" "I would say English," he said. "When you fail at your writing, you can always teach English." "All right, I'll take that," I said.

For the next two years at San Francisco State and a year at Stanford, I tried to write about Louisiana. I wrote every free moment I had, and many times I disregarded my textbooks in order to write. There was something deep in me that I wanted to say—something that had been boiling in me ever since I left the South—and maybe even before then. My instructors at San Francisco State and Stanford thought I would say it all one day—but it would take time. "It will take time and work, time and work," they said. "Now you ought to read this," they said, "and read it carefully. Do you see how Turgenev handles this same kind of situation? Bazorov's relationship to his old people in *Fathers and Sons* is the same as what you're trying to do to Jackson and Aunt Charlotte. Now, take Joyce—see how he handles Stephen and his discussion with the priest. Sherwood Anderson—how he handles the people of Winesburg, Ohio. Faulkner—and his Yoknapatawpha County. Read, read, read it carefully. You'll get it. But it will take time—time and work. Much work."

In 1962, I realized that to write a novel about Louisiana, then I, too, should go back to the source that I was trying to write about. It was then that I decided to go to Baton Rouge to stay awhile and to work. I stayed six months, beginning in January 1963. I'd work five or six hours during the day, then take a nip or two at night—and I had much fun. I met some of the most wonderful people in the world. I talked to many people, but most of the time I tried listening—not only to what they had to say but also to the way they said it. I visited the plantation that I had tried to write about while I was in San Francisco. Many of the people whom I had left nearly fifteen years before were still on the plantation. Some were dead, but the ones living could talk about them and did talk about them as though they had simply walked into another room only a few minutes before. I stayed in Baton Rouge six months, and six months after I went back to San Francisco, I finished the novel that I had been so long trying to write. The novel was *Catherine Carmier*.

In the beginning the novel was twice as long as it was when it was finally published. I had put everything into those seven hundred pages that I could think of. I wanted everything that I had experienced, that I knew or had heard of about Louisiana. There were house fairs, with gumbos and fried fish, soft drinks and beer; there was much lovemaking, and, of course, there had to be illegitimate children; there were deaths, wakes, funerals, baptisms, even threats of race violence. But my editor thought I had a little too much and that the book ought to be cut in half. Stick to the simple love story between the boy from the North and the girl in the South and leave everything else out. After we had exchanged a few bitter words through letters and over the telephone, and after I had called him a few choice names that I think all writers call all editors, I finally took his advice. The book was then published, but just as soon forgotten.

Now where would I go from here?

Most of what was published in *Catherine Carmier* had taken place in the late fifties or early sixties. But what about my life before then? What about the people I really loved and knew? And what about the language—that language that is like no other?

It seemed that I could not think of another novel about Louisiana no matter how hard I tried, so I tried to write about San Francisco— the bohemian life in San Francisco, which I knew a little about. I wrote one novel in six months, another in about the same amount of time—and another novel about six months later. Within a year and a half or two years, I had written three of the worst novels that have ever been written by a published writer. I realized from those efforts that I was not a San Francisco writer—or at least not yet. And if I was not, then what—what then? Since I could not think of another Louisiana novel, what could I do? I got a job working with a printer. And when anyone asked me what I was doing, I told them I was learning the printing business. "What about your writing?" they asked me. "I don't know. Maybe I'll put it down," I said. But even when I was saying this, my mind was only on writing—writing something else about Louisiana. I knew that I had more to say—and eventually it would come—but when and how, I didn't know.

Then one day I was playing some of my records, and a particular verse caught my attention. I should note here that I'm an avid record collector. I have over five hundred LPs of all kinds of music—jazz, blues, spirituals, European and African folk music, American Indian music, etc., etc. I think I have learned as much about writing about my people by listening to blues and jazz and spirituals as I have learned by reading novels. The understatements in the tenor saxophone of Lester Young, the crying, haunting, forever searching sounds of John Coltrane, and the softness and violence of Count Basie's big band—all have fired my imagination as much as anything in literature. But the rural blues, maybe because of my background, is my choice in music. So, I was sitting around listening to a record by Lightnin' Hopkins, and these words stuck in my mind: "The worse thing this black man ever done—when he moved his wife and family to Mr. Tim Moore's farm. Mr. Tim Moore's man don't stand and grin; say 'If you stay out the graveyard, nigger, I'll keep you out the pen'" [sic]. These words haunted me for weeks, for months—without my knowing why, or what I would ever do with them.

Then I came back here in 1965, and a friend of mine and I were talking, and during our conversation he told me that someone we knew had been killed by a man in Baton Rouge, and that the person who had killed him was sent to prison for only a short time and then released. When I heard this, I had no idea that this incident could have any connection with Lightnin' Hopkins's blues verse. But the two things—the murder and the song—stayed in my mind, stayed in mind so much that I began to wonder what I could do with them. Then I recalled hearing about two other incidents in which blacks had murdered blacks. In Case One, when a white lawyer offered his services for a small fee, the prisoner told him that he would rather go to the pen and pay for his crime. But in Case Two, the prisoner left with his white employer. Remembering the first incident, I wrote the long story "Three Men," which was published in my *Bloodline* collection. But the second incident would require much more time and thinking. What would I do with my young killer once I got him out of prison? It took about a year, I suppose, before it all jelled in my mind, and then I started writing, in the summer of 1966, the novel *Of Love and Dust*. The novel takes place the summer I left the South. The action takes place on a plantation along False River. I used that particular place and that time because I knew more about them than I did about Baton Rouge. And I think I also used that time and place because, again, I was trying to say something about my past, something of what I had left out in *Catherine Carmier*. I wanted to talk about the fields a little bit more, about the plantation store, the river, the church, the house fairs, etc., etc., etc. And yet, when that novel, *Of Love and Dust*, was finished, I realized that I had done only a small part of what I had intended to write. I still had not gone far enough back. Jim, my narrator—who was a man thirty-three years old—though good, was not able to say all that I wanted him to say. Even when I brought Aunt Margaret, someone twice his age, to help him out, they, both together, could not say it all.

Before I wrote *Of Love and Dust*—sometime around 1963 or 1964—I wrote a short story titled "Just Like a Tree." The story was about an old woman who had to move from the South during the civil rights demonstrations. The story was told from multiple points of view—that is, several people telling a single story from different angles. Most of the people were her age, and while they were telling you the reason she had to leave, they were also telling you something about themselves. But they were only touching on their lives; they were not going into any great detail. In the case of Aunt Fe, the protagonist in the story, you only hear snatches of conversation about her life. You know that she must leave the South because they are bombing near her home and she could be killed. But you don't know her life—where she comes from, her children, her husband—her life, in general, before that particular day.

Now, I did not know when I wrote the short story "Just Like a Tree" in 1963 or 1964 that four years later I would start out from that idea and write a novel, *The Autobiography of Miss Jane Pittman*. As I've said before, at this time I still had not published *Catherine Carmier*; nor did I have any idea that I would write another novel,

titled *Of Love and Dust*. But after these two books had been published, as well as the collection of stories *Bloodline*, I realized that I
was writing in a definite pattern. One, I was writing about a definite
area; and two, I was going farther and farther back into the past. I
was trying to go back, back, back into our experiences in this country
to find some kind of meaning to our present lives. No, Miss Jane is
not the end of my traveling into the past—she is only another step
back so that I can see some meaning in the present.

I knew at least two years before I started writing *The Autobiography of Miss Jane Pittman* that eventually I would write it. Maybe
I had known it all my life, because it seems that I started writing
it many, many years before, when I used to sit on the porch or the
steps and write letters for the old people. But it took me at least two
years after I first conceived the idea to start working on the book. I
held back as long as I could because I knew I did not know enough.
I had an idea of what I wanted to say—I wanted to continue from
"Just Like a Tree"—where a group of people tell the life story of a
single woman. But this woman in "Just Like a Tree" would live to
be 100 years old—110, to be exact—with her life extending over
the last half of the nineteenth century through the first half of the
twentieth. But did I know enough to try such a project? The narrative technique would be easy—I had done it already in "Just Like a
Tree"—but what in the world would these people talk about that
could possibly fill five hundred pages?

After the *Bloodline* stories, I realized that in order to tell what
I wanted to say about the people and the place, I had to go much
farther back in time. *Catherine Carmier*, *Of Love and Dust*, and
the *Bloodline* stories were easy writing, and I was writing about
things that could have happened in the South during my lifetime,
but I wanted to go farther back now, to a time before I, my parents,
even my grandparents were born.

In the fall of 1967, I visited Alvin Aubert, a friend at Southern
University in Baton Rouge. We sat in the living room while his wife
prepared dinner in the kitchen. I said to him, "Al, what were those

old people talking about when they visited my aunt and when they talked all day on the porch around the fireplace and at night? I can remember that they talked and talked, but I cannot remember what they talked about. You see, Al, I have this idea for a novel; it is about a 110-year-old woman who is born into slavery. I want the people to talk about her and in their rambling to reveal her story as well as their own. The story will happen between 1852 and 1962—from slavery to the civil rights demonstrations of the 1960s. What do you think they would have talked about?"

Where to start? With slavery, what the old people could have heard from their parents and great-grandparents about slavery. Next we discussed Reconstruction, the hard times. We discussed the Freedmen's Bureau. We discussed Lincoln, and Douglass, and Booker T. Washington because I could remember as a child a photo collage of the three hanging over the mantel in my aunt's room, just as I would see photo collages of John and Bobby Kennedy and Martin Luther King hanging on the walls of other African Americans in the 1970s. We talked about national heroes such as Jack Johnson, Joe Louis, and Jackie Robinson, about President Franklin D. Roosevelt, about the First and Second World Wars. After the national events we discussed state events—the great floods of 1912 and 1927, the cholera epidemic in New Orleans, the voodoo queen Marie Levaux, Huey P. Long and his men, the insane asylum in Jackson, the state penitentiary at Angola.

So we covered the nation and the state; next we came to the parish. We talked about the towns, the sheriff, the river, the people who lived along the river; we talked about the black professor who had been killed in 1903 for trying to teach young African Americans to read and write and to look after their health. His grave is on the bank of False River, about five miles from where I was born. My wife, Dianne, and I go by there all the time to stand in silence a moment.

After we discussed the parish we discussed the plantation and the quarter. We discussed the crops and the seasons and the work. We talked about the big house where my own grandmother worked for so many years; we talked about the store where the people bought their food and clothes. We talked about long days, dark nights, little pay, and mean overseers. We talked about hunting and fishing and gathering fruit that grew wild along the ditches and bayous. We talked about the church, about baptisms, about the cemetery, about unmarked graves. We talked about one-room schoolhouses and the teacher who came to the plantation to teach us children six months out of the year. We talked about a distant sound, the marching of the men and women for civil rights and their spokesman, a young Baptist minister from Georgia.

Al and I must have talked eight or nine hours that day and on into the night. After dinner when I got ready to leave, Al said to me, "Now this is what they could have talked about; now you have to convince the readers that this is what they did talk about." I remembered that the old people spoke of seasons and not the name of the month. They spoke of cold, cold winters and hot, hot summers when it rained or did not rain, when the pecan and cane crops were plentiful and when they were not. When I asked them for the year, they would tell me, "Well, I ain't for sure." As a child I remember hearing them talk about the great flood and the boll weevils that came after the flood, but they could not remember the year. Yes, they knew the horror of the flood: they knew how swift the water moved one day, how slow the next. They could tell you the color of the water, they could describe the trash and the dead animals that the water brought, but they could not tell you what year except that it happened around the time that Huey Long was just beginning.

But I needed more; I needed dates, months, years. I needed to know whether it happened during the week or the weekend, whether it was spring, summer, fall, or winter. I had visited LSU in Baton Rouge several times to talk to professors in the English department and to give readings, but I had never been to the library. Louis Simpson at LSU recommended I go to the Louisiana room and speak to Mrs. Evangeline Lynch. When I gave Mrs. Lynch a list of all the information I needed, she said, "My God, are you sure?" I said, "Yes, ma'am." She had heard of me through the *Bloodline* stories, and she was happy to meet me, but she thought I was taking on a task much too big for me to handle. "Well, let's start looking around," she said; "we have a lot in here, my, my." When I received the Louisiana Library Association Award for *The Autobiography of Miss Jane Pittman* in 1972, Mrs. Evangeline Lynch was in the audience. She stood and waved as I told the people how she had helped me find information and how she had sent information to me in San Francisco, where I was writing the book. Twenty-two years later, when I received the same award for *A Lesson Before Dying*, she was again in the audience. She had long since retired and was a bit frail, but she stood up and waved as I told the people what she had done for me so many years before.

Mrs. Evangeline Lynch helped me get material from books, periodicals, magazines, newspapers, but I still had to go to the people. I still had to go out to the field. Mr. Walter Zeno liked his vodka and he liked his wine, and whenever I came back to Louisiana from San Francisco I would rent a car in Baton Rouge and go out to the old place with one of his favorite bottles. He would squat, not sit, on the porch by the door and drink and talk while I would lean back against a post, listening to him. He knew my grandparents' grandparents and all the others, white and black, who lived on that plantation the first eighty years of the twentieth century. Either by being directly involved or by getting this information vicariously, he knew everything that had happened in the parish during that same period. But he dated events by seasons, not by the calendar, and I had to go back to Mrs. Lynch or to one of the other libraries to find out exactly when it had happened.

Many of the local things could not be found in books or in newspapers. For instance, I have never found any written information about the professor who was killed in the parish in 1903; but when you asked about him, the braver ones—white or black—could tell you exactly how the weather was that day, and they could tell you it happened at the turn of the century, but they did not know the exact year. His tombstone, placed on the grave some seventy years after he was murdered, gave me that information.

I started writing *Miss Jane Pittman* with this idea of narration in mind: that different characters would tell the story of her life in their own way. The story was to begin on the day that she was buried—the old people who had followed her body to the cemetery would later gather on the porch of a lady who had never walked in her life, and there they would start talking. In the beginning there would be only three or four of them, but around midnight, when they were still talking, there would be a dozen or more. And by now they would be talking about almost anything—Miss Jane would be only part of their conversation.

I followed this multiple-point-of-view technique for a year—then I discarded it. (I should mention here—I should have mentioned earlier—that the original title was *A Short Biography of Miss Jane Pittman*, and that it was changed to *The Autobiography of Miss Jane Pittman* when I decided to tell the story from a single voice—Miss Jane's own.) I decided to change the way of telling the story because I had fallen in love with my little character, and I thought she could tell the story of her life much better than anyone else. The others were making her life too complicated in that they had too many opinions, bringing in too many anecdotes. I thought a single voice (Miss Jane's) would keep the story in a straight line. (Though, even here, I had trouble with her when she got wound up. Once the story really got moving, Miss Jane did and said pretty much whatever she wanted, and all I could do was act as her editor, never her adviser.)

Who is Miss Jane? What does she represent? I've heard all kinds of interpretations. More than one reviewer has said that she is a capsule history of black people of the rural South during the past hundred years. I must disagree, and I'm sure Miss Jane would, too. Miss Jane is Miss Jane. She is not my aunt, she is not any one person—she is Miss Jane. Maybe I had my aunt in mind when I was writing about her, but I had other old people in mind as well—those who sat on our gallery in the 1940s and those whom I've met on the road since then. You have seen Miss Jane, too. She is that old lady who lives up the block, who comes out every Sunday to go to church when the rheumatism does not keep her in. She is the old lady who calls a child to her door and asks him to go to the store for a can of coffee. She sits on a screened-in porch fanning herself in the summer, and in the winter she sits by the heater or the stove and thinks about the dead. Even without turning her head, she speaks to the child lying on the floor watching television, or to the young woman lying across a bed in another room. She knows much—she has lived long. Sometimes she's impatient, but most times she's just the opposite. If you take time to ask her a question you will find her to be quite dogmatic. You will say, "But that's not it, that's not it, that's not it." And she will stick to her beliefs. If you go to the history books, you will find that most of them would not agree with what she has told you. But if you read more closely you will also notice that these great minds don't even agree with one another.

Truth to Miss Jane is what she remembers. Truth to me is what people like Miss Jane remember. Of course, I go to the other sources, the newspapers, magazines, the books in libraries—but I also go back and listen to what Miss Jane and folks like her have to say.

This I try to do in all my writing.

I begin with an idea, this point, this fact: sometime in the past we were brought from Africa in chains, put in Louisiana to work the rice, cane, and cotton fields. Some kind of way we survived. God? Luck? Soul food? Threats of death? Superstition? I suppose all of these have played their part. If I asked a white historian what happened, he would not tell it the same way a black historian would. If I asked a black historian, he would not tell it the same way a black field-worker would. So I ask them all. And I try in some way to get the answer. But I'm afraid I have not gotten it yet. Maybe in the next book, or the one after, or the one after. Maybe.

Alice Walker
(1944–)

ALICE WALKER WAS BORN in rural Eatonville, Georgia, and attended Spelman College in Atlanta. She later transferred to and graduated from Sarah Lawrence College. Alice Walker is an accomplished writer in several genres. She has written poetry, essays, short stories, and novels. Over the years, she has also been, for literary and other reasons, a controversial figure. She was an activist in the civil rights movement and an early womanist/feminist critic. She was, for example, a contributing editor to *Ms.* magazine. One controversy beyond the literary involved her denunciations of the ritual and practice of female circumcision in various African countries.

The Color Purple (1982) remains her most controversial and successful work. The book brought her national and international fame. It was awarded the Pulitzer Prize, the National Book Award, and the American Book Award.[32] The novel was highly praised and reviewed as an original work that highlights the violent abuse of young women, especially in the African American community. It was also criticized for the same reason. Some critics read it as an example of the public bashing of African American men. Others read it as a scathing repudiation of traditional Christianity and a celebration of lesbianism. Yet the book, beyond its initial publication and controversy, has brought Walker additional fame and good fortune. It was produced as a Hollywood film, featuring Whoopi Goldberg and Oprah Winfrey. More recently, it was produced as a Broadway play.

Walker is a formidable writer. To date, she has published at least fifteen books, including novels, short story collections, and poetry collections. Her first publication was a collection of poems titled

Once (1968). In 1970, Walker published her first novel, *The Third Life of Grange Copeland*.

Four years later, she published "In Search of Our Mothers' Gardens: The Legacy of Southern Black Women," which became the title essay in the collection *In Search of Our Mothers' Gardens: Womanist Prose*, published in 1983. This collection includes several remarkable essays. In the title essay, Walker celebrates a long line of unknown but highly creative black women who were forced to find unconventional places to express their creativity. For example, she refers to a quilt that hangs in the Smithsonian Institution, crafted by an anonymous black woman, that is a kind of tableau of the crucifixion. In "Beauty: When the Other Dancer Is the Self," Walker candidly reveals her memory of the loss of eyesight in one of her eyes and the resulting consequences of the loss. The moment had a definitive impact on her personality. "Looking for Zora" shows Walker's early recognition of the power of Zora Neale Hurston's novel *Their Eyes Were Watching God*. Moreover, Walker understands the significance of Hurston's role as a woman writer who, during the period before Walker's rediscovery of her, was largely neglected. The essay tells the story of Walker's search for Hurston's unmarked grave.[33]

In "Writing *The Color Purple*," taken from *In Search of Our Mothers' Gardens*, Walker reveals the challenge of getting her novel going, as well as the pleasant surprise of its unexpected completion.

Writing *The Color Purple* (1982)

I don't always know where the germ of a story comes from, but with *The Color Purple* I knew right away. I was hiking through the woods with my sister, Ruth, talking about a lovers' triangle of which we both knew. She said: "And you know, one day The Wife asked The Other Woman for a pair of her drawers." Instantly the missing piece of the story I was mentally writing—about two women who felt married to the same man—fell into place. And for months—through illnesses, divorce, several moves, travel abroad, all kinds of heartaches and revelations—I carried my sister's comment delicately balanced in the center of the novel's construction I was building in my head.

I also knew *The Color Purple* would be a historical novel, and thinking of this made me chuckle. In an interview, discussing my work, a black male critic said he'd heard I might write a historical novel someday, and went on to say, in effect: Heaven protect us from it. The chuckle was because, womanlike (he would say), my "history" starts not with the taking of lands, or the births, battles, and deaths of Great Men, but with one woman asking another for her underwear. Oh, well, I thought, one function of critics is to be appalled by such behavior. But what woman (or sensuous man) could avoid being intrigued? As for me, I thought of little else for a year.

When I was sure the characters of my new novel were trying to form (or, as I invariably thought of it, trying to contact me, to speak *through* me), I began to make plans to leave New York. Three months earlier I had bought a tiny house on a quiet Brooklyn street, assuming—because my desk overlooked the street and a maple tree in the yard, representing garden and view—I would be able to write. I was not.

New York, whose people I love for their grace under almost continual unpredictable adversity, was a place the people in *The Color Purple* refused even to visit. The moment any of them started to form—on the subway, a dark street, and especially in the shadow of very tall buildings—they would start to complain.

"What is all this tall shit anyway?" they would say.

I disposed of the house, stored my furniture, packed my suitcases, and flew alone to San Francisco (it was my daughter's year to be with her father), where all the people in the novel promptly fell silent—I think, in awe. Not merely of the city's beauty, but of what they picked up about earthquakes.

"It's pretty," they muttered, "but us ain't lost nothing in no place that has earthquakes."

They also didn't like seeing buses, cars, or other people whenever they attempted to look out. "Us don't want to be seeing none of this," they said. "It makes us can't think."

That was when I knew for sure these were country people. So my lover and I started driving around the state looking for a country house to rent. Luckily I had found (with the help of friends) a fairly inexpensive place in the city. This too had been a decision forced by my characters. As long as there was any question about whether I could support them in the fashion they desired (basically in undisturbed silence) they declined to come out. Eventually we found a place in northern California we could afford and that my characters liked. And no wonder: it looked a lot like the town in Georgia most of them were from, only it was more beautiful and the local swimming hole was not segregated. It also bore a slight resemblance to the African village in which one of them, Nettie, was a missionary.

Seeing the sheep, the cattle, and the goats, smelling the apples and the hay, one of my characters, Celie, began, haltingly, to speak.

But there was still a problem.

Since I had quit my editing job at *Ms.* and my Guggenheim Fellowship was running out, and my royalties did not quite cover expenses, and—let's face it—because it gives me a charge to see people who appreciate my work, historical novels or not, I was accepting invitations to speak. Sometimes on the long plane rides Celie or Shug would break through with a wonderful line or two (for instance, Celie said once that a self-pitying sick person she went to visit was "laying up in the bed trying to look dead"). But even these vanished—if I didn't jot them down—by the time my contact with the audience was done.

What to do?

Celie and Shug answered without hesitation: Give up all this travel. Give up all this talk. What is all this travel and talk shit anyway? So, I gave it up for a year. Whenever I was invited to speak I explained I was taking a year off for Silence. (I also wore an imaginary bracelet on my left arm that spelled the word.) Everyone said, Sure, they understood.

I was terrified.

Where was the money for our support coming from? My only steady income was a three-hundred-dollar-a-month retainer from *Ms.* for being a long-distance editor. But even that was too much distraction for my characters.

Tell them you can't do anything for the magazine, said Celie and Shug. (You guessed it, the women of the drawers.) Tell them you'll have to think about them later. So, I did. *Ms.* was unperturbed. Supportive as ever (they continued the retainer). Which was nice.

Then I sold a book of stories. After taxes, inflation, and my agent's fee of ten percent, I would still have enough for a frugal, no-frills year. And so, I bought some beautiful blue-and-red-and-purple fabric, and some funky old secondhand furniture (and accepted donations of old odds and ends from friends), and a quilt pattern my mama swore was easy, and I headed for the hills.

There were days and weeks and even months when nothing happened. Nothing whatsoever. I worked on my quilt, took long walks with my lover, lay on an island we discovered in the middle of the river and dabbled my fingers in the water. I swam, explored the redwood forests all around us, lay out in the meadow, picked apples, talked (yes, of course) to trees. My quilt began to grow. And, of course, everything was happening. Celie and Shug and Albert were getting to know each other, coming to trust my determination to serve their entry (sometimes I felt *re*-entry) into the world to the best of my ability, and what is more—and felt so wonderful—we began to love one another. And, what is even more, to feel immense thankfulness for our mutual good luck.

Just as summer was ending, one or more of my characters—Celie, Shug, Albert, Sofia, or Harpo—would come for a visit. We would sit wherever I was sitting, and talk. They were very obliging, engaging, and jolly. They were, of course, at the end of their story but were telling it to me from the beginning. Things that made me sad often made them laugh. Oh, we got through that; don't pull such a long face, they'd say. Or, You think Reagan's bad, you ought've seen some of the rednecks us come up under. The days passed in a blaze of happiness.

Then school started, and it was time for my daughter to stay with me—for two years.

Could I handle it?

Shug said, right out, that she didn't know. (Well, her mother raised *her* children.) Nobody else said anything. (At this point in the novel, Celie didn't even know where *her* children were.) They just quieted down, didn't visit as much, and took a firm Well, let's us wait and see attitude.

My daughter arrived. Smart, sensitive, cheerful, at school most of the day, but quick with tea and sympathy on her return. My characters adored her. They saw she spoke her mind in no uncertain terms and would fight back when attacked. When she came home from school one day with bruises but said, You should see the other guy, Celie (raped by her stepfather as a child and somewhat fearful of life) began to reappraise her own condition. Rebecca gave her courage (which she *always* gives me)—and Celie grew to like her so much she would wait until three-thirty to visit me. So, just when Rebecca would arrive home needing her mother and a hug, there'd be Celie, trying to give her both. Fortunately I was able to bring Celie's own children back to her (a unique power of novelists), though it took thirty years and a good bit of foreign travel. But this proved to be the largest single problem in writing the exact novel I wanted to write between ten-thirty and three.

I had planned to give myself five years to write *The Color Purple* (teaching, speaking, or selling apples, as I ran out of money). But, on the very day my daughter left for camp, less than a year after I started writing, I wrote the last page.

And what did I do that for?

It was like losing everybody I loved at once. First Rebecca (to whom everyone surged forth on the last page to say goodbye), then Celie, Shug, Nettie, and Albert. Mary Agnes, Harpo and Sofia. Eleanor Jane. Adam and Tashi Omatangu. Olivia. Mercifully, my quilt and my lover remained.

I threw myself in his arms and cried.

Ernest J. Gaines

JEFFERSON, IN *A Lesson Before Dying*, refuses to speak. He has been charged and convicted of murder and sentenced to death via the electric chair. Day after day, he awaits his execution in surly silence. The narrative challenge Gaines faced was finding a convincing way to get Jefferson to start talking.

Writing *A Lesson Before Dying* (2005)

I was teaching at the University of Louisiana at Lafayette when I came up with the idea for *A Lesson Before Dying*. And that would be around 1983 or 1984. Now, the original idea was that the story would occur in the early 1980s. I wrote a letter to the warden at Angola, the state prison here in Louisiana, and informed him who I was—that I was a teacher here at UL, and that I was the author of *The Autobiography of Miss Jane Pittman* and several other books, and that I had another novel in mind about a prisoner on death row, and would he, the warden, mind if I asked him a few questions. Question number one: Would it be possible for someone not kin to the condemned man who was not a minister of religion or his legal adviser to visit him on death row? About a week later, I received a letter from the warden's office informing me that the warden would not be able to guarantee me that kind of security. I immediately wrote a second letter, assuring the warden that I, Ernest J. Gaines, had no intention of visiting Angola on a regular basis, but that I was writing a novel (and I emphasized the word *novel*), and I was wondering if it was possible that such a person—a teacher, for example—could visit a condemned man. Well, the warden's office never did answer my second letter, and maybe that was a blessing in disguise.

Being a writer-in-residence on any university campus, you're constantly being asked how's the writing coming along, and when can we expect the next book, etc., etc., etc. *A Gathering of Old Men* had been published in 1983, so between '83 and '85 I was between books. That is, I was not writing. When a colleague of mine asked me what I was doing, I told him I had a novel in mind and that I had written the warden at Angola. I told him the results of my second letter. I gave him the general plot of the novel, of a young man being in the wrong place at the wrong time, and he was charged with murder. Paul Nolan, my colleague, told me that he knew of a case I might be interested in reading about. The case Paul was referring to concerned a young man, a seventeen-year-old boy, who had been sentenced to be electrocuted in the electric chair here in Louisiana. Something happened that day with the chair. It did not work properly, and the boy was *not* executed, but put back into his cell to await what next step the governor would take. Paul told me he realized that the two cases didn't sound the same—sound alike—but I might benefit by reading his case and that he had a lot of material about the case if I would like to do so.

This particular case he spoke of having happened about '46 or '47 appeared familiar to me, and around a time I had written about in previous stories—"The Sky Is Gray," "Three Men"—and the novel *Of Love and Dust*. Besides that, the case Paul Nolan referred to happened only a few miles from where I was now teaching and no more than seventy miles from where I had lived as a child and the area where most of my previous stories had taken place. There were so many similarities—the work, religion, the food that people ate, everything. The case Paul recommended could have happened in the parish where I grew up. The stories are different, still I would use some of the information from the previous case. Both young men are black. Both nearly illiterate. Both were involved in the murder of a white man. In Paul's case, the young man confessed to the murder. My young man would maintain his innocence to the end. No defense witnesses were called in either case. Only white men served on the juries. This was the forties, so there were no women and, of course, no blacks on the juries. After reading all the material that Paul had given me, I asked myself, "Why not bring my story back to the forties?" If I put the story in the forties, there was so much material I could use. I could use the plantation as home for my characters. I knew life on the plantation because I had written about it in several other books—*The Autobiography of Miss Jane Pittman*, *Of Love and Dust*, and the stories in *Bloodline*. I could use the church school for background, the church where generations of my folks had worshipped and where I had attended school my first six years. I could use the crop as background—when it was planted, when it was harvested. I knew the food the people ate, knew the kind of clothes they wore, knew the kind of songs they sang in the fields and in the church.

So the best thing to do was to bring my story back to the forties, the period I knew and where I was most comfortable. I read everything Paul Nolan gave me to read and all he recommended. His young man would lose and be executed a year and a week from the day when he was first placed in that chair. The case went all the way to the Supreme Court in Washington, where it lost by a decision of 5 to 4.

Because I teach creative writing at the university and because I teach at night, I have a chance to draw people from outside the university, and I always get attorneys. I've had one or more in each class since I started teaching in the university in 1981. All have a dream of being a Scott Turow or a John Grisham. One of my students had a condemned man on death row. And I would always ask him questions about his client, especially what emotions did he show knowing that he was going to die on a certain date, at a certain hour. I could always tell when my student had visited with his client because of the tired and painful look he brought into the classroom. He was much older than this young man, and through the years he had gotten very close to him. He had gotten too emotionally involved, and he knew it, and it showed.

He, the student of mine, helped me in many ways. He brought me pictures of the state prison, pictures of the electric chair—"Gruesome Gerty." I asked him more questions. I asked him what kind of wood was the chair made of, how much does the chair weigh, how wide and thick were the straps that went around the arms and legs of the condemned. And I kept a picture of the chair on my desk, especially while writing the last chapters of the novel.

Another colleague of mine knew someone whose father-in-law was the sheriff of a small town. She asked me if I would like to meet the sheriff. I think he was an ex-sheriff by then, but everyone still called him sheriff. When we arrived at the house, I was introduced to the sheriff, to his wife, and to another man. The sheriff's wife served us coffee. I was served last, and I saw how much her hands shook when she served me. I was certain that she had never served coffee to a black man before, but after all, I had written *The Autobiography of Miss Jane Pittman* and also knew someone who knew her daughter-in-law. So she, of course, could show some of her Southern hospitality. The sheriff and the other man wanted to know where I came from, did I like the South, how long had I been teaching at the university. I told them I was born and raised about sixty miles from where we now sat, that my people had been there since the time of slavery, and that I had been teaching at the university for about five years, and I liked it very much. That relaxed them a bit, and we finished our coffee. I asked the sheriff the same questions I had proposed to the warden in my letter: "Could someone who was not a close relation, a minister of religion, or a legal adviser visit someone on death row?" The sheriff told me that in the case of a parish jail it would be entirely up to the discretion of the sheriff. He told me that the sheriff of the jail was totally in charge and that he made all the decisions. Now, that bit of information was extremely vital. I had to find a reason to pressure the sheriff into allowing someone whom he may not even like into visiting the prisoner.

Some of my colleagues at the university would ask me how the novel was coming along. When I would tell them that I was still trying to get everything straight in my mind, some of them would offer advice. One fellow who considered himself a writer, too, said find something on the sheriff that he would not want people to know about. I told him it sounded like blackmail, and I didn't want to have anything to do with that. He told me he had another idea—the sheriff's wife had had an abortion in the past, and you know how these Southerners felt about that. I told him I didn't care for that idea either. He said, Well, let's say the sheriff's wife had had a relationship with a black man and your character threatens to expose it. By God, that would light his fire—"and more than likely get my character killed before he ever got to the jail. No thanks," I said.

The original idea of the novel, when I thought the story would take place in the eighties, was that Grant, the narrator, would have been living in California, and he would come to Louisiana one summer to visit his aunt and eventually get involved in visiting the young man on death row. That was the original reason for the questions about whether someone other than a legal adviser or a minister could visit him, because I'm sure the sheriff would not want an outsider, especially someone from the North, interfering with his business. It was not until I decided that the story would take place in the forties that I would make Grant a teacher who had gone away for his education and then returned to teach on the same plantation where he was born and raised and where all of his people had lived for several generations. However, because he was educated, the sheriff still may not have wanted him to be there.

My colleague at the university had given me an idea about how to solve my problem when he mentioned the sheriff's wife several times. I would not cause her to have an abortion or a black lover, but I would put her in a position where she would pressure her husband into allowing Grant to visit Jefferson in prison.

On the plantation where I was born, my maternal grandmother worked at the big house as a cook for many years, and I myself had worked in the yard there on several occasions, collecting eggs from where chickens had laid in the grass, gathering pecans, and picking fruit from the different trees. Now, suppose I made the sheriff's wife a member of the family where my grandmother had worked all these years. Wouldn't she, my grandmother, have done favors, extra favors, for members of the family? Would that be enough reason for her to feel that she could go to them for a favor, which I thought would be a better reason—and more convincing to the reader—to get the sheriff to allow the narrator to visit the prisoner? So I created two elderly women. They were Tante Lou, the narrator's aunt, and Miss Emma, the prisoner's godmother. And those two would apply the pressure.

I have said that I wanted the story to take place in the eighties and that the narrator, Grant, would come from California. Once I decided that the story would take place in the forties, and that Grant had lived on the plantation all his life, had gone away to be educated, and had returned to teach, all this adds another element to the story. I didn't want just another story of someone waiting to be executed; that had been done many times before. To make my story different I had to do something else, and make Grant also a prisoner of his environment. Grant teaches in a church. As I said, I went to a church school the first six years of my education. Grant hates teaching. He hates the South. He hates everything around him. This is the forties, remember, and the professions for blacks to enter were extremely limited. You could be a teacher and teach black children. You could be an undertaker, a barber, an insurance collector from other blacks. You could own a small grocery store or a nightclub. But you could *not* be an attorney or a doctor. You could not be a banker or a politician and certainly you could not run for political office. Not in a small place like this in the South at that time. Grant wishes to run away. He's been well educated and he knows there's a better world somewhere else. But he has an aunt, Tante Lou, and just as she and Miss Emma exert pressure on the sheriff, they do the same to him to keep him in the South. Eventually he would become involved in Jefferson's plight, and in the end it would benefit both of them. He would teach Jefferson to live for a while and to die with dignity. Jefferson in turn would help him find himself.

In 1986, a young female attorney in my class asked me if I would like to meet the lawyer who had defended the young man whom Paul Nolan had spoken about. I told her I certainly would. She brought the old man to my house—a Cajun fellow, probably in his seventies, bent, frail. My student and I made coffee, and she had brought cookies, and we sat on the porch. It was this man who told me about the traveling electric chair. I had heard about it, read about it, but I had not spoken to anybody who knew about it firsthand. He told me about the generator that accompanied the chair because sometimes our Louisiana weather causes the electricity to be erratic. To avoid that problem, the state prison sent its own generator. We don't have the electric chair in Louisiana now, but some type of lethal injection is instead used for execution.

But let's go back to the late forties, when it did travel from one parish to the other. At that time the execution was administered in the parish where the crime was committed, not necessarily at the state prison, as it is today. This attorney told me about how the chair with the generator was delivered in a truck, a special truck that delivered it the morning of or the night before the execution. He told me that the time of day for execution in that particular parish was between noon and 3:00 p.m. on Friday. He told me the generator had to be tested before the hour of execution to be sure it was working in time. He told me you could hear the generator at least two city blocks away from the jail. He had witnessed the execution of the young man who had been sent to the chair a year earlier. During that year, this attorney had argued the case before the Appellate Court of Louisiana, the Supreme Court in Louisiana, and the Supreme Court in Washington. His argument was that it would be cruel and unusual punishment to send this young man back to that chair. But he failed in each court, and a year and a week from that first date, the young man was executed. Suddenly the attorney became silent and brought his hands up to his face. My student moved closer to him and held him. He laid his head on her shoulder and wept. Forty years later, he could still remember that generator, that chair.

Students are always asking me, "Do you know the ending of your novel when you start writing?" And I have always used the analogy of getting on a train from San Francisco to go to New York. It takes three or four days to get there. I know some facts. I'm leaving San Francisco for New York. I also know the states I'll travel through and some of the things I'll do. I know that I'll go to the dining car to eat. I'll go to the club car for a drink. I'll read the book I brought with me. I'll get so many hours of sleep. These things I know. What I don't know is how the weather will be the entire trip. I don't know who will get on the train and how they'll be dressed or where they'll sit. I don't know all the valleys and hills that I'll cross during my trip. I don't know all the different colors of nature, the colors of the leaves on the trees, the color of the different crops in the different fields. I don't know all the turnings and twists of the rail or when the train will make a sudden stop. In other words, I can't anticipate everything that will happen on the trip, and sometimes I don't even get to New York, but end up in Philadelphia.

When I started *A Lesson Before Dying*, I knew that Jefferson would be sentenced to die. Because in Louisiana in the forties, if he had been caught on the premises where a white man had been killed with a bottle of liquor in his hand and money in his pocket, that added up to guilt. But would he be executed? I didn't know for certain. Maybe the governor at the last moment would pardon him when the state could not definitely prove his guilt. The story could have ended there, because by now Grant could have reached him, convinced him that he was not the animal he had been so described in court, but that he was as much human as any of them and probably even more so. Because the story is not whether Jefferson is innocent or guilty but how he feels about himself at the end. However, the Cajun attorney gave me a different alternative. After he described that tarpaulin-covered truck delivering that chair and that generator on an early foggy morning, I knew that I had no other ending but that Jefferson would be executed. I wanted the reader to see that truck and that chair and to hear that generator.

Two things I had not anticipated when I began the novel and that would be vital in the story are the radio and the notebook. After I had gone so far into the novel and Jefferson still refused to communicate with anyone, I knew I had to find some way to make him talk. On that plantation where I lived as a child, on Saturday night the people of one or two of the homes in the quarter would give a house party—or a "supper," as we also called them. At these suppers, there would be food and drinks and music, the music coming from an old gramophone. On one of his visits to the jail, Grant mentions the music to Jefferson. When Jefferson shows some sign of interest, Grant promises to get him a radio so he can have some music to listen to. The idea of the radio was not planned, but it turned out to be a most important turn in the story. From that moment on, there was some communication, although limited, between the two of them. Still, Jefferson refuses to open up completely to Grant or his godmother, Miss Emma, or the minister of the church. So we know little of what he's thinking about or what he thinks about life. And I felt we had to know him better. Once I decided he would be executed, I knew, since he would not reveal his thoughts to someone, still in some way he had to give the reader some information. I didn't want any last efforts, speaking on the walk to the chair. I needed the information long before then.

Thus, the notebook. Grant would bring him a notebook and a pencil and tell him to write down anything he wished. His least little thoughts. When Grant visits again, he sees that Jefferson has written in the notebook and erased. And Grant tells him not to erase, never to erase, just go on and write his first thoughts the best way he can, which he does from then on. Jefferson is barely literate. He has never written a letter in his life. He was barely able to write his elementary school assignments. But now, with his pencil and notebook, he tries to define his humanity—in the few days he has left to live. He does not know whether to write above the lines or across the lines, so he does both. He does not erase. He does not capitalize. He uses no punctuation marks. He writes what comes into his mind. He writes at night when he has light because he does not want others to see him doing so during the day. He writes the night before his execution because the sheriff promises him that he can have all the light he wants on his last night. His diary is made up of small things, about the people he knew and how they affected his life, about insignificant incidents. He thinks about justice and injustice. And he wonders about God. All of this is written above and across the lines of his notebook, without capitalization and punctuation.

Grant does not attend the execution. Though he has worked hard with Jefferson, he does not have the courage to be there at his death. The young deputy brings Jefferson's notebook to him and tells him that Jefferson was the strongest man in that room when he came to die. The young deputy gives Grant this information outside the schoolhouse. When Grant returns to his class, his students are waiting, standing at attention, their shoulders back, heads high, to hear of the execution. Grant, cynical to this moment, looks at them, crying.

Writing for me is discovery. If I knew everything when I began a novel, I'm afraid it would be boring to write. I do not know everything that's going to happen in the book. I don't want to know everything. I want to discover, as you, the reader, want to discover, what it's all about. Those little unknown things that happen on the train between San Francisco and New York keep me writing and you, the reader, turning the pages.

Oprah Winfrey asked what I try to reach for in my writing. And I said something to this effect: I try to create characters with character to help develop my own character and maybe the character of the reader who might read me.

Toni Morrison
(1931–)

WHEN *NEWSWEEK* PLACED Toni Morrison on its cover on March 30, 1981, with the words "Black Magic" at the top of the page, the novelist was well on her way to being awarded the 1993 Nobel Prize for Literature. She is the first and only African American writer to receive the coveted award and the second American woman, joining Pearl S. Buck, who was awarded the prize in 1938.

Born Chloe Wofford in Lorrain, Ohio, Toni Morrison graduated from Howard University and later earned an M.A. in English from Cornell University. Morrison worked for years as a senior editor at Random House before she started writing full-time. During that period, she edited the books of other writers who would become well known—including Angela Davis, Huey Newton, June Jordan, Gayl Jones, and Toni Cade Bambara. In addition, she edited several collections, notably *The Black Book* (1974), a thick picture book (without commentary) composed of photos, blackface ads, and compelling images and artwork of African Americans.

When Morrison appeared on *Newsweek*'s cover, she had recently published *Tar Baby* (1981), her fourth novel. To date, Morrison has published ten novels, including her latest, *Home* (2012). Morrison has also written two plays, a libretto, and a book of nonfiction: *Playing in the Dark: Whiteness and the Literary Imagination* (1991).

In 2012, D. G. Myers used the latest MLA International Bibliography to count "the top 25 American writers as determined by the amount of scholarship" written since 1987 (25 years) about each writer. Toni Morrison was number eight with 1,950 items—below Henry James (3,188) and William Faulkner (2,955), numbers one and two. Nathaniel Hawthorne (1,751) and Walt Whitman trailed

Morrison as numbers nine and ten.[34] In her Nobel Lecture, Morrison addresses the transformative power as well as the abusive employment of language.

Nobel Lecture (December 7, 1993)

"Once upon a time there was an old woman. Blind but wise." Or was it an old man? A guru, perhaps. Or a griot soothing restless children. I have heard this story, or one exactly like it, in the lore of several cultures.

"Once upon a time there was an old woman. Blind. Wise."

In the version I know the woman is the daughter of slaves, black, American, and lives alone in a small house outside of town. Her reputation for wisdom is without peer and without question. Among her people she is both the law and its transgression. The honor she is paid and the awe in which she is held reach beyond her neighborhood to places far away; to the city where the intelligence of rural prophets is the source of much amusement.

One day the woman is visited by some young people who seem to be bent on disproving her clairvoyance and showing her up for the fraud they believe she is. Their plan is simple: they enter her house and ask the one question the answer to which rides solely on her difference from them, a difference they regard as a profound disability: her blindness. They stand before her, and one of them says, "Old woman, I hold in my hand a bird. Tell me whether it is living or dead."

She does not answer, and the question is repeated. "Is the bird I am holding living or dead?"

Still she doesn't answer. She is blind and cannot see her visitors, let alone what is in their hands. She does not know their color, gender or homeland. She only knows their motive.

The old woman's silence is so long, the young people have trouble holding their laughter.

Finally she speaks and her voice is soft but stern. "I don't know," she says. "I don't know whether the bird you are holding is dead or alive, but what I do know is that it is in your hands. It is in your hands."

Her answer can be taken to mean: if it is dead, you have either found it that way or you have killed it. If it is alive, you can still kill it. Whether it is to stay alive, it is your decision. Whatever the case, it is your responsibility.

For parading their power and her helplessness, the young visitors are reprimanded, told they are responsible not only for the act of mockery, but also for the small bundle of life sacrificed to achieve its aims. The blind woman shifts attention away from assertions of power to the instrument through which that power is exercised.

Speculation on what (other than its own frail body) that bird-in-the-hand might signify has always been attractive to me, but especially so now thinking, as I have been, about the work I do that has brought me to this company. So I choose to read the bird as language and the woman as a practiced writer. She is worried about how the language she dreams in, given to her at birth, is handled, put into service, even withheld from her for certain nefarious purposes. Being a writer she thinks of language partly as a system, partly as a living thing over which one has control, but mostly as agency—as an act with consequences. So the question the children put to her: "Is it living or dead?" is not unreal because she thinks of language as susceptible to death, erasure; certainly imperiled and salvageable only by an effort of the will. She believes that if the bird in the hands of her visitors is dead the custodians are responsible for the corpse. For her a dead language is not only one no longer spoken or written, it is unyielding language content to admire its own paralysis. Like statist language, censored and censoring. Ruthless in its policing duties, it has no desire or purpose other than maintaining the free range of its own narcotic narcissism, its own exclusivity and dominance. However moribund, it is not without effect for it actively thwarts the intellect, stalls conscience, suppresses human potential. Unreceptive to interrogation, it cannot form or tolerate new ideas, shape other thoughts, tell another story, fill baffling silences. Official language smitheryed to sanction ignorance and preserve privilege is a suit of armor polished to shocking glitter, a husk from which the knight departed long ago. Yet there it is: dumb, predatory, sentimental. Exciting reverence in schoolchildren, providing shelter for despots, summoning false memories of stability, harmony among the public.

She is convinced that when language dies, out of carelessness, disuse, indifference and absence of esteem, or killed by fiat, not only she herself, but all users and makers are accountable for its demise. In her country children have bitten their tongues off and use bullets instead to iterate the voice of speechlessness, of disabled and disabling language, of language adults have abandoned altogether as a device for grappling with meaning, providing guidance, or expressing love. But she knows tongue-suicide is not only the choice of children. It is common among the infantile heads of state and power merchants whose evacuated language leaves them with no access to what is left of their human instincts for they speak only to those who obey, or in order to force obedience.

The systematic looting of language can be recognized by the tendency of its users to forgo its nuanced, complex, mid-wifery properties for menace and subjugation. Oppressive language does more than represent violence; it is violence; does more than represent the limits of knowledge; it limits knowledge. Whether it is obscuring state language or the faux-language of mindless media; whether it is the proud but calcified language of the academy or the commodity driven language of science; whether it is the malign language of law-without-ethics, or language designed for the estrangement of minorities, hiding its racist plunder in its literary cheek—it must be rejected, altered and exposed. It is the language that drinks blood, laps vulnerabilities, tucks its fascist boots under crinolines of respectability and patriotism as it moves relentlessly toward the bottom line and the bottomed-out mind. Sexist language, racist language, theistic language—all are typical of the policing languages of mastery, and cannot, do not permit new knowledge or encourage the mutual exchange of ideas.

The old woman is keenly aware that no intellectual mercenary, nor insatiable dictator, no paid-for politician or demagogue; no counterfeit journalist would be persuaded by her thoughts. There is and will be rousing language to keep citizens armed and arming; slaughtered and slaughtering in the malls, courthouses, post offices, playgrounds, bedrooms and boulevards; stirring, memorializing language to mask the pity and waste of needless death. There will be more diplomatic language to countenance rape, torture, assassination. There is and will be more seductive, mutant language designed to throttle women, to pack their throats like paté-producing geese with their own unsayable, transgressive words; there will be more of the language of surveillance disguised as research; of politics and history calculated to render the suffering of millions mute; language glamorized to thrill the dissatisfied and bereft into assaulting their neighbors; arrogant pseudo-empirical language crafted to lock creative people into cages of inferiority and hopelessness.

Underneath the eloquence, the glamor, the scholarly associations, however stirring or seductive, the heart of such language is languishing, or perhaps not beating at all—if the bird is already dead.

She has thought about what could have been the intellectual history of any discipline if it had not insisted upon, or been forced into, the waste of time and life that rationalizations for and representations of dominance required—lethal discourses of exclusion blocking access to cognition for both the excluder and the excluded.

The conventional wisdom of the Tower of Babel story is that the collapse was a misfortune. That it was the distraction, or the weight of many languages that precipitated the tower's failed architecture. That one monolithic language would have expedited the building and heaven would have been reached. Whose heaven, she wonders? And what kind? Perhaps the achievement of Paradise was premature, a little hasty if no one could take the time to understand other languages, other views, other narratives period. Had they, the heaven they imagined might have been found at their feet. Complicated, demanding, yes, but a view of heaven as life; not heaven as post-life.

She would not want to leave her young visitors with the impression that language should be forced to stay alive merely to be. The vitality of language lies in its ability to limn the actual, imagined and possible lives of its speakers, readers, writers. Although its poise is sometimes in displacing experience it is not a substitute for it. It arcs toward the place where meaning may lie. When a President of the United States thought about the graveyard his country had become, and said, "The world will little note nor long remember what we say here. But it will never forget what they did here," his simple words are exhilarating in their life-sustaining properties because they refused to encapsulate the reality of 600,000 dead men in a cataclysmic race war. Refusing to monumentalize, disdaining the "final word," the precise "summing up," acknowledging their "poor power to add or detract," his words signal deference to the uncapturability of the life it mourns. It is the deference that moves her, that recognition that language can never live up to life once and for all. Nor should it. Language can never "pin down" slavery, genocide, war. Nor should it yearn for the arrogance to be able to do so. Its force, its felicity, is in its reach toward the ineffable.

Be it grand or slender, burrowing, blasting, or refusing to sanctify; whether it laughs out loud or is a cry without an alphabet, the choice word, the chosen silence, unmolested language surges toward knowledge, not its destruction. But who does not know of literature banned because it is interrogative; discredited because it is critical; erased because alternate? And how many are outraged by the thought of a self-ravaged tongue?

Word-work is sublime, she thinks, because it is generative; it makes meaning that secures our difference, our human difference—the way in which we are like no other life.

We die. That may be the meaning of life. But we do language. That may be the measure of our lives.

"Once upon a time, . . ." visitors ask an old woman a question.

Who are they, these children? What did they make of that encounter? What did they hear in those final words: "The bird is in your hands"? A sentence that gestures towards possibility or one that drops a latch? Perhaps what the children heard was "It's not my problem. I am old, female, black, blind. What wisdom I have now is in knowing I cannot help you. The future of language is yours."

They stand there. Suppose nothing was in their hands? Suppose the visit was only a ruse, a trick to get to be spoken to, taken seriously as they have not been before? A chance to interrupt, to violate the adult world, its miasma of discourse about them, for them, but never to them? Urgent questions are at stake, including the one they have asked: "Is the bird we hold living or dead?" Perhaps the question meant: "Could someone tell us what is life? What is death?" No trick at all; no silliness. A straightforward question worthy of the attention of a wise one. An old one. And if the old and wise who have lived life and faced death cannot describe either, who can?

But she does not; she keeps her secret; her good opinion of herself; her gnomic pronouncements; her art without commitment. She keeps her distance, enforces it and retreats into the singularity of isolation, in sophisticated, privileged space.

Nothing, no word follows her declaration of transfer. That silence is deep, deeper than the meaning available in the words she has spoken. It shivers, this silence, and the children, annoyed, fill it with language invented on the spot.

"Is there no speech," they ask her, "no words you can give us that helps us break through your dossier of failures? Through the education you have just given us that is no education at all because we are paying close attention to what you have done as well as to what you have said? To the barrier you have erected between generosity and wisdom?

"We have no bird in our hands, living or dead. We have only you and our important question. Is the nothing in our hands something you could not bear to contemplate, to even guess? Don't you remember being young when language was magic without meaning?

When what you could say, could not mean? When the invisible was what imagination strove to see? When questions and demands for answers burned so brightly you trembled with fury at not knowing?

"Do we have to begin consciousness with a battle heroines and heroes like you have already fought and lost leaving us with nothing in our hands except what you have imagined is there? Your answer is artful, but its artfulness embarrasses us and ought to embarrass you. Your answer is indecent in its self-congratulation. A made-for-television script that makes no sense if there is nothing in our hands.

"Why didn't you reach out, touch us with your soft fingers, delay the sound bite, the lesson, until you knew who we were? Did you so despise our trick, our modus operandi you could not see that we were baffled about how to get your attention? We are young. Unripe. We have heard all our short lives that we have to be responsible. What could that possibly mean in the catastrophe this world has become; where, as a poet said, "nothing needs to be exposed since it is already barefaced." Our inheritance is an affront. You want us to have your old, blank eyes and see only cruelty and mediocrity. Do you think we are stupid enough to perjure ourselves again and again with the fiction of nationhood? How dare you talk to us of duty when we stand waist deep in the toxin of your past?

"You trivialize us and trivialize the bird that is not in our hands. Is there no context for our lives? No song, no literature, no poem full of vitamins, no history connected to experience that you can pass along to help us start strong? You are an adult. The old one, the wise one. Stop thinking about saving your face. Think of our lives and tell us your particularized world. Make up a story. Narrative is radical, creating us at the very moment it is being created. We will not blame you if your reach exceeds your grasp; if love so ignites your words they go down in flames and nothing is left but their scald. Or if, with the reticence of a surgeon's hands, your words suture only the places where blood might flow. We know you can never do it properly—once and for all. Passion is never enough; neither is skill. But try. For our sake and yours forget your name in the street;

tell us what the world has been to you in the dark places and in the light. Don't tell us what to believe, what to fear. Show us belief's wide skirt and the stitch that unravels fear's caul. You, old woman, blessed with blindness, can speak the language that tells us what only language can: how to see without pictures. Language alone protects us from the scariness of things with no names. Language alone is meditation.

"Tell us what it is to be a woman so that we may know what it is to be a man. What moves at the margin. What it is to have no home in this place. To be set adrift from the one you knew. What it is to live at the edge of towns that cannot bear your company.

"Tell us about ships turned away from shorelines at Easter, placenta in a field. Tell us about a wagonload of slaves, how they sang so softly their breath was indistinguishable from the falling snow. How they knew from the hunch of the nearest shoulder that the next stop would be their last. How, with hands prayered in their sex, they thought of heat, then sun. Lifting their faces as though it was there for the taking. Turning as though there for the taking. They stop at an inn. The driver and his mate go in with the lamp leaving them humming in the dark. The horse's void steams into the snow beneath its hooves and its hiss and melt are the envy of the freezing slaves.

"The inn door opens: a girl and a boy step away from its light. They climb into the wagon bed. The boy will have a gun in three years, but now he carries a lamp and a jug of warm cider. They pass it from mouth to mouth. The girl offers bread, pieces of meat and something more: a glance into the eyes of the ones she serves. One helping for each man, two for each woman. And a look. They look back. The next stop will be their last. But not this one. This one is warmed."

It's quiet again when the children finish speaking, until the woman breaks into the silence.

"Finally," she says, "I trust you now. I trust you with the bird that is not in your hands because you have truly caught it. Look. How lovely it is, this thing we have done—together."

List of Contributors' Novels and Short Stories

*The list does not include science fiction, erotica,
or books written for young adults or children.*

JAMES BALDWIN
Go Tell It on the Mountain (1953)
Giovanni's Room (1956)
Another Country (1962)
Going to Meet the Man (1965) (short stories)
Tell Me How Long the Train's Been Gone (1968)
If Beale Street Could Talk (1974)
Just Above My Head (1979)

ARNA BONTEMPS
God Sends Sunday (1931)
Black Thunder (1936)
Drums at Dusk (1939)
*The Old South: "A Summer Tragedy" and Other Stories of
the Thirties* (1973) (short stories)

W. E. B. DU BOIS
The Quest of the Silver Fleece (1911)
Dark Princess: A Romance (1928)
The Ordeal of Mansart (1957)
Mansart Builds a School (1959)
Worlds of Color (1961)

RALPH ELLISON
Invisible Man (1952)
Flying Home and Other Stories (1996) (short stories)
Juneteenth (1999)
Three Days Before the Shooting (2010)

ERNEST J. GAINES

Catherine Cormier (1964)
Of Love and Dust (1967) (short stories)
Bloodline (1968) (short stories)
The Autobiography of Miss Jane Pittman (1971)
In My Father's House (1978)
A Gathering of Men (1983)
A Lesson Before Dying (1993)
Mozart and Leadbelly (2005) (stories and essays)

CHESTER HIMES

If He Hollers Let Him Go (1945)
Lonely Crusade (1947)
Cast the First Stone (1952)
The Third Generation (1954)
The End of Primitive (1955)
For Love of Imabelle (1957)
The Crazy Kill (1959)
The Real Cool Killers (1959)
All Shot Up (1960)
The Big Gold Dream (1960)
Run Man Run (1960)
Pink Toes (1961)
Cotton Comes to Harlem (1965)
The Heat's On (1966)
Blind Man with a Pistol (1969)
Black on Black (1973)
A Case of Rape (1980)
The Collected Stories of Chester Himes (1990) (short stories)
Plan B (1993)
Yesterday Will Make You Cry (1998)

LANGSTON HUGHES

Not Without Laughter (1930)
The Ways of White Folks (1934)
Simple Speaks His Mind (1950) (short stories)
Laughing to Keep from Crying (1952)
Simple Takes a Wife (1953) (short stories)

Sweet Flypaper of Life (1955)
Simple Stakes a Claim (1957) (short stories)
Tambourines to Glory (1958)
The Best of Simple (1961) (short stories)
Something in Common and Other Stories (1963) (short stories)
Simple's Uncle Sam (1965) (short stories)
Short Stories of Langston Hughes (1996) (short stories)

ZORA NEALE HURSTON

Jonah's Gourd Vine (1934)
Their Eyes Were Watching God (1937)
Moses, Man of the Mountain (1939)
Seraph on the Suwanee (1948)

CHARLES JOHNSON

Faith and the Good Thing (1974)
Oxherding Tale (1982)
The Sorcerer's Apprentice (1986) (short stories)
Middle Passage (1990)
Dreamer (1998)
Soul Catcher and Other Stories (2001)
Dr. King's Refrigerator and Other Bedtime Stories (2005)

JAMES WELDON JOHNSON

The Autobiography of an Ex–Colored Man (1912)

GAYL JONES

Corregidora (1975)
Eva's Man (1976)
White Rat (1977) (short stories)
The Healing (1998)
Mosquito (1999)

TERRY McMILLAN

Mama (1987)
Disappearing Acts (1989)
Waiting to Exhale (1992)
How Stella Got Her Groove Back (1996)

A Day Late and a Dollar Short (2002)
The Interruption of Everything (2006)
Getting to Happy (2010)
Who Asked You? (2013)

JAMES ALAN McPHERSON
Hue and Cry (1968) (short stories)
Elbow Room (1977) (short stories)

TONI MORRISON
The Bluest Eye (1970)
Sula (1973)
Song of Solomon (1977)
Tar Baby (1981)
Beloved (1987)
Jazz (1992)
Paradise (1998)
Love (2003)
A Mercy (2008)
Home (2012)

WALTER MOSLEY
EASY RAWLINS MYSTERIES
Devil in a Blue Dress (1990)
A Red Death (1991)
White Butterfly (1992)
Black Betty (1994)
A Little Yellow Dog (1996)
Gone Fishin' (1997)
Bad Boy Brawly Brown (2002)
Six Easy Pieces (2003)
Little Scarlet (2004)
Cinnamon Kiss (2005)
Blonde Faith (2007)
Little Green (2013)
Rose Gold (2014)

FEARLESS JONES MYSTERIES
Fearless Jones (2001)
Fear Itself (2003)
Fear of the Dark (2006)

LEONID MCGILL MYSTERIES
The Long Fall (2009)
Known to Evil (2010)
When the Thrill Is Gone (2011)
All I Did Was Shoot My Man (2012)

SOCRATES FORTLOW BOOKS
Always Outnumbered, Always Outgunned (1997)
Walkin' the Dog (1999)
The Right Mistake (2008)

OTHER NOVELS
RL's Dream (1995)
The Man in My Basement (2004)
Walking the Line (2005) (a novella in the *Transgressions* series)
Fortunate Son (2006)
The Tempest Tales (2008)
The Last Days of Ptolemy Grey (2010)
Parishioner (2012)
Debbie Doesn't Do It Anymore (2014)

ISHMAEL REED
The Freelance Pallbearers (1967)
Yellow Back Radio Broke-Down (1969)
Mumbo Jumbo (1972)
The Last Days of Louisiana Red (1974)
Flight to Canada (1976)
The Terrible Twos (1982)
Reckless Eyeballing (1986)
The Terrible Threes (1989)
Japanese by Spring (1993)
Juice (2011)

MARTHA SOUTHGATE

Another Way to Dance (1997)
The Fall of Rome (2002)
Third Girl from the Left (2005)
The Taste of Salt (2011)

ALICE WALKER

The Third Life of Grange Copeland (1970)
In Love and Trouble: Stories of Black Women (1973) (short stories)
Meridian (1976)
The Color Purple (1982)
You Can't Keep a Good Woman Down (1982) (short stories)
The Temple of My Familiar (1989)
Possessing the Secret of Joy (1992)
The Complete Stories (1994) (short stories)
The Light of My Father's Smile (1998)
The Way Forward Is with a Broken Heart (2000) (short stories)
Now Is the Time to Open Your Heart (2004)

MARGARET WALKER

Jubilee (1966)

JOHN EDGAR WIDEMAN

A Glance Away (1967)
Hurry Home (1970)
The Lynchers (1973)
Damballah (1981) (short stories)
Hiding Place (1981)
Sent for You Yesterday (1983)
Reuben (1987)
Fever (1989) (short stories)
Philadelphia Fire (1990)
The Stories of John Edgar Wideman (1992) (short stories)
The Cattle Killing (1996)
Two Cities (1998)
God's Gym (2005) (short stories)
Fanon (2008)
Briefs (2010) (short stories)

RICHARD WRIGHT
Uncle Tom's Children (1938) (short stories)
The Man Who Was Almost a Man (1939)
Native Son (1940)
The Outsider (1953)
Savage Holiday (1954)
The Long Dream (1958)
Eight Men (1961) (short stories)
Lawd Today (1963)
Rite of Passage (1994)
A Father's Law (2008)

Notes

PREFACE

1. Horace Porter, *The Making of a Black Scholar: From Georgia to the Ivy League* (Iowa City: University of Iowa Press, 2003), 53.

2. Malcolm Cowley, *Writers at Work: The Paris Review Interviews* (New York: Viking Press, 1960), 7–9.

3. John Hersey, *The Writer's Craft* (New York: Alfred A. Knopf, 1974), 332.

4. Tillie Olsen, *Silences* (New York: Dell, 1978), 6.

5. Hersey, *The Writer's Craft*, 273.

INTRODUCTION

6. John O' Brien, *Interviews with Black Writers* (New York: Liveright, 1973); Mari Evans, *Black Women Writers (1950–1980)* (New York: Doubleday, 1984); Claudia Tate, *Black Women Writers at Work* (New York: Continuum, 1988).

7. James Baldwin, *The Cross of Redemption: Uncollected Writings*, edited by Randall Kenan (New York: Pantheon, 2010), 53–56.

JAMES BALDWIN (1924–1987)

8. Horace Porter, *Stealing the Fire: The Art and Protest of James Baldwin* (Middletown, CT: Wesleyan University Press, 1989), 22–37.

ARNA BONTEMPS (1902–1973)

9. Charles H. Nichols, ed., *Arna Bontemps–Langston Hughes Letters, 1925–1967* (New York: Dodd, Mead, 1980).

LANGSTON HUGHES (1902–1967)

10. Arnold Rampersad, *The Life of Langston Hughes*, vol. 1, *1902–1941: I, Too, Sing America* (New York: Oxford University Press, 1986).

RICHARD WRIGHT (1908–1960)

11. Margaret Walker, *Richard Wright: Daemonic Genius* (New York: Warner Books, 1988), 121–150.

CHESTER HIMES (1909–1984)

12. Lawrence P. Jackson, *The Indignant Generation: A Narrative History of African American Writers and Critics, 1934–1960* (Princeton, NJ: Princeton University Press, 2011), 138–139.

ISHMAEL REED (1938–)

13. Michael DeRell Hill, *The Ethics of Swagger: Prizewinning African American Novels, 1977–1993* (Columbus: Ohio State University Press, 2013), 16–17.

JAMES ALAN MCPHERSON (1943–)

14. Horace A. Porter, "James Alan McPherson," in *The Columbia Companion to the Twentieth-Century American Short Story*, edited by Blanche H. Gelfant (New York: Columbia University Press, 2000), 377–380.

TERRY MCMILLAN (1951–)

15. Terry McMillan, *Breaking Ice: An Anthology of Contemporary African-American Fiction* (New York: Penguin, 1990).

JOHN EDGAR WIDEMAN (1941–)

16. Michael DeRell Hill, *The Ethics of Swagger: Prizewinning African American Novels, 1977–1993* (Columbus: Ohio State University Press, 2013), 144–145.

W. E. B. DU BOIS (1868–1963)

17. Lena Hill, *Visualizing Blackness and the Creation of the African American Literary Tradition* (New York: Cambridge University Press, 2014), 59.

18. Ibid., 58–66.

GAYL JONES (1949–)

19. Peter Manso, "Chronicle of a Tragedy Foretold," *New York Times*, July 19, 1998.

JAMES WELDON JOHNSON (1871–1938)

20. Miriam Thaggert, *Images of Black Modernism: Verbal and Visual Strategies of the Harlem Renaissance* (Amherst: University of Massachusetts Press, 2010), 51–64.

21. James Weldon Johnson, *The Essential Writings of James Weldon Johnson*, edited by Rudolph P. Byrd (New York: Modern Library, 2008), xxii.

ZORA NEALE HURSTON (1891–1960)
22. Lena Hill, *Visualizing Blackness and the Creation of the African American Literary Tradition* (New York: Cambridge University Press, 2014), 145–147.

MARTHA SOUTHGATE (1960–)
23. Martha Southgate, "Writers Like Me," *New York Times Book Review*, July 1, 2007.

CHARLES JOHNSON (1948–)
24. Rudolph P. Byrd, ed., *I Call Myself An Artist: Writings by and about Charles Johnson* (Bloomington: Indiana University Press, 1999), 7–8.

WALTER MOSLEY (1952–)
25. Walter Mosley, *This Year You Write Your Novel* (Boston: Little, Brown, 2007).

RALPH ELLISON (1913–1994)
26. Ralph Ellison, *The Collected Essays of Ralph Ellison*, edited by John F. Callahan (New York: Random House, 1995).

27. Horace Porter, *Jazz Country: Ralph Ellison in America* (Iowa City: University of Iowa Press, 2001).

28. Ralph Ellison, *Three Days Before the Shooting*, edited by John F. Callahan and Adam Bradley (New York: Random House, 2010).

MARGARET WALKER (1915–1998)
29. Margaret Walker, *How I Wrote "Jubilee" and Other Essays on Life and Literature*, edited by Maryemma Graham (New York: Feminist Press, 1990), xiii–xxi.

30. Margaret Walker, *Richard Wright: Daemonic Genius* (New York: Warner Books, 1988), 93.

ERNEST J. GAINES (1933–)
31. Ernest Gaines, *Mozart and Leadbelly: Stories and Essays*, edited by Marcia Gaudet and Reggie Young (New York: Knopf, 2005).

ALICE WALKER (1944–)

32. Michael DeRell Hill, *The Ethics of Swagger: Prizewinning African-American Novels, 1977–1993* (Columbus: Ohio State University Press, 2013), 47–52.

33. Alice Walker, *In Search of Our Mothers' Gardens: Womanist Prose* (San Diego: Harcourt Brace Jovanovich, 1983), 93–116.

TONI MORRISON (1931–)

34. D. G. Myers, "MLA Rankings of American Writers," *Commentary,* March 26, 2012, www.commentarymagazine.com/2012/03/26/mla-rankings/.

Sources and Permissions

JAMES BALDWIN, "Why I Stopped Hating Shakespeare," copyright 1964 by James Baldwin, originally published in *The Observer*. Collected in *The Cross of Redemption: Uncollected Writings by James Baldwin*, edited by Randall Kenan and published by Vintage Books. Used by arrangement with the James Baldwin Estate.

ARNA BONTEMPS, "Introduction to the 1968 Edition," in *Black Thunder* by Arna Bontemps. Copyright 1936 by The Macmillan Company, renewed 1963 by Arna Bontemps. Introduction copyright 1968 by Arna Bontemps. New Introduction copyright 1992 by Arnold Rampersad. Used by permission of Beacon Press, Boston, and Harold Ober Associates.

LANGSTON HUGHES, excerpts from "The Mother of Gracchi" and "Patron and Friend," in *The Big Sea: An Autobiography* by Langston Hughes. Copyright 1940 by Langston Hughes. Copyright renewed 1968 by Arna Bontemps and George Houston Bass. Reprinted by permission of Farrar, Straus and Giroux, LLC, and Harold Ober Associates Incorporated.

RICHARD WRIGHT, excerpts from *Black Boy* by Richard Wright. Copyright 1937, 1942, 1944, 1945 by Richard Wright; renewed 1973 by Ellen Wright. Reprinted by permission of HarperCollins Publishers, The Random House Group Limited, John Hawkins & Associates, Inc., and The Estate of Richard Wright.

JAMES BALDWIN, excerpted from *The Devil Finds Work* by James Baldwin. Copyright 1976 by James Baldwin. Copyright renewed. Published by Vintage Books. Used by agreement with the James Baldwin Estate.

CHESTER HIMES, from *The Quality of Hurt: The Early Years: The Autobiography of Chester Himes*. Paragon House. Copyright 1971 and 1972. Used with permission of the Himes Estate.

Index

About the Author

Horace A. Porter, F. Wendell Miller Professor of English & American Studies, is chair of the American Studies department and African American Studies program at the University of Iowa. He is also the author of *Stealing the Fire: The Art and Protest of James Baldwin* (Wesleyan University Press, 1989); *Jazz Country: Ralph Ellison in America* (University of Iowa Press, 2001); and *The Making of a Black Scholar: From Georgia to the Ivy League* (University of Iowa Press, 2003).